CRESCENT AND STAR

CRESCENT AND STAR

TURKEY BETWEEN TWO WORLDS

STEPHEN KINZER

FARRAR, STRAUS AND GIROUX

NEW YORK

Farrar, Straus and Giroux
19 Union Square West, New York 10003

Copyright © 2001 by Stephen Kinzer
All rights reserved
Distributed in Canada by Douglas and McIntyre Ltd.
Printed in the United States of America
First edition, 2001

Fifth printing, 2001

Library of Congress Cataloging-in-Publication Data
Kinzer, Stephen.
    Crescent and star : Turkey between two worlds / Stephen Kinzer.— 1st
ed.
    p.   cm.
    Includes index.
    ISBN 0-374-13143-0 (hardcover : alk. paper)
    1. Turkey—Politics and government—20th century.   2. Turkey—Ethnic
relations—History—20th century.   3. Civil society—Turkey—
History—20th century.   4. Turkey—Armed Forces—Political
activity—History—20th century.   5. Turkey—Social life and customs—
20th century.   I. Title: Turkey between two worlds.   II. Title.

DR576 .K56 2001
956.1—dc21

                                                2001023298

Designed by Jonathan D. Lippincott

Maps by Jane Simon

TO THE PEOPLE OF TURKEY

The past has vanished,

Everything that was uttered belongs there.

Now is the time to speak of new things.

—Jelaluddin Rumi (1207–1273)

CONTENTS

NOTE ON TURKISH PRONUNCIATION

The Turkish alphabet uses Latin letters, and most words are pronounced as they look. There are a few peculiarities, however:

c is spoken as the English j, so *cirit* is pronounced "jirit."

ç is spoken as ch, so *Çiller* is pronounced "Chiller."

ı is spoken as a short u, like the u in sun, so *rakı* is pronounced "raku."

ğ is silent but slightly extends the preceding vowel, so *Çırağan* is pronounced "Churaan."

ş is spoken as sh, so *Ateş* is pronounced "Atesh."

ö is spoken as in German or like the French eu, so *Özal* is pronounced "Oezal."

ü is spoken as in German or like the French u (*lune*), so *Atatürk* is pronounced "Atatuerk."

CRESCENT AND STAR

*It is late at night when a royal messenger rouses Othello from his mar-
riage bed to tell him that his sovereign, the duke of Venice, is in counsel
with other Venetian lords and demands to see him immediately. Walking
briskly toward the palace, he wonders what business could be so urgent
as to bring these "most potent, grave, and reverend signors" to gather at
such an extraordinary hour. He arrives to find them waiting for him. Before he has a chance to ask what the matter is, the duke speaks: "Valiant
Othello, we must straight employ you / Against the general enemy Ottoman."*

In Shakespeare's day and for centuries thereafter, Christians in Europe could hear no more urgent summons. Generations of them considered "the general enemy Ottoman," better known simply as "the Turk,"
to be the scourge of civilization. His chief characteristics were thought to
include mendacity, unbridled lust, sudden violence and a passion for
gratuitous cruelty. Religion was fundamental to this stereotype. Few Europeans knew anything about Islam, but nearly all considered it a sa-
tanic affront to everything a Christian held sacred.

Arabs had conquered the Holy Land in the seventh century and were
later displaced by another Muslim people, the Turks, who swept into the
region from Central Asia. As the age of chivalry dawned, tens of thou-

sands of Europeans found themselves so profoundly outraged by Islamic control of the places where Christ was born and died that they joined the Crusades, bloody campaigns that gave an entire continent an image of Muslims, especially Turkish Muslims, as God's enemy. The first Crusade began in 1095 at the call of Pope Urban II; when the last one ended two centuries later, Turks were still ascendant and the balance of political and religious power was essentially unchanged. But in the course of these wars, Europeans came to perceive Turks as the epitome of evil. They were presumed to be not only bent on destroying Christianity but also determined to kill or enslave every man, woman and child in Christendom. "The Turks," Martin Luther declared, "are the people of the wrath of God."

Had the Turks been simply a faraway focus of evil, they would not have struck any more fear in the European heart than did the heathen Chinese. What made them such an awful thing to contemplate was that their forces were battering down doors across Europe itself. When the most successful Turkish clan, founded by Sultan Osman and known in English as the Ottomans, conquered Constantinople in 1453, it won possession of a Christian city that had once been capital of the Roman Empire and then, for more than a thousand years, capital of the Byzantine Empire. That conquest made Turks at least the geographic heirs to two of the most powerful and culturally influential kingdoms in all human history. Not just Greeks, who were once the rulers of Byzantium, but countless other European and Middle Eastern Christians have had great trouble coming to grips with this truth. Many of them still consider Constantinople, which the Turks renamed Istanbul, to be under lamentable but perhaps reversible occupation by a hostile people.

With this incomparable prize in their hands, the Ottoman Turks set out to build a great empire of their own. They captured Athens in 1458, Tabriz in 1514, Damascus in 1516, Cairo in 1517, Belgrade in 1521, Rhodes in 1522, Baghdad in 1534, Buda in 1541, Tripoli in 1551 and Cyprus in 1571. They nearly took Vienna in 1529 and continued to threaten it for more than a century. Muslim pirates captured European seamen in the Mediterranean and raided towns in Italy, Spain, France, even Britain. For many years the great question hanging over Europe was not whether Protestantism or Catholicism would prevail, but whether the Ottomans would sweep into Paris and claim the entire continent for Islam. They never did, but the fears they aroused in their military campaigns, some of which were marked by episodes of barbarous cruelty on both sides, left a deep impression on the European consciousness.

Turks consider the Ottoman period to have been a golden age of ethnic harmony and cultural diversity. In many ways it was. Ottoman sultans allowed their subject nations almost complete religious freedom and considerable political autonomy. While much of Europe was being shaken by anti-Semitic pogroms, the Ottomans were accepting thousands of Jews from Spain and other oppressive nations, allowing them not only to live peacefully but also to rise to positions of wealth and influence. But the Ottoman age was also one of almost unbroken warfare, first as Turks fought to capture territory in Europe and then as they fought to keep from losing it. In the more than six centuries between the coronation of the first Ottoman sultan around 1300 and the fall of the last one in 1922, the longest period of peace lasted just twenty-four years. Older people in some parts of Europe can still remember being warned as children that if they did not behave, Turks would come to get them.

For centuries European literature overflowed with dire warnings of the Turkish peril. King James VI of Scotland, later James I of England, wrote a vivid poem describing the world as locked in conflict "betwixt the baptiz'd race and circumcised Turban'd Turks." The sixteenth-century Italian historian Augustino Curio warned that "even at our doors and ready to come into our houses, we have this arrogant and bragging hellhound." Christopher Marlowe, in his play Tamburlaine the Great, saw the same peril for the nations of Europe: "Now Turks and Tartars shake their swords at thee / Meaning to mangle all thy provinces."

Europeans considered the Ottomans cruel sinners even after the tide of history began to turn aginst them. "I shall always hate the Turks," Voltaire wrote to King Frederick II of Prussia. "What wretched barbarians!" Jane Austen mused in one of her novels about "the turban'd Turk who scorns the world." In The Brothers Karamazov one brother tells another: "These Turks, among other things, have also taken a delight in torturing children, starting with cutting them out of their mothers' wombs with a dagger and ending with tossing nursing infants up in the air and catching them on their bayonets before their mothers' eyes. The main delight comes in doing it before their mothers' eyes."

Yet throughout the long period when the Turk was considered to embody everything savage and unholy, many Westerners also found him an object of fascination. He seemed to have a wholly different approach to life, symbolized most vividly by the harem, which was seen as a seat of depravity but also of pleasure. Here began the duality of the Western view of Turks, the creeping suspicion that for all their savagery, they might have something to teach the Christian world.

This view spread as more Europeans began to visit Istanbul and Ottoman provinces. Many came back with startlingly positive reports. "There are many in Christendom who believe that the Turks are great devils, barbarians, and people without faith, but those who have known them and have talked with them have quite a different opinion," a French traveler wrote in 1652. "It is certain that the Turks are good people who follow very well the commandment given to us by nature, only to do to others what we would have done to us."

Another Frenchman, the philosopher Jean Bodin, returned home several decades later to tell his countrymen that the Turkish sultan "constrains no one, but on the contrary permits everyone to live as his conscience dictates. What is more, even in his seraglio at Pera he permits the practice of four diverse religions, that of the Jews, the Christians according to both the Roman and Greek rites, and that of Islam."

Perhaps the most perceptive of all the Europeans who wrote about Turkish life was Lady Mary Wortley Montagu, whose husband became British ambassador to the Ottoman court in 1716. She immersed herself in her "new world" and recorded her impressions in a series of witty and incisive letters that were published in England in 1763 and are still read today.

"Thus you see, sir, these people are not as unpolish'd as we represent them," she wrote at the end of one letter. "'Tis true their magnificence is of a different taste from ours, and perhaps of a better. I am almost of the opinion they have a right notion of life; while they consume it in music, gardens, wine and delicate eating, we are tormenting our brains with *some scheme of politics or studying some science to which we can never attain, or if we do, cannot persuade people to set that value upon it we do our selves . . . I allow you to laugh at me for the sensual declaration that I had rather be a rich Effendi with all his ignorance, than Sir Isaac Newton with all his knowledge."*

Among those who were struck by Lady Mary's letters was the French painter Ingres, who after reading them began to produce brilliant works depicting the harem as a haven of pure and uplifting beauty. Soon afterward Mozart wrote his opera Abduction from the Seraglio, whose plot was equally subversive of conventional stereotypes. In the climactic scene the Turkish sultan is revealed to be tender and benevolent despite having been grossly abused by Europeans.

This confusion of images persisted through the nineteenth century. Lord Byron's impossibly romantic death in Greece, where he was fighting against Ottoman forces in the cause of Greek independence, set off a new wave of anti-Turkish feeling throughout Europe, especially because it was accompanied by reports that the Turks had committed atrocities during their campaign. But only five years after Byron died, the future British prime minister Benjamin Disraeli was able to describe Istanbul in terms that made the Turks seem the most civilized people on earth.

"I confess to you that my Turkish prejudices are very much confirmed by my residence in Turkey," Disraeli wrote home to a friend. "The life of this people greatly accords with my taste, which is naturally somewhat indolent and melancholy, and I do not think would disgust you. To repose on voluptuous ottomans, and smoke superb pipes, daily to indulge in the luxuries of a bath which requires half a dozen attendants for its perfection, to court the air in a curved caique by shores which are a continual scene and to find no greater exertion than to canter on a barb, is I think a far more sensible life than all the bustle of clubs, and all the boring of saloons—all of this without coloring and exaggeration is the life which may be here commanded accompanied by a thousand sources of calm enjoyment and a thousand modes of mellow pleasure, which it would weary you to relate, and which I leave to your own lively imagination."

Pit of barbarism or seat of wisdom and tolerance? As the Ottoman Empire gave way to the Turkish Republic in the early years of the twen-

*tieth century, the outside world was uncertain which of these two per-
ceptions to believe. It still is. Many people, including more than a few
statesmen, view modern Turkey as a backward land plagued by vast
social inequalities, grotesque human-rights violations and a callous, corrupt and militaristic regime. Others, believing that Turks have contributed to civilization rather than having sought to destroy it, hope they
will overcome their problems and soon emerge as a powerfully modern
nation. And the Turks themselves? For centuries they shaped world history, and the not-so-distant memory of Ottoman glory allows them to believe they can again.*

ONE

DREAMING IN TURKISH

My favorite word in Turkish is *istiklal*. The dictionary says it means "independence," and that alone is enough to win it a place of honor in any language. It has special resonance in Turkey because Turkey is struggling to become independent of so much. It wants to break away from its autocratic heritage, from its position outside the world's political mainstream, and from the stereotype of the terrifying Turk and the ostracism which that stereotype encourages. Most of all, it is trying to free itself from its fears—fear of freedom, fear of the outside world, fear of itself.

But the real reason I love to hear the word *istiklal* is because it is the name of Turkey's most fascinating boulevard. Jammed with people all day and late into the night, lined with cafés, bookstores, cinemas and shops of every description, it is the pulsating heart not only of Istanbul but of the Turkish nation. I go there every time I feel myself being overwhelmed by doubts about Turkey. Losing myself in Istiklal's parade of faces and outfits for a few minutes, overhearing snippets of conversation and absorbing the energy that crackles along its mile and a half, is always enough to renew my confidence in Turkey's future. Because Istanbul has attracted millions of migrants from other parts of the country—several hundred new ones still arrive every day—this street is the ultimate melting pot. The country would certainly take a huge leap forward if people could be grabbed there at random and sent to Ankara to replace the members of Parliament. Istiklal is perfectly named because its human panorama reflects Turkey's drive to break away from claustrophobic provincialism and allow its people to express their magnificent diversity.

That drive has been only partly successful. Something about the concept of diversity frightens Turkey's ruling elite. It triggers the deep insecurity that has gripped Turkish rulers ever since the Republic was founded in 1923, an insecurity that today prevents Turkey from taking its proper place in the modern world.

No nation was ever founded with greater revolutionary zeal than the Turkish Republic, nor has any undergone more sweeping change in such a short time. In a very few years after 1923, Mustafa Kemal Atatürk transformed a shattered and bewildered nation into one obsessed with progress. His was a one-man revolution, imposed and steered from above. Atatürk knew that Turks were not ready to break violently with their past, embrace modernity and turn decisively toward the West. He also knew, however, that doing so would be the only way for them to shape a new destiny for themselves and their nation. So he forced them, often over the howling protests of the old order.

The new nation that Atatürk built on the rubble of the Ottoman Empire never could have been built democratically. Probably not a single one of his sweeping reforms would have been approved in a plebiscite. The very idea of a plebiscite, of shaping a political system according to the people's will, would have struck most Turks of that era as not simply alien but ludicrous.

In the generations that have passed since then, Turkey has become an entirely different nation. It is as vigorous and as thirsty for democracy as any on earth. But its leaders, who fancy themselves Atatürk's heirs, fiercely resist change. They believe that Turks cannot yet be trusted with the fate of their nation, that an elite must continue to make all important decisions because the people are not mature enough to do so.

Atatürk's infant Turkish Republic was a very fragile creation. Sheiks and leaders of religious sects considered its commitment to secularism a direct assault on all they had held sacred for centuries. Tribal chieftans and local warlords realized that a strong centralized state would undermine their authority. Kurds who dominated eastern provinces sought to take advantage of the new state's weakness by staging military uprisings. European powers hoped it would collapse so that they could divide its territory among themselves. The new Soviet Union actively sought to subvert it and turn it into a vassal state.

In this hostile climate, Atatürk and his comrades came to think of themselves as righteous crusaders slashing their way through a world filled with enemies. They ruled by decree and with a rubber-stamp Parliament, equating criticism with treason. During their first years in power, arrest and execution were the fate of their real and imagined opponents.

Three-quarters of a century has passed since then, and in that time Turkey has changed beyond recognition. The nation that faced Atatürk when he took power was not only in ruins but truly primitive. Nearly everyone was illiterate. Life expectancy was pitifully short, epidemics were accepted as immutable facts of life and medical care was all but nonexistent. The basic skills of trade, artisanry and engineering were unknown, having vanished with the departed Greeks and Armenians. Almost every citizen was a subsistence farmer. There were only a few short stretches of paved road in a territory that extended more than a thousand miles from Iran to Greece. Most important of all, the Turkish people knew nothing but obedience. They had been taught since time immemorial that authority is something distant and irresistible, and that the role of the individual in society is submission and nothing more.

If Atatürk could return to see what has become of his nation, he undoubtedly would be astonished at how far it has come. Muddy villages have become bustling cities and cow paths have become superhighways. Universities and public hospitals are to be found in even the most remote regions. The economy is unsteady but shows bursts of vitality. Turkish corporations and business conglomerates are making huge amounts of money and competing successfully in every corner of the globe. Hundreds of young men and women return home every year from periods of study abroad. People are educated, self-confident and eager to build a nation that embodies the ideals of democracy and human rights.

The ruling elite, however, refuses to embrace this new nation or even admit that it exists. Military commanders, prosecutors, security officers, narrow-minded bureaucrats, lapdog newspaper editors, rigidly conservative politicians and other members of this sclerotic cadre remain psychologically trapped in the 1920s. They see threats from across every one of Turkey's eight borders and, most dangerously, from within the country itself. In their minds Turkey is still a nation under siege. To protect it from mortal danger, they feel obliged to run it themselves. They not only ignore but actively resist intensifying pressure from educated, worldly Turks who want their country to break free of its shackles and complete its march toward the democracy that was Atatürk's dream.

This dissonance, this clash between what the entrenched elite wants and what more and more Turks want, is the central fact of life in modern Turkey. It frames the country's great national dilemma. Until this dilemma is somehow resolved, Turkey will live in eternal limbo, a half-democracy taking half-steps toward freedom and fulfilling only half its destiny.

The most extraordinary aspect of this confrontation is that both sides are seeking, or claim to be seeking, the same thing: a truly modern Turkey. Military commanders and their civilian allies, especially the appointed prosecutors, judges and governors who set the limits of freedom in every town and province, consider themselves modernity's great and indispensable defenders. They fear democracy not on principle, but because they are convinced it will unleash forces that will drag Turkey back toward ignorance and obscurantism. Allowing Turks to speak, debate and choose freely, they believe, would lead the nation to certain catastrophe. To prevent that catastrophe, they insist on holding ultimate political power themselves and crushing challenges wherever they appear.

Yet what this means in practice is that state power is directed relentlessly against the very forces in society that represent true modernity. Writers, journalists and politicians who criticize the status quo are packed off to prison for what they say and write. Calls for religious freedom are considered subversive attacks on the secular order. Expressions of ethnic or cultural identity are banned for fear that they will trigger separatist movements and ultimately rip the country apart. When foreign leaders remind Turkey that it can never become a full member of the world community as long as its government behaves this way, they are denounced for harboring secret agendas whose ultimate goal is to wipe Turks off the face of history.

These attitudes have turned Turkey's ruling elite into the enemy of the ideal that gave it life. Originally dedicated to freeing a nation from dogma, this elite now defends dogma. Once committed to liberating the mind, today it lashes out against those whose minds lead them to forbidden places. It has become the "sovereign" against which its spiritual ancestors, the Young Turks, began rebelling in the nineteenth century.

"Our sovereign and our government do not want the light to enter our country," the Young Turk theorist Abdullah Cevdet wrote in 1897. "They want all people to remain in ignorance, on the dunghill of misery and wretchedness; no touch of awakening may blaze in the hearts of our compatriots. What the government wants is for the people to remain like beasts, submissive as sheep, fawning and servile as dogs. Let them hear no word of any honest lofty idea. Instead, let them languish under the whips of ignorant gendarmes, under the aggression of shameless, boorish, oppressive officials."

The Young Turks were members of insurgent groups that defied the absolutism of Ottoman rule during the nineteenth and early twentieth centuries. These groups built a rich tradition of dissent that shaped the intellectual and political life of the late Ottoman period and laid the foundation for Atatürk's revolution. Their principles were admirable, but most of their leaders believed instinctively that the state, not popular will, was the instrument by which social and political change would be achieved. They bequeathed to Atatürk the conviction that Turkish reformers should seize state power and then use it ruthlessly for their own ends, not try to democratize society in ways that would weaken the centralized state.

Turkey's effort to rid itself of this authoritarian mind-set has been difficult and scarred by trauma. Not until 1950 did military commanders, the vanguard of Atatürk's new class, allow free multiparty elections for Parliament. To this day they watch politicians closely. Three times they have staged coups to depose elected governments. After the last one, in 1980, they ruled the country for three years, and before returning to their barracks they wrote a new constitution and called a national referendum to ratify it. Criticizing the document or campaigning for a "no" vote was illegal, and in the end ninety-one percent of voters approved. This constitution, which remains in force, was written to embody the needs of Turkey's military-dominated elite. The article guaranteeing freedom of speech and the press stipulates that "the exercise of these freedoms may be restricted for the purposes of preventing crime." Another article bans "any news or articles that threaten the internal or external security of the state." A third asserts: "Fundamental rights and freedoms may be restricted by law, in conformity with the letter and spirit of the Constitution, with the aim of safeguarding the indivisible integrity of the state with its territory and nation, national sovereignty, the Republic, national security, public order, general peace, the public interest, public morals and public health."

These articles and a series of laws passed to bolster them have been used very effectively to prevent the flowering of Turkish democracy. In the 1990s, however, it became clear that the true core of the constitution was Article 118, which established a body called the National Security Council, composed of five elected officials (the president, prime minister and ministers of defense, interior and foreign affairs) and five generals (the chief of staff and the commanders of the army, navy, air force and gendarmerie). Article 118 stipulates that the government must give "priority consideration" to its decisions.

For most of the 1980s Turkey was dominated by Turgut Özal, an energetic visionary whose rise to power the departing generals had tried to prevent. He managed to impose a measure of civilian control over the armed forces, and during his years as prime minister and then president, the National Security Council remained in the background. But after Özal's death in 1993, Turkey entered a period of political upheaval in which small-minded politicians bickered while the country drifted toward social and political fragmentation and a new Kurdish revolt in the eastern provinces reached an alarming peak. The politicians' failure to confront these challenges created a vacuum, and to the relief of many Turks, military officers stepped in to fill it. They became Turkey's true rulers, assuming the power to veto every government policy of which they disapproved. The vehicle they used to exercise this power, and use to this day, is the National Security Council. It is not a forum for debate or discussion but a place where generals come to tell the country's elected leaders what to do.

The council usually meets once a month, and although its deliberations are private, television reporters are admitted for a few minutes to film the members as they arrive and settle into their seats. The pictures they take perfectly convey the balance of power within the council. Elected government leaders sit on one side of a long table, shifting uncomfortably like guilty schoolboys. The military commanders, ribbon-bedecked and unsmiling, sit opposite, glowering at their charges as they pull folders from their briefcases and prepare to deliver their decrees. Always they speak with a single voice, and always it is understood that their will must be done.

In 1997 I visited the Islamic Republic of Iran to write about the election that brought Mohammed Khatami to that country's presidency. On the plane trip back to Turkey, I reflected on the curious system by which Iran is ruled. There is a fully functioning government headed by an elected president and including a parliament and various local authorities. But there is also a second center of power, the Council of Guardians, composed of religious figures and headed by a mullah they choose for a life term. The government is elected by the people, who are human and therefore fallible, but the Council of Guardians is guided by God, who is infallible. Whenever there is a conflict between the two branches, therefore, the Council of Guardians must be right. What it decides must be done, regardless of what the people or their elected representatives want.

As my plane entered Turkish airspace, my thoughts slowly drifted from the country I was leaving to the one to which I was returning. Comparing Iran's political system to that of Turkey, I saw a remarkable similarity. Turkey has a diverse and often feisty Parliament that chooses a prime minister according to the outcome of free elections, as well as a cabinet and all the trappings of bureaucratic state. Ultimate power, however, rests with the National Security Council, dominated by military commanders accountable only to each other. The commanders draw their authority from Atatürk, who though long dead remains Turkey's secular god. Because they defend Atatürk's principles and believe they know instinctively what he would do in any situation, their decisions must take precedence over those of fallible politicians. To allow civilians to overrule them, they believe, would be an unforgivable betrayal of both duty and the nation's sacred guiding spirit.

There is one glaring difference, of course, between the roles of Iranian mullahs and Turkish generals. The mullahs use their power to enforce a reactionary theocratic order based on hatred of the modern world. Turkish officers detest that order, and wield their power in an unrelenting battle to assure that it can never take hold in their country. They want what most Turks want: a society that is free, democratic and secular. The great question they now face is whether the tactics they have used to promote those ideals for four generations are still appropriate or whether it is time for them to relax their grip and let civil society bloom.

To portray Turkey's political system as a form of military dictatorship would be unfair. Certainly military commanders, like many powerful civilians, harbor a deep mistrust of the people and an abiding fear that if given the chance to do so, the people would make disastrous mistakes and bring Atatürk's magnificent edifice crashing to the ground. But these commanders and the system by which they exercise power also provide a measure of stability that Turkish politicians have been unable to offer. In the absence of a strong constitutional tradition or a long-established social consensus, they are a bulwark against Islamic fundamentalism and other threats to Atatürk's modern state. Turks are acutely aware of this uncomfortable reality, and many sleep soundly at night because they know the generals will not allow anything to go too badly wrong.

For years, Turkish officers took great pride in public-opinion surveys that showed the armed forces to be the country's most trusted institution. This was not so great a compliment as it seems. It is illegal to criticize the armed forces, so no newspaper may publish stories about waste, corruption, brutality, abuses of power or other negative aspects of military life. Being thus protected, military institutions naturally seem to exist on a higher moral plane than others. Yet in their hearts, many Turks feel a sincere respect, admiration and even affection for their men in uniform.

Part of the reason for this is historical. It was, after all, the army that established the Turkish Republic against the will of European powers, rallying behind Atatürk to rescue the nation from impending doom. The Republic's first leaders rose from military ranks, and it was their collective act of will that ripped Turks away from their old ways, reversed their long decline as a people and set them on the road toward freedom and prosperity. It is frightening to imagine what Turkey would look like today without the influence of its army. Quite possibly it would be somnolent and isolated, like Syria, Iraq and other Middle Eastern countries where democracy and individual rights are concepts about which citizens dare not even dream.

All young Turkish men must serve in the army, which means that virtually every adult male is a veteran and that most families have had the experience of seeing sons in uniform. Turks do not fear their army or consider it oppressive, the way terrified Africans and Latin Americans did when cruel military dictatorships dominated their societies. Most see it as a benevolent force that has successfully defended Turkey against foreign and domestic enemies, and that truly has the national interest at heart.

Some things the army has done are widely viewed as tragic errors—such as its decision after the first military coup in 1960 to convene a tribunal that convicted Prime Minister Adnan Menderes and two of his cabinet ministers of treason and then sent them to the gallows. Other stains on its record, like the imprisonment and torture of thousands of political activists following the 1980 coup or the brutish tactics used to suppress Kurdish rebels in the 1990s, are not much discussed outside intellectual circles. People understand that these excesses occurred, but choose either not to dwell on them or to believe they were necessary to preserve the nation. In much of Turkish society there is a desire to believe the best about the armed forces and their commanders.

Turks have a vivid collective memory of the chaos out of which their nation was forged. Over the years they have also watched several nearby countries—Yugoslavia, the Soviet Union, Lebanon, Iraq, Afghanistan—dissolve into fratricidal conflict. These experiences have convinced them of the supreme value of stability. In Turkey it is not hard to find thoughtful, worldly people who believe their country is not ready for full democracy. They know that once Turks are allowed to speak and write freely, to form political parties that advocate unorthodox ideas and to challenge long-held principles in the court of public opinion, Turkey will become more turbulent. That is something they deeply fear. They doubt their society can withstand the clash of ideas that is the essence of democratic life.

"You in the West also had long periods of backwardness and intolerance," a Turkish diplomat once told me as we walked along a quiet corridor in the foreign ministry in Ankara. "You had dictatorships, civil wars, religious fanaticism, the Inquisition, all kinds of horror. Then, over a period of centuries, you climbed out of that hole. You had the Enlightenment. You had philosophers who wrote books about democracy. Very slowly, people started to understand and accept these new ideas. You began to have governments based on democratic principles. Now, because you went through all that, you can give your people complete freedom. Your societies are stable enough to handle it. But it's not the same here. Our Enlightenment began only seventy-five years ago. It's too soon to lift every restriction. The risk is too great. We could lose everything."

This rationale for limiting democracy is repeated constantly in Turkey. After a while it begins to sound like what an overprotective mother might say about her child. No mother would allow her four-year-old to cross the street alone or handle knives or play with matches, but there must come a time when, however reluctantly, she accepts that her child has grown up and is able to handle the responsibilities of adulthood. The fear of popular will that underpins Turkey's political system is like that of a mother whose child turns fifteen and then eighteen and then twenty-five and older, but is still not trusted to leave home alone.

When I asked my diplomat friend how long he thought it would take before Turks grow wise enough to assume the responsibilities of freedom, he stopped in his tracks and turned to me, a very serious expression on his face. Obviously he had pondered this question before. "It's been three-quarters of a century since this process started," he said. "Maybe after a century has passed we'll be far enough along." Then, after another pause, he repeated the key word with emphasis: "*Maybe.*"

Many Turks, especially the impatient young, feel profoundly insulted by this contempt for their intelligence. Why, then, do they not rebel against the army's insistence on guiding the political system? One reason, at least during the 1990s, was the widely held belief that without a strong military hand, Kurdish rebels and religious fanatics would plunge the country into crisis. But with the rebellion over and fundamentalists in retreat, another unpleasant reality still hangs over the body politic. No matter how committed one may be to the principles of democracy, the inescapable reality in Turkey is that the political class deserves its poor reputation. Military schools are far superior to those most civilians attend, and as a result the average officer is considerably more likely than the average politician to understand history, speak foreign languages and grasp the principles of effective government. It is no wonder, then, that many Turks like the idea of a military hand on the tiller of state.

Most developed countries are overflowing with people qualified to serve as legislators or public administrators, and as a result they are run relatively well. At the other end of the spectrum are countries that are a mess partly because their educational and social systems have, for one reason or another, failed to produce a capable political class. Turkey is caught uniquely between these two extremes. Its writers, thinkers, university professors and business executives are as talented, highly trained and broadly experienced as any in the world. But its political system has been very effectively designed to exclude these people from positions of power, and as a result Turkish democracy remains stunted. In no country is the gap between the quality of the educated elite and the quality of the political class as great as it is in Turkey.

For decades, each of Turkey's important political parties has been run by a single individual, sometimes with a tiny coterie of coconspirators. These few figures choose candidates for public office by using a single criterion: blind obedience. Only sycophants need apply, and independent thinkers are avoided as if they carry the virus of a deadly plague. The political system has become ossified, dominated by a handful of phlegmatic reactionaries whose only true allegiance is to the status quo.

In Turkey, as in any democracy, the defense minister is supposed to be responsible to civilian leaders. Interviewing one, however, is a revealing experience. During my years in Turkey I did so only once, and the folly of it quickly became clear. The minister's office is located inside the walled complex in Ankara where the general staff has its headquarters, vividly symbolizing his position as a prisoner of his generals. It is the generals who make military policy, usually without even consulting the civilians who are their titular superiors. The defense minister I interviewed was almost blissfully ignorant and took great pains to avoid saying anything that might offend his uniformed masters. A colonel sat beside him, serving not simply as chaperone and note-taker but also as keeper of correct answers. Every time I asked a substantive question, the minister leaned his head toward the colonel and listened to whispered advice. Then he straightened up and repeated what he had been told.

Commanders of the Turkish army, navy, air force and gendarmerie are appointed as a group along with the chief of the general staff, normally serving in top command posts for three years and then, always in August, turning power over to the next group. They choose their own successors, with the principal qualification being absolute loyalty to the established order. Each group has its own attitude toward the press, so there are periods when they welcome journalists and other periods, often years long, when they view us as lepers or worse. During one interlude of openness, I was able to meet them regularly. Once I sat transfixed as a top commander launched into an astonishingly frank monologue full of contempt for politicians and their system.

"Idiots!" he began, shaking his head slowly and sounding almost as sad as he was outraged. "Those people in the Parliament are idiots! They don't know anything about government or Turkey or the world. The only thing they want is to steal money in their own little ways, to build their own little empires. Public good? Forget it. Planning for the future? Never think about it. Duty or integrity? Unknown. You should see the defense ministers they send us! They hardly know a tank from a plane. And those are the *ministers*! The rest are even worse. Their intellectual level is incredibly low. How can anyone expect us to take orders from people like that? Turkey would never forgive us if we did."

My first reaction to this tirade was horror, coupled with a sinking feeling that this country was doomed to live a very long time under military dominance. But my indignation and outrage were soon overwhelmed by unwelcome thoughts. Against my will, I had to admit that much of what this general was telling me was true. Of course the Turkish Parliament and other elected bodies include men and women of intelligence and character, but not nearly enough of them.

Although the generals are justified in lamenting this unfortunate situation, their outrage is a bit disingenuous. They themselves are the ones who dictate the outlines of the political system, and they have shaped it so that parties reflect military ideas of order and discipline. Conditioned by their training, they like dealing with a handful of autocrats and are repelled by the brawling untidiness of open politics. Laws that govern Turkish political parties, including those that make it all but impossible to challenge or depose party leaders, were inspired by the generals themselves. So was Article 68 of the constitution, which allows the banning of any party whose program is found to conflict with "the democratic and secular order." And beyond these laws is the memory of three coups staged by the military, the execution of a prime minister and the jailing and humiliation of hundreds of politicians, along with the knowledge that dissidents have little legal protection from the vengeance of the ruling elite. With its array of spoken and unspoken laws, this system allows generals to control politicians and, ultimately, the course of the nation.

To ensure that the public does not stray too far from the ruling ideology, not only the political system but also the press must be brought to heel. In Turkey this is done with marvelous efficiency. The most potent weapon in the state's hand is a set of laws that allow reporters and editors to be imprisoned, newspapers to be closed and radio or television stations to be silenced if they challenge any aspect of the ruling dogma. Beyond those laws is the structure of the press itself, which functions not as an independent watchdog or critic but as a conscious part of the ruling system. Publishers readily accept guidance from the state about what should and should not be published, even to the point of suspending or firing columnists about whom the generals complain.

Eighty percent of the total circulation of Turkish newspapers and many of the country's most powerful broadcast outlets have traditionally been controlled by two industrial groups that together function very much like a cartel. Under a gentlemen's agreement between these groups, no reporter or columnist fired by one may be hired by the other.

Their collaboration with each other and with the ruling elite is dictated not simply by misguided patriotism but also by crude economic interests. The cartel that runs the news business is also involved in a host of other enterprises, from real estate to power generation, that succeed or fail according to Ankara's whim. Thus do press barons join generals and leaders of political parties as key figures in the maintenance of the status quo.

Turks do not torment themselves by asking endlessly how they can push the army and its allies away from politics. They know the answer. All they need to do is elect a capable and united government that could assert civilian power. Such a government would be able to act without much resistance. Certainly the army is not willing to surrender its power to make key decisions, and someday that may lead to a confrontation. But today military commanders would give up much of their political power without a fight. Unlike commanders in countries under military dictatorship, they are not grasping to dominate every aspect of society. They seem genuinely to regret that they must intervene so often, and would welcome a strong civilian regime that would allow them to concentrate on military matters. Such a regime, however, is only beginning to take shape.

The larger reason for this state of affairs, beyond the structural weakness of Turkey's political system, lies in the nation's deep uncertainty about its identity and future. Should it look east or west, turn toward its Asian or its European heritage, take the risks of democracy or remain wrapped in comfortable paternalism? Many of today's Turkish leaders believe the Ottoman Empire was brought down by treacherous citizens who joined with foreign powers to extract special privileges from the state or to break away from it entirely. They fear that if they yield to the rising demand for recognition of Turkey's political, social, religious and ethnic diversity, the Republic will ultimately be dismembered and collapse just as the empire did.

One day, especially if Turkey moves closer to joining the European Union, the ruling elite will have to embrace democracy fully and without reservation. That will mean abandoning the system under which the Republic has been governed since its foundation. Most important, it will require that military commanders surrender all their influence over pol-

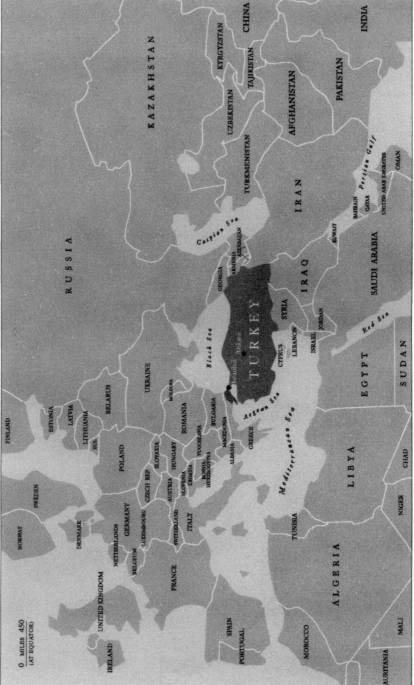

itics and, by extension, abandon their belief that they know what is best for Turkey. Before that can happen, Turks must finally succeed in building the civic consensus that has eluded them for so long. If they are able to do so, they will have the political and moral authority to demand that they finally be set free to shape their own destiny.

This would be a grand challenge for any country, but it is especially important that Turkey succeed because that success would have such profound effects in Europe, the Middle East and beyond. Though Turkey has looked inward for most of its short life, it has begun to share its cultural riches and make a serious mark on geopolitics and the world economy. A truly modern Turkey governed by the rule of law would raise the Turkish people to levels of prosperity and self-confidence they have never known before. Despite this country's political and psychological underdevelopment, it has the resources to become a towering power. If it can liberate itself from its paralyzing fears and embrace true democracy, it will also serve as a magnetic example of how the ideals of liberty can triumph over enormous obstacles. By adding moral strength to its military strength, Turkey could become a dominant force in the Middle East, encouraging peace and pulling Arab countries away from the social backwardness and feudal dictatorship under which most of them now suffer. It could exert a mighty and stabilizing influence westward to the Balkans and eastward to the Caucasus and Central Asia, becoming the key power in a region that is strategically vital, overwhelmingly rich in oil and other resources and now ruled mostly by tyrants who are dragging it toward chaos.

As a result of geography and because of their Ottoman past, Turks occupy a singular position in the Islamic consciousness. If any country is going to prove that Islam can coexist with modernity and democracy, it will almost certainly be Turkey. That achievement would make Turkey an invaluable countervailing force against religious fundamentalism everywhere. As a real democracy, Turkey would be a shining beacon not only for Muslims in nearby countries but for the entire Islamic world. Its example would be immensely important to the more than one billion people who live in the fifty-six predominantly Muslim countries stretching from Morocco to Indonesia. If Turkey can entice those countries toward democracy, it will reshape the entire world.

By embracing democratic principles Turkey would also qualify for membership in the European Union, which would be a historic breakthrough for Turkey itself and also bring Europe a badly needed injection of youthful energy. By embracing rather than denying its ethnic diversity, it would show the world, as the United States has done, what great benefits accrue to richly diverse societies. Once again, as during the Ottoman centuries, it would stand like a colossus at the point where two continents come together, drawing riches from both and offering itself as a meeting point for civilizations that might otherwise drift toward calamitous confrontation.

Whenever I sit in a café beside the Bosphorus I sense the power of Turkey's geography. Behind me lie Paris, Berlin and London. Across the narrow waterway is Asia, an unbroken land mass stretching from the streets of Istanbul to Baghdad, Delhi and Beijing. The Black Sea, gateway to Russia and the Slavic world, is a few miles to the north. To the south lies the wine-dark Mediterranean, most storied of seas, which washes the shores of Europe and Africa. Turkey's own heartland, Anatolia, is a paradise of dreamy coasts and coves, vast fruited plains, thick forests, deep lakes, raging rivers and soaring mountain ranges. This country is the great bridge between East and West, North and South. Seen another way, it is a barrier protecting Europe from the tides of political upheaval and religious extremism.

Turkey is an easy country to appreciate, but not such an easy country to help. Its leaders are proud, sensitive and quick to take offense. They don't make things easy for their friends. So the great question facing Americans and others who sympathize with Turkey is: What can we do to encourage Turkey to become the kind of country we can help without reservation?

Outside pressure on Turkey has proven effective. The United States has applied it discreetly, maintaining a strong military relationship while seeking gently to promote the values of tolerance and free choice. European leaders have taken a more direct approach, denouncing Turkey's human-rights abuses and publicly lamenting its failure to meet modern democratic standards. For many years this approach seemed unproductive, but now that Turkey has been officially designated as a candidate for membership in the European Union, there is a very concrete reason for its leaders to listen. If they can meet Europe's high standards, they will be rewarded with a huge prize that will guarantee them generations of freedom and fulfillment.

Turkey's success in creating a genuinely democratic space in a part of the world where there has traditionally been very little democracy is a historic achievement. It is, however, still incomplete. To fulfill its destiny, Turkey must create a democracy that shines not just by regional standards but by world standards.

This transformation will require more than mere political reform. It will require Turks to change the way they view themselves and their relationship to society. In Turkey the individual is considered less important than the collective, but the collective is the family or village or clan rather than the nation. There is little civic or environmental consciousness. Few people feel that they have a stake in society or care much about contributing to it.

Time and again I have stepped off an ugly or dirty Turkish street, passed through a portal and entered an immaculate and lovingly kept home. The contrast is striking, often amazing. Whether because of their nomadic past in Central Asia or as a response to their centuries of life under autocratic rule, many Turks still believe that life is to be lived within the family or clan. They feel no true allegiance to national goals and aspirations.

A classic Turkish village has no central plaza or square. In other parts of the world such public spaces encourage people to come together to crystallize their ideas and realize their collective power, to speak out, argue and protest. But in Turkey, allowing people to do that has always seemed vaguely dangerous. Turks gather to eat, drink and smoke, and sometimes to chat in front of the local mosque, but most of them do not enjoy the public space that has been the incubator of popular movements in other parts of the world.

Turkish leaders have sought to bind their people together by creating a concept called *devlet*. Over the years this has become my least favorite Turkish word. The dictionary says it means "state," but it also means something much uglier. *Devlet* is an omnipotent entity that stands above every citizen and every institution. Loyalty to it is held to be every Turk's most fundamental obligation, and questioning it is considered treasonous. No one ever defines what *devlet* means; everyone is supposed to know. Its guardians are a self-perpetuating elite—the generals, police chiefs, prosecutors, judges, political bosses and press barons who decide what *devlet* demands of the citizenry. This elite has written many laws to help it do what it perceives as its duty, and when necessary it acts outside the law. In its collective mind, serving *devlet* is a responsibility so transcendent and sublime that not even law may be allowed to obstruct it.

The reason that freethinkers must be imprisoned in Turkey is not simply because they speak against hallowed principles but because they threaten *devlet*. This *devlet* is much more than an abstract concept, much more than a focal point for national unity. It is Turkey's apocalyptic swordsman, the repressive mentality that overwhelms, constricts and suffocates the citizenry.

Many Turks who serve *devlet* are truly selfless. They consider themselves Atatürk's heirs and servants and are utterly convinced that their ceaseless vigilance is all that stands between Turkey and disaster. One of them, Vural Savaş, who for much of the 1990s was the country's most zealous prosecutor, was once asked why he worked so tirelessly to close political parties and imprison politicians and journalists. He replied, "One simply has to know how to say no." That was a wonderfully precise answer, because saying no is the main duty of *devlet*. Saying yes to *devlet* means saying no to dissent, no to iconoclasm, no to new ideas, no to the kind of boldness and daring that propelled Atatürk to greatness. In the end, it means saying no to the possibility of Turkey rising to fulfill what could be a glorious historic mission.

Another fervent member of this secular priesthood, General Doğu Silahcıoğlu, once met with elected officials in Samsun, a provincial capital on the Black Sea coast, as they were making plans for a patriotic celebration. One city councillor ventured the opinion that since Samsun is home to people from various ethnic groups and Muslims of various persuasions, the celebration should emphasize the value of tolerance. That suggestion touched the general's rawest nerve.

"Tolerance!" he shouted. "Tolerance is the password of those people with a certain ideology. You cannot use this word here!"

That too was a perfectly concise expression of *devlet*. Its defenders detest the notion of tolerance because they believe tolerance will allow the spread of ideas that will ultimately kill Turkey. They consider themselves the truest defenders of Turkish democracy because they work day and night to suppress ideas and forces and people who want to destroy that democracy. More than a few Turks, conditioned as they are to obey and not protest, agree that although *devlet* is an arbitrary and often unfair institution, it is also indispensable.

In today's Turkey, no two words are as fundamentally contradictory as *istiklal* and *devlet*. The first stands not just for national independence but for the freedom and progress that independent thought brings to any society that encourages it. The second is a dark force that represents fear, mistrust and arrogance. It keeps Turkey in chains. For Turkey to live, *devlet* must die.

Without surrendering its unique identity, Turkey must find a way to break out of its political immobility. The world has changed radically since the fall of the Berlin Wall, and in many ways so has Turkey. It is an incomparably freer and more open society than it was a generation ago. But still it lags behind the countries that are its natural friends and allies. More and more of its citizens chafe under the restrictive order that so relentlessly limits their progress as a nation. If they can find a way to break free, Turkey will astonish the world by becoming the most audaciously successful nation of the twenty-first century.

The first friends I made in Turkey told me that if I really wanted to understand their country, I would have to drink a lot of rakı. These were wise people, so I took their advice. Every year the annual level of rakı consumption in Turkey rises by slightly more than one million liters, and my contribution to the increase has not been inconsiderable.

In the bottle rakı is absolutely clear, but it is rarely consumed that way. Instead it is mixed with water, which turns it translucent. Drinking it has the same effect on one's perception of Turkey. After a glass or two, what at first seemed clear becomes obscure. By the time the bottle is empty, everything appears murky and confused. Yet through this evocative haze, truths about Turkey may be most profoundly understood.

Many countries have national drinks, but rakı is much more than that because it embodies the very concept of Turkey. The mere fact that a Muslim land would fall under the spell of a powerful distilled drink is enough to suggest this nation's unexpected and tantalizing appeal. Do not speak to a Turk about ouzo or other anise-based drinks supposed to reflect the characters of other lands. The careful mix of natural ingredients in rakı and the loving process by which it is distilled, they believe, make it gloriously unique.

History books say that Mustafa Kemal Atatürk died from the effects *of overindulgence in* rakı. *That is only partly true. In fact he died from an overdose of Turkey. His involvement with Turkey, like his involvement with* rakı, *was so passionate and so intense that it ultimately consumed him.*

The same almost happened to me. I had admired Turkey from afar, but it was only after long nights drinking rakı *with friends that I came to understand the true audacity of the Turkish idea. Its grandeur and beauty filled me with awe. My excitement rose with each glass as I realized how much Turkey has to share with the world, to give the world, to teach the world.*

I should have stopped there, but you never do with rakı. *That is its blessing and its curse. As months and years passed,* rakı *began to work subtly on my mind. Slowly the delight I had found in discovering Turkey became mixed with other, more ambiguous emotions. No longer did my evenings end with the exhilarating sensation that I had found a jewel of a country poised on the brink of greatness.* Rakı *led me inexorably toward frustration and doubt. It never shook my conviction that Turkey is a nation of unlimited potential, but it did lead me to wonder why so much of its potential remains unrealized. Turkey is undoubtedly the country of the future, but will it always be? Can it ever become what it hopes to be, or is it condemned to remain an unfulfilled dream, an exquisite fantasy that contains within it the seeds of its own failure?*

There are as yet no answers to those questions, and therein lies the Turkish conundrum. This nation is still very much a work in progress, a dazzling kaleidoscope of competing images and ideas. Born of trauma and upheaval, it remains deeply insecure, shrouded in old fears and uncertain which direction it should take.

This identity crisis led to a near-collapse of the rakı *tradition in the 1960s and 1970s. Turkey was opening itself to the world, and a class of educated and sophisticated Turks was emerging. These people considered* rakı *anathema because it symbolized the primitive mentality of rural peasants. If illiterate hillbillies wanted to drink it in their broken-down shacks, that was one thing, but no modern Turk would do so; much better to sip wine, cognac or some other drink with a European pedigree.*

Fortunately, those days are past. Turks no longer feel embarrassed to embrace their heritage and identity. Drinking rakı is an ideal way to do so while at the same time enjoying a sublime pleasure.

Rakı is the key to Turkey, not because of the drink itself but because of the circumstances in which one consumes it. This is not a drink like whiskey, useful for solitary reflection; not like beer, good for drinking in a noisy bar while munching on pretzels; and not like gin or vodka, lubricants for cocktail-party chatter. Bars and cocktail parties are, in fact, mortal enemies of the Turkish drinking tradition. Resistance to these pernicious influences is centered around the meyhane, a sort of bistro created especially for rakı drinking. The meyhane is a temple of Turkish cuisine, but it is also a place where people meet, talk, debate, embrace and lament. Turkey's diversity is most tangible at the meyhane because it is spread out on tables for all to see.

An evening at a meyhane is centered around rakı, but rakı never stands alone. It is only one component, albeit the essential one, of a highly stylized ritual. With rakı always come meze, small plates of food that appear stealthily, a few at a time. Theoretically, meze are appetizers leading to a main course, but often the main course, like Turkey's supposedly great destiny, never materializes. No one complains about that because eating meze while sipping rakı is such a supreme pleasure in itself. The path is so blissful that the idea of a destination seems somehow sacrilegious.

Meze usually come in waves. The first will include salad, thick slabs of white cheese, smoked eggplant purée and honeydew melon. What comes next depends on the chef's whim. There might be a selection of cooked, cooled vegetables in olive oil, each presented on its own miniature platter, or small dolma, which are peppers stuffed with rice, currants and pine nuts, and their close cousins, sarma, made from grape or cabbage leaves. After the next pause might come spicy red lentil balls, mussels on the half shell, mashed beans with lemon sauce, puréed fish roe, yogurt seasoned with garlic and dill, raw tuna fillets, poached mackerel with hazelnut paste or an explosively flavorful dish made of baby eggplants stuffed with garlic cloves, tomatoes, sliced onion and parsley. This last is called Imam Bayıldı, meaning "the Imam fainted."

After these come piping-hot börek, delicate pastries filled with feta cheese and sometimes also spinach, diced chicken, ground lamb or veal, pistachios, walnuts or whatever else is lying around the kitchen. Some are layered, others triangular and still others cylindrical or crescent-shaped. Often they are served with squid rings fried in a light batter, which are to be dipped in a white sauce made from wine vinegar, olive oil and garlic.

Turkey's ethnic vitality shines through as the evening proceeds. Kebabs and other meze made from meat recall the Central Asian steppes from which nomadic Turkic tribes migrated to Asia Minor, now called Anatolia, a thousand years ago. With them come hummus from Arabia, shredded chicken with walnuts from the Caucasus, diced liver from Albania and cooked cheese thickened with corn flour from coastal villages along the Black Sea. Then comes the crowning glory, the seafood, a gift from the Greeks, who for millennia did all the cooking along what is now Turkey's Aegean coast. Rakı sharpens the taste of all food, but its magic works best with fish. An old proverb calls rakı the pimp that brings fish and men together for acts of love.

The variety of fish in Turkey seems endless. It changes according to what body of water is nearest and also according to the season. Always the fish is very fresh, and always it is prepared very simply, grilled or pan-fried and served with no sauce, only a lemon wedge and perhaps a slice of onion or sprig of parsley.

Such a meal is a microcosm of Turkey. It is an astonishingly rich experience but yields its secrets slowly. Patrons at a meyhane, like all Turks, confront an ever-changing mosaic, endless variations on a theme. Each meze tastes different, has its own color, aroma, texture and character. The full effect is comparable to that of a symphony, complete with melodies, different rhythms, pacing and flashes of virtuosity, all contained within an overarching structure.

Meze make a feast, but drinking rakı with them raises the experience to a truly transcendent level. "All the senses are involved," my friend Aydın Boysan, an architect and bon vivant who had been drinking rakı for more than sixty years when I met him, told me during a long night we spent at a meyhane overlooking the Bosphorus. "First you watch the water being poured into the glass and mixing with the rakı. Then you pick up the glass and inhale the aroma. When you drink it, you take a small sip, feel the pleasure of it flowing down your throat, take another small sip, then put the glass down."

Aydin demonstrated this ritual to me, seeming to enjoy it every bit as much as he might have half a century earlier, and then closed his eyes for a moment. "The best part is feeling it go down your throat," he said lovingly. "A giraffe—that's an animal ideally made to appreciate rakı."

The meyhane *culture tells a great deal about Turkey. Like the country, it offers almost infinite possibilities because it blends the heritage of so many different peoples. It encourages discourse and deepens friendship, but because the food is brought unbidden by a waiter instead of ordered from a menu, it does not require any action, any decision, any act of choice other than turning away dishes that do not strike one's fancy. Rakı can evoke either determination or resignation, a desire to rebel or an acceptance of the inevitability of submission.*

At a meyhane, *the world can either be invited in or shut out. Turks have not yet decided which is the wisest path. By the time they drain their final glasses and step out into the darkness, they have often concluded that their country is either the "golden nation" destined to shape world history or a hopeless mess certain to remain mired in wretched mediocrity.*

TWO

THE HERO

C⋆

One of my Turkish friends is a proud father who has saved the first essay his son ever wrote. The boy was a third-grader when his teacher explained to the class what an essay is, read a few simple ones aloud and then assigned her pupils the topic "love" for their first try. His essay began like this: "Love means love for Atatürk. Love means love for Atatürk's mother, Zübeyde Hanim. Love means love for Atatürk's father, Ali Rıza Bey."

By instinctively associating the deepest human emotion with the person of Mustafa Kemal Atatürk, this young boy showed how fully he had already absorbed the holy creed of the Turks. According to its constitution, Turkey is a secular state with no official religion. But the truth is that Turks profess, and must profess, a highly developed faith enveloping and defining every aspect of their lives. It is the cult of Atatürk, founder of the Turkish Republic and now a virtual deity.

The Atatürk faith, known as Kemalism, has its churches, dozens of houses and rooms around the country where the Great Man slept, spoke or ate; its holy writ, scores of adoring books, poems and films in which his exploits are recounted; its icons, countless portraits, busts, plaques and statues that are to be seen even in the remotest corners of the country; and its clergy, the military and political elite, faithful beyond measure and ceaselessly on the watch for apostates. It also has its holy center, its Vatican, its Mecca. On a hillside near the center of Ankara, imposing and lugubrious behind a wall of forbidding quadrangular columns, stands a combination mausoleum, museum and cathedral beneath whose marble floor Atatürk's body lies interred. On national holidays, the gravest of which is November 10, the day on which he departed this world, huge throngs gather to pay tearful homage to his memory and pledge eternal fidelity to his cause. Visiting heads of state are expected to lay wreaths upon the tomb before they begin their official business. Generals come regularly to rededicate themselves to their role as Kemalism's high priests. Politicians and others who fall under suspicion of heresy unfailingly turn up as a way of proving that they do, in fact, embrace the true faith.

"In this country it is allowed to say bad things about God," one young man told me confidentially soon after I arrived in Turkey, "but it is not allowed to say bad things about Atatürk."

There is much to justify Turkey's reverence for Atatürk. He is the force that allowed Turkey to rise from the ashes of defeat and emerge as a vibrant new nation. Without Atatürk's vision, without his ambition and energy, without his astonishing boldness in sweeping away traditions accumulated over centuries, today's Turkey would not exist and the world would be much poorer.

Kemalism emerged at a time when new ideologies were being born from the rubble of a world laid waste by the Great War of 1914–18. Fascism, national socialism and bolshevism have been swept away by history, leaving behind a heritage of immeasurable suffering and pain, but Kemalism remains triumphant, modern Turkey its crowning glory. Trying to understand Turkey without understanding Atatürk would be like studying European history without considering Christianity.

Yet a century after Atatürk began his rise to power, the Kemalist faith is in crisis. Its promise of liberation, so vividly fulfilled at the beginning, is fading. Once it embodied reason and progress, the purest principles of the Enlightenment. "For everything in the world—for civilization, for life, for success—the truest guide is knowledge and science," Atatürk declared in one famous speech. But today, many Turks who seek knowledge find themselves victims of Kemalism rather than its paragons.

The man around whom this passionate faith was built remains largely unknown outside his homeland. Perhaps that is because upon assuming power, he concentrated his efforts on building his own nation rather than on conquest. Perhaps it is simply because Turkey has remained for so long on the fringes of the world's consciousness. Whatever the reason, Atatürk's obscurity is unfortunate. He deserves to be recognized and celebrated as one of the twentieth century's most successful revolutionaries. The story of his life and the story of what has become of his legacy embody both Turkey's greatest glories and its most daunting challenges.

This titanic figure was born in 1880 or 1881 to a humble family in Salonika, now the Greek city of Thessaloniki, a thriving port on the outer edge of the crumbling Ottoman Empire. His father was a minor clerk in government service who died young and unhappy. His mother was the family's guiding force, and like many Turkish mothers, Zübeyde Hanim doted on her son. At first he seemed a difficult case, truculent and rebellious, often in trouble at school. Zübeyde, a traditional Muslim woman who spent most of her time at home and was never seen without her head scarf, hoped that he would become a religious teacher or Koran reader. Young Mustafa never showed the slightest interest in following that path. An uncle suggested that he pursue a military career, and with the help of a retired officer who had been a friend of his father, he arranged to take the entrance examination that led to his admission into the local academy. There he took a surname, Kemal, supposedly after the radical nineteenth-century poet Namık Kemal, one of whose couplets was later to spur him into action:

The enemy has pressed his dagger to the breast of the motherland.
Will no one arise to save his mother from her black fate?

As Mustafa Kemal rose rapidly through military ranks, the decadent Ottoman monarchy was in its death throes. The reigning sultan, Abdülhamid II, was an intolerant and narrow-minded tyrant who countenanced no talk of reform. His empire was shrinking steadily, and in 1912 Kemal himself had the chance to watch Balkan rebels win their independence after easily defeating a demoralized Turkish force twice their size. Even the city of his birth fell to advancing Greek patriots shouting "Christ is risen!"

During postings in Istanbul, Tripoli, Cairo, Damascus and Sofia, and in trips to Germany and Austria, Kemal became aware of the wider world and the currents that were surging through it. He learned French and devoured the works of Voltaire and Rousseau, together with translations of Thomas Hobbes and John Stuart Mill. They helped him grasp the great challenge that was to shape his life. "The Turkish nation has fallen far behind the West," he told a German officer he met in the Balkans. "The main aim should be to lead it to modern civilization."

While still a young officer, Kemal became a clandestine operative for a subversive group founded in the 1890s and known as the Committee of Union and Progress; the world called its members Young Turks. In 1913 the Committee managed to seize key posts in the Ottoman regime, but war broke out before its work could begin in earnest. Some Young Turks believed that if their country allied itself with Germany, the two powers could ride a wave of re-colonization that would allow both to pursue their imperial dreams. One of them, Minister of Defense Enver Pasha, whose irredentist passion was later to lead the Ottoman Empire to its end and himself to ignominious death while fighting to reclaim Central Asia for the Turks, met secretly with German envoys in a mansion on the shore of the Bosphorus and signed a pact of alliance.

Turkey's experience as an ally of Kaiser Wilhelm's Germany was disastrous, with one shining exception. To the astonishment of Europe and the world, in 1915 a Turkish force managed to resist and then repel British-led invaders whose battle plan had been drawn up by no less a personage than First Lord of the Admiralty Winston Churchill. The battle was fought on the Gallipoli Peninsula overlooking the crucial Dardanelles strait, which the Allies needed to capture if they hoped to control Istanbul and the Black Sea beyond. In fierce fighting that lasted eight months and cost tens of thousands of lives, Turkish soldiers managed to hold their peninsula, keep their strait and ultimately overwhelm the Allied expeditionary force. The commander who achieved this, thereby winning the only important Turkish victory of the war, was Mustafa Kemal. Alone among Turkish officers, he emerged from the Great War as a hero.

With the war ending in defeat for the Germans and their Turkish allies, the German imperial monarchy was overthrown and the once-glorious Ottoman Empire lay prostrate. Triumphant Allied leaders presumed they had won the right to carve up its rich carcass, a huge tract of land stretching from southeastern Europe to the frosty Caucasus and parched Arabian deserts. Under the guidance of Prime Minister Lloyd George of Great Britain, they decreed that all Turkish territory in Europe, together with most of the lush Aegean coast, where Hellenic civilization had flourished for millennia, would be given to Greece. Armenians and Kurds would be given the chance to form new states in the east. France was awarded a vast "zone of influence" in the south, abutting its territory in what is now Syria. Italy won an even larger zone that encompassed the entire Mediterranean coast and thousands of square miles inland. Istanbul, along with the Bosphorus and the Dardanelles, for which Kemal had fought so brilliantly, was to be placed under international control. All that remained for the Turks themselves was a swath of central Anatolia, much of it mountainous and inhospitable. This was a settlement even more punishing than the one imposed on Germany at Versailles. Three emissaries from the sultan signed it without protest at a ceremony in the Paris suburb of Sèvres on August 10, 1920.

There seemed no way the Turks could resist. Their army was defeated and leaderless, their sultan dispirited and willing to accept the victorious Allies' every dictate. Foreign troops occupied their most historic cities. A French commander had ridden into Istanbul on a white horse, just as Sultan Mehmet the Conqueror had when his Ottoman army captured the city nearly five centuries earlier. Italian forces had landed at Antalya, gateway to the Turkish Mediterranean, and the Greek army had occupied Smyrna, the jewel of Turkey's Aegean coast, and begun annexing the land around it.

As the only Turkish commander with a major battlefield victory to his credit, and a magnificent one at that, Mustafa Kemal was the logical figure around whom this defeated nation could rally. He eagerly embraced the savior's role, winning the loyalty of disaffected officers and denouncing the dying regime in terms so contemptuous that its courts sentenced him to death in absentia. "Cowards, criminals! You are engaged in treasonable conspiracies with the enemy against the nation," he wrote in one telegram to the Ottoman interior minister. "I did not doubt that you would be incapable of appreciating the strength and will of the nation; but I did not want to believe that you would act in this traitorous and murderous way against the fatherland and the nation."

Seeing their homeland on the brink of dismemberment, Turks by the thousands flocked to Kemal's side. He established a National Assembly and shadow government of his own, built an army of eager volunteers and declared war on the foreign powers occupying Anatolia. A chastened Winston Churchill later wrote:

> Loaded with follies, stained with crimes, rotted with misgovernment, shattered by battle, worn down by long disastrous wars, his Empire falling to pieces around him, the Turk was still alive. In his breast was beating the heart of a race that had challenged the world, and for centuries had contended victoriously against all comers. In his hands was once again the equipment of a modern army, and at his head a Captain, who with all that is learned of him, ranks with the four or five great figures of the cataclysm. In the tapestried and gilded chambers of Paris were assembled the law-givers of the world. In Constantinople, under the guns of the Allied Fleets there functioned a puppet Government of Turkey. But among the stern hills and valleys of "the Turkish homeland" in Anatolia, there dwelt that company of poor men . . . who would not see it settled so; and at their bivouac fires at this moment sat in the rags of a refugee the august Spirit of Fair Play.

Kemal's first assaults on positions held by his main adversaries, the Greeks, did not go well. Later he and his growing force returned, better armed and organized, and won several important victories. Finally, in the summer of 1922, the tide turned decisively in their favor. Whipped into a patriotic frenzy by their gifted commander, Turkish troops stormed from their Anatolian heartland toward the Aegean, driving the Greek force before them in frantic retreat and finally pushing it into the sea. Allied contingents posted at the Dardanelles withdrew rather than face this newly self-confident army. French and Italian units along the Mediterranean wisely followed suit. In one of the most astonishing military reversals of modern history, Kemal had turned utter defeat into brilliant triumph, ripping to shreds the Sèvres treaty under which modern Turkey was to have been aborted before it could be born.

A new treaty recognizing new realities now had to be negotiated to replace the one that had been imposed at Sèvres. Its signing in 1922 at Lausanne signaled the arrival on the world scene of two powerful new phenomena: the Republic of Turkey and Mustafa Kemal. Turkey emerged with all the land that the Sèvres treaty had awarded to Greece, Italy, the Kurds and the Armenians, along with most of what had been the French zone. Kemal did not insist on taking Greek islands, many of which are far from Greece and within sight of the Turkish mainland, but he did win a good-size chunk of land on the western side of the Bosphorus, giving the new nation a firm foothold in Europe, where the Ottoman Empire had once controlled much territory. The country he took over was in ruins, devastated not only by war but by the horrible consequences of a "population exchange" agreed upon by Greek and Turkish leaders, in which hundreds of thousands of ethnic Greeks were forced to leave their homes in Turkey, taking their skills with them. Nonetheless, after Lausanne Turks had a homeland where they could work, build and begin to rise again.

With this amazing victory, Kemal had summoned his nation out of the coffin in which it was about to be buried. That alone would have been enough to earn him a secure place in history. But after emerging as Turkey's liberator, he went on to even more extraordinary achievements. The first of them was not something he did, but something he chose not to do: build on his triumph in Anatolia to push farther. He might well have sought to retake European parts of the old empire, at least seizing the city of his birth back from the exhausted Greeks. Or he might have turned eastward, joining with Muslims in Central Asia who were resisting assimilation into the nascent Soviet Union. Instead he renounced pan-Islamic and pan-Turkic ideologies, resisted the expansionist temptation that has brought down so many leaders and took off his military uniform once and forever. Looking about him, he saw a backward nation of twelve million people mired in poverty and ignorance. "The civilized world is far ahead of us," he proclaimed, echoing the view he had first expressed as a cadet. "We have no choice but to catch up."

Perhaps alone in Turkey and even the world, Mustafa Kemal believed that Turks could become everything they had never been: modern, secular, prosperous and, above all, truly European. He became a one-man revolution, pushing and dragging a baffled and sometimes resistant nation toward the radical vision that blazed in his imagination. Earthquake, bomb, whirlwind, cyclone, tornado, tidal wave—none of these metaphors can capture the force of Kemal's impact on his nation.

With no official power, using only the moral authority he had won on the battlefield, Kemal in 1922 ordered his rubber-stamp National Assembly to abolish the Ottoman monarchy. Not even his closest comrades had ever contemplated such a step. "It was by force that the sons of Osman seized the sovereignty and sultanate of the Turkish nation," he told the astonished Assembly. "They have maintained this usurpation for six centuries. Now the Turkish nation has rebelled, has put a stop to these usurpers, and has effectively taken sovereignty and sultanate into its own hands."

On October 29, 1923, the Assembly proclaimed the Turkish Republic and unanimously elected Kemal as its first president. He was forty-two years old, a dashing figure with fair hair and piercing blue eyes, always dressed impeccably from his dandy cravat down to his imported French underwear. His pleasures, like his politics, were Western: dancing, drinking, smoking cigarettes, visiting restaurants and night clubs, swimming, yachting and seducing women. Since childhood he had been absolutely convinced that he was destined for greatness. "History has proven incontrovertibly," he asserted after taking power, "that success in great enterprises requires the presence of a leader of unshakable capacity and power."

Having abolished the Ottoman regime with the stroke of a pen, Kemal set his sights on an even more sacred institution, the Islamic caliphate. For centuries the caliph had been revered by Muslims everywhere as "God's shadow on earth," and had used his power for political as well as religious ends. For many years the sultan had served simultaneously as caliph, embodying the Ottoman theocracy and ruling with divine as well as earthly authority. But late on the night of March 3, 1924, only sixteen months after the last sultan, Mehmet VI Vahidettin, had fled Istanbul on a British warship, his cousin Abdülmecid, who had been

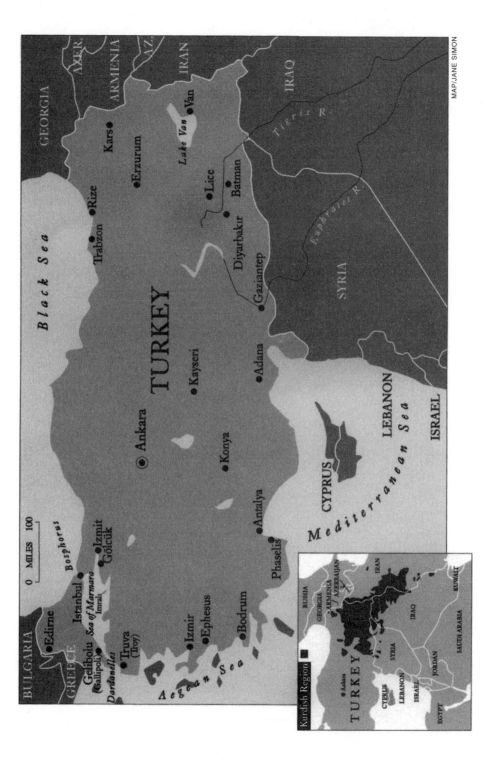

chosen to succeed him as caliph, was visited by an emissary from Atatürk, told that the National Assembly had voted to abolish the caliphate, put aboard a train and packed into exile. This crushing blow to religious power was quickly followed by the dissolution of Islamic courts and a ban on religious brotherhoods. With the same reckless daring he had shown on the battlefield, Kemal had torn down the central pillars of Ottoman political and religious tradition.

After moving his new government to Ankara, a small Anatolian town far from the pleasure domes of Istanbul and infinitely closer to the masses in whose name he was ruling, Kemal continued his demolition work. His next target was the fez, the crimson headgear with a flat top designed to resemble a prayer mat and a tassel meant to symbolize the prospect of escape to Heaven. The fez had been a symbol of Muslim identity in the Ottoman world, but to Kemal it was "an emblem of ignorance, negligence, fanaticism, and hatred of progress and civilization." His will, as ever, was quickly translated into law, and in November 1925 the fez was banned.

"A civilized, international dress is worthy and appropriate for our nation, and we will wear it," Kemal declared. "Boots or shoes on our feet, trousers on our legs, shirt and tie, jacket and waistcoat—and, of course, to complete these, a cover with a brim on our heads. I want to make this clear. This head-covering is called 'hat.'"

Shock waves from this act spread across Turkey and beyond. The chief mufti of Egypt, who since the abolition of the caliphate had become a leading voice of orthodox Islam, proclaimed that any Muslim who wore a hat was an infidel and a sinner, and asserted that the wearing of hats would lead to "the annihilation of our own identity." Such challenges only stirred Kemal to new vigor. Why stop with banning the garb that Islamic men had worn for centuries? The veil must also go, and with it the subservience of women.

"In some places I have seen women who put a piece of cloth or a towel or something like it over their heads to hide their faces, and who turn their backs or huddle themselves on the ground when a man passes by," Kemal said in one speech. "What are the meaning and sense of this behavior? Gentlemen, can the mothers and daughters of a civilized nation adopt this strange manner, this barbarous posture? It is a spectacle that makes the nation an object of ridicule. It must be remedied at once."

Although the veil was not officially banned for several more years, by attacking it Kemal had made clear that he considered nothing sacred simply because it was long-established. Indeed, the opposite seemed to be true. At the end of 1925 he decreed that the Muslim calendar should be replaced with the European one, which dates years from the birth of Christ. The next year he imposed a version of the Swiss civil code that banned polygamy, permitted the marriage of Muslim women to non-Muslim men, gave all adults the right to change their religion and replaced the Muslim practice of "repudiation" with civil divorce (though not before he took advantage of it to "repudiate" his own wife). Later he shifted the weekly day of rest from Friday to Sunday. Finally, in case the point was lost on anyone, his Assembly repealed the constitutional clause stipulating that "the religion of the Turkish state is Islam."

One of the last tangible links connecting Turkey to its Ottoman past and to the rest of the Muslim world, while at the same time separating it from the West, was Arabic script. Turks had always had their own language, but for many centuries had written it with Arabic characters. Breaking with that tradition would mean cutting Turks off from the rich cultural heritage of their ancestors, making it impossible for them to read the words of their own poets, scientists and philosophers. This disturbed Kemal not a whit. He convened a group of specialists to transliterate the Turkish language into Latin letters, and introduced the new alphabet himself at a gala party to which he invited the country's leading figures.

"We must free ourselves from these incomprehensible signs which for centuries have held our minds in an iron vice," he told them. "Our nation will show, with its script and with its mind, that its place is with the civilized world."

Kemal took fewer years to wipe away the defining traditions of Turkish life than centuries had been spent building them. Some of the steps he took were relatively innocuous, such as introducing the metric system and opening a conservatory under the direction of the German composer Paul Hindemith. Others were momentous but grudgingly accepted, such as giving women the rights to vote and hold office. A few were so bitterly resisted that they were ultimately repealed, including a ban on the broadcast of Oriental music and a decree that the *ezan*, the Muslim call to prayer, must be chanted in Turkish rather than Arabic. None of them, however, could have been imposed if Turkey had been a democracy. Great as Kemal's personal prestige was, it alone could not have made his revolution possible. Demolishing the legacy of an ancient nation so suddenly, and imposing such a completely new order on the rubble, required the use of much raw power. Kemal did not shrink from using it.

During the War of Liberation, as Kemal's uprising against the Sèvres treaty came to be known, everyone who wanted to fight against foreign occupiers was welcomed into the revolutionary army. After the war was won, however, Kemal did not hesitate to crush former allies who opposed his radical program. The first challenge came in 1925 from Kurdish tribesmen in the east, who rose up in the name of Islam and called upon God to help them chase the infidels from Ankara. Immediately a "law for the maintenance of order" was pushed through the National Assembly, giving Kemal's government dictatorial powers and establishing "independence courts" with powers of summary execution. Among the first victims were leaders of the Kurdish rebellion; forty-seven were captured, tried and hanged at Diyarbakır, the main Kurdish city. A year later, plotters who sought to assassinate Kemal in the Aegean port of Izmir, formerly known as Smyrna, were sentenced and executed in the same manner. Later the web spread to more peaceful opponents. In all, the "independence courts" dispatched several hundred enemies and critics of the regime. Some victims did not even enjoy its dubious justice. Eighteen leaders of the Turkish Communist party were put aboard a ship in Trabzon for deportation across the Black Sea to the Soviet Union, but they disappeared somewhere along the way. By 1927 all opposition to Kemalism had been crushed.

Twice Kemal arranged for friends of his to form opposition parties, but both times the parties disappointed him by trying to behave like true opponents. Convinced that his reforms were too important to be debated and delayed, and probably realizing that they horrified many Turks, he banned these parties before they could build popular bases.

With the same conflicting impulses, he praised freedom of the press as a cornerstone of liberty but did not hesitate to silence critical journalists and close their newspapers. "His dictatorship—a benevolent, educating, guiding dictatorship—was the only form of government possible at the moment," concluded one of his first biographers, the British historian H. C. Armstrong. A later historian, Bernard Lewis, elaborated the same conclusion:

> An autocrat by personal and professional bias, dominating and imperious by temperament, he yet showed a respect for decency and legality, for human and political standards, that is in astonishing contrast with the behavior of lesser and more pretentious men. His was a dictatorship without the uneasy over-the-shoulder glance, the terror of the door-bell, the dark menace of the concentration camp. Force and repression were certainly used to establish and maintain the Republic during the period of revolutionary changes, but no longer; and after the executions of 1926 there was little danger to life and personal liberty. . . . At the darkest moment in their history, the Kemalist revolution brought new life and hope to the Turkish people, restored their energies and self-respect, and set them firmly on the road not only to independence, but to that rarer and more precious thing that is freedom.

Toward the end of his life, Kemal recognized one more element of Turkish life that reminded him of the hated past. Since time immemorial, Turkish life had been centered on villages and clans small enough that in each there was likely to be only one Abdullah, one Hikmet and one Fatma. Those days were gone, and as a logical result of his Westernizing impulse, Kemal decreed that each citizen must have a last name. The head of every family was ordered to choose one. Some thought first of their fathers, so today there are names like Berberoğlu (barber's son), Karamehmetoğlu (Black Mehmet's son), and even Yarımbıyıkoğlu (son of the man with the half-mustache). Others took martial names like Eraslan (brave lion) or Demirel (iron hand). For those who had trouble choosing, books of names were sent to every town hall. Many people selected lyrical ones like Sarıgül (yellow rose) or Akyıldız (pale star). Only one name was forbidden: Atatürk (Father of the Turks). That was the name Kemal chose for himself. He embraced it, even dropping his first name, Mustafa, which he considered too Arab-sounding. From then until his death of cirrhosis in 1938, he called himself Kemal Atatürk. Under that name, for good and ill, he has become the overwhelming presence in every aspect of Turkish life.

After Atatürk's premature death at the age of fifty-eight, his successors had to make a difficult choice: whether to cling to his program as sacred dogma or adjust it to meet the demands of new times and new generations. That the Hero laid down clear principles and fought for them all his life is indisputable. Yet his central belief was in reason and progress. Certainly he hoped that his successors would march in the vanguard of humanity rather than fight endless rear-guard actions to keep Turks in the political straitjacket into which they had been bound during the 1920s and 1930s.

When Atatürk's successors introduced multiparty democracy in 1950, they gave Turks the right to elect a parliament and by extension a prime minister, as well as mayors and city councils (though not governors, who to this day are appointed from Ankara). With this step, the country began to embrace the creed of the Western world to which Atatürk so passionately wanted Turkey to belong. Human rights, tolerance, free speech and unity in diversity are its pillars. Turkey's Kemalist faith should lead it to embrace those principles, but not all Kemalists do. Some in the ruling elite believe that for Turkey, full democracy would lead to increases in ethnic tension, religious devotion and every form of social conflict. Even more profoundly, they believe it would become a weapon for those who seek to drag Turkey back to the pre-Kemalist era and turn it into a fundamentalist theocracy. With the stakes so high, they prefer to limit democracy, to parcel it out in what they consider digestible doses. By doing so they keep Turkey the way they like it and guarantee their own continued power.

Yet because Turkey is so open to currents from the outside world, the demand for European- and American-style democracy is growing. Civil society is emerging as a potent force. A new generation chafes at old restrictions and taboos. If the power structure fails to respond creatively to these challenges, it risks polarizing the country.

It is one of the great ironies of modern Turkish life that the name of the heroic figure who devoted his life to destroying taboos is now used to enforce taboos. The authority of the great Westernizer is invoked to justify policies that keep Turkey isolated from the West. Atatürk devoted his life to bringing his country into the world's mainstream, but some of his self-appointed heirs are preventing this dream from becoming real. In so doing they are rejecting Atatürk's own passionate belief in progress and ignoring one of his last pleas.

"I am leaving no sermon, no dogma, nor am I leaving as my legacy any commandment that is frozen in time or cast in stone," he said shortly before his death. "Concepts of well-being for countries, for peoples and for individuals are changing. In such a world, to argue for rules that never change would be to deny the reality found in scientific knowledge and reasoned judgment."

The hero-worship that has raised Atatürk to secular sainthood began during his own lifetime and with his blessing. During his early years in power, he approved the erection of monuments to independence that were actually monuments to him. By the end of the 1920s, statues depicting him on horseback or in other martial poses had assumed commanding positions in Ankara, Istanbul, Izmir, Konya and Samsun. In later years, and especially after his death, they became such a common feature of the Turkish landscape that today they are hardly noticed. No town or village or neighborhood is without one. At every school in the country, every day begins with pupils assembling before one of these icons and pledging eternal loyalty to Kemalism. The cult has even come to embrace Atatürk's mother, who by the act of giving birth to him is now held up as the ideal of Turkish womanhood.

The sanctity of Atatürk's person is protected not just by tradition and social pressure but also by law. Statute 5816 establishes the crime of "cursing Atatürk's memory," punishable by up to three years in jail, and that of damaging or destroying statues or busts of him, punishable by up to five years at hard labor. In many communities the police also enforce regulations, especially odd in light of Atatürk's own habits, that ban the serving of alcohol anywhere near monuments dedicated to him.

Trying to count the images of Atatürk in Turkey would be akin to counting the stars in the sky. His gaze is quite literally inescapable. It stares sternly from every coin and banknote and from the wall of virtually every shop, office, restaurant, *meyhane*, hotel lobby, bank, cinema and tea house. Judges, prosecutors, provincial bureaucrats, military commanders, school principals and others who consider themselves part of the Kemalist vanguard often display five or ten or more, not just photographs but also paintings, etchings, busts, engraved paperweights, ceramic plates and whatever else they can find. No form of veneration is considered too extreme or too vulgar. In Kars, near the Armenian border, an enormous silhouette of Atatürk dominates the ruins of a twelfth-century citadel. Another is painted in white on the side of a mountain near the Anatolian city of Erzurum. In Gaziantep, a provincial capital in the south, the governor's conference room is decorated with no less than fifty images, truly a blinding spectacle.

There is a ludicrous quality to this excess, and a dark side too, since anyone who does not join the ostentation is immediately suspected of insufficient patriotism or worse. But pressure to conform to the official ideology is not the only reason Turks surround themselves with these graven images. Respect and grateful admiration for Atatürk, and even a mystical attachment to him that resembles love, are widespread and genuine.

I too succumbed to these feelings, and although I came to question some tenets of the Kemalist faith, I keep two pictures of the old man on my office wall. They are not the usual portraits, most of which show him frowning like a harsh schoolmaster. In one he is on a swing, dressed in a natty three-piece suit but with what looks like a mischievous smile on his face, his legs extended in front of him. The other is even more subversive, showing him as a young man at a costume ball. For the occasion he chose to dress as a member of the Janissary corps, the elite guard that had protected Ottoman sultans, with an elaborate headdress and two richly embroidered vests. In his right hand he holds the hilt of a sword that he seems ready to pull from its scabbard at the slightest provocation.

Both of these images depict the Atatürk I like to imagine: the transgressor, the adventurer, the lover of life. Unlike many of those who today claim his mantle, Atatürk eagerly grasped the opportunities presented by a rapidly changing world. He understood that Turkey can become modern only by embracing modern values. It is in his true image, not in the distorted one promoted by the modern Kemalist elite, that the new Turkey must be shaped.

A charge of emotion surged through my body as I placed my hand against a crumbling wall on a field near Turkey's Aegean shore. Poseidon claimed to have built it: "Indeed I built a wall around their city for the Trojans, a broad and very beautiful wall to make the place impregnable." It was below this wall that the enraged Achilles chased Hector "three times around the city of Priam" before overtaking and killing him. Afterward he tied Hector's body to his chariot and dragged it around the citadel while Priam and other Trojan heroes watched in horror. Within sight of this wall, events unfolded that serve as the wellspring of Western civilization. On the day I stood beside it there was not a soul in sight on Homer's "vast, untilled and mountain-shirted plain." It was several minutes before I could bring myself to pull back my hand.

Skeptics have long argued that Homer's epics were fiction. In 1796 a professor at Cambridge University published "A Dissertation Concerning the War of Troy and the Expedition of the Grecians as described by Homer, showing that no such expedition was ever taken and that no such city of Phrygia existed." Slowly, however, as the science of archaeology began to develop, curious seekers combed Homer's epics for clues and compared what they found to the topography of what is now Turkey's northwest coast. In the 1870s a German businessman named Heinrich

Schliemann, an amateur archaeologist whose main experience with digging had been during the California gold rush, found what he believed was the true site. He even discovered a hoard of jewelry and other artifacts that he quickly announced was "Priam's Treasure." Much of what Schliemann found, including the treasure, turned out not to have been what he believed it to be, but he had indeed found Troy.

Several later expeditions built on Schliemann's work, and in 1988 American and German archaeologists launched an intensive new excavation project at the site. On my visits to their dig I found them reluctant to answer my questions about the historical accuracy of Homer's epics. They are, after all, scientists whose business is uncovering verifiable secrets of the past, not speculating on the relationship between literature and truth. Nonetheless, they cannot help being acutely aware that they are not digging at the site of just another ancient settlement. Their work and that of their predecessors has proven conclusively that there was a Troy and that they have found it. It also strongly suggests that a great battle was fought there around 1250 B.C., exactly the period of Homer's Trojan War. Since I allow myself to draw conclusions that go slightly beyond what scientists might accept, and since, like so many people over the eons, I have been thrilled by the Homeric epics, these findings persuade me that Achilles, Odysseus, Agamemnon and their noble comrades all gazed upon the very wall I touched.

Ever since Homer composed his epics twenty-seven centuries ago, an unbroken though not unchallenged tradition has held that his "meadow of Asia" was at the edge of a cape overlooking the southern entrance to the Dardanelles, the strait then known as the Hellespont, and that his "well-walled city of Troy" stood on a floodplain near the coast. Both Herodotus and Thucydides wrote of the city and of a great war fought there. Although no one knew the city's exact location, it has long been presumed not only that the Trojan War was a historical event but that it crystallized the age-old conflict between Asia and Europe.

Before Xerxes led his Persian army against Greece in 480 B.C., he stopped at the peninsula where Troy had stood and sacrificed a thousand oxen to Athena in the hope that she would bless his campaign. When Alexander the Great, who supposedly carried a copy of The Iliad with him on campaigns, set off from Macedonia to reverse the tide of

Persian conquest in 334 B.C., he visited the same site to pray to the spirit of Achilles, his greatest hero and role model. Julius Caesar considered moving his capital there from Rome, but the move was aborted by his assassination. Constantine also thought of making it the capital of his empire before choosing Byzantium, which he renamed Constantinople in his own honor.

Crusaders later justified their wars partly on their desire to bring Troy, or at least the land on which it had stood, back under European control. "Troy belonged to our ancestors, and they escaped and went to live in the land from whence we have come; and it is because they were our ancestors that we have come hither to conquer their land," the crusader Peter of Bracheaux told an opposing commander during the Fourth Crusade, which lasted from 1202 to 1204. Two and a half centuries later, after taking Constantinople for the Turks in 1453, Sultan Mehmet the Conqueror traveled to the plain and declared that his triumph was Asia's long-delayed vengeance for Greece's defeat of the Trojans.

Archaeologists have identified nine distinct cities that existed on these "proud heights" over a period of more than three thousand years. The one they call Troy VI is probably the one that existed when the Trojan War was supposedly fought. As early as 1902 the archaeologist Wilhelm Dörpfeld, who spent years excavating Troy VI, had found enough evidence to convince him that it "was thoroughly destroyed by enemy action." Discoveries since then have lent much support to his view. The wall of Troy VI, which was excavated in 1995, was the one on which I laid my hand.

Some have suggested that the Trojan War may have been nothing more than a minor pirate raid, or that Homer drew on accounts of various conflicts to invent a single great one. I choose not to believe that, though admittedly my reasons are emotional rather than scientific. Like most romantics, I want there to have been a Trojan War and am overjoyed that so much evidence has emerged to suggest that there was. I hope Manfred Korfmann, Brian Rose and the other archaeologists who guided me on my visits to the site, or perhaps their successors, will find what even they can accept as conclusive proof.

Compared to other ancient sites that have been uncovered in Turkey,

Troy is only modestly impressive. Without the timeless aura that Homer gave it, it might not even rank among the hundred most interesting ones. But there is something quite extraordinary about the entrance to the Dardanelles that would make the place fascinating even if Homer had never written about it. This strait, together with the Bosphorus to the north, is the greatest strategic prize in a region over which nations have fought for ages. In ancient times sailors had to put ashore at the southern entrance to the Dardanelles to wait for favorable winds. Troy was then on the coast rather than two and a half miles inland, as it is today, and those who controlled it could extort whatever tribute they wanted in exchange for allowing these sailors free passage toward the Black Sea. Simple geography explains why so many battles have been fought for control of the Dardanelles. The Trojan War was probably one of them.

Each time I visit Troy I take time to stop at a spot on the other side of the strait that is equally pregnant with memories of war, death and heroism. It is Gallipoli, the place where rivers of blood were spilled during one of the fiercest battles of World War I. Since most of the fighting there took place in an area of only two or three square miles, everywhere a visitor treads is likely to be a soldier's grave. There are thirty-one cemeteries on this narrow spit of land, fields of gravestones with inscriptions like this one: "Trooper G. R. Seager. 7 August 1915. Age 17. He Died a Man & Closed His Life's Brief Day Ere It Had Scarce Begun."

When Winston Churchill planned the Allied assault on Gallipoli, he had every reason to be confident of victory. Britain was at the peak of its imperial might, and the ragged Turks who held the peninsula were the last gasp of dying Ottoman power. But the invading force, which included many soldiers from Australia and New Zealand, found Turkish defenders astonishingly tenacious and willing to take staggering casualties. For most of 1915 the two armies fought from trenches that were often less than ten yards apart. Finally the invaders were forced to withdraw in defeat, many of them recording in letters and diaries their newfound respect for Turkish fighting men.

Today many Australians and New Zealanders consider Gallipoli to have been a crucible in which the identities of their young nations were forged. Hardly a day passes without visitors from one country or the other walking somberly over its gentle hills, and each year on April 25, the anniversary of the Allied landing, diplomats from Australia, New Zealand, Britain and Turkey gather there for solemn memorial services. But perhaps the most significant result of the campaign was the emergence of Mustafa Kemal, the victorious commander who went on to become President Kemal Atatürk.

In 1934 Atatürk learned that a ship carrying relatives of fallen Allied soldiers had docked near Gallipoli and that its passengers were mourning at the site. He sent them a moving message that is now chiseled, in English translation, into a memorial stone there. "Those heroes that shed their blood and lost their lives," he wrote, "you are now lying in the soil of a friendly country. Therefore rest in peace. There is no difference between the Johnnies and the Mehmets to us, where they lie side by side in this country of ours . . . You, the mothers who sent their sons from faraway countries, wipe away your tears. Your sons are now lying in our bosom and are in peace. After having lost their lives on this land, they have become our sons as well."

The Trojan War and the Battle of Gallipoli were fought on fields almost within sight of each other. Churchill wanted the Dardanelles so that Britain could send Allied warships through to supply Russia's Black Sea ports, perhaps giving Russia enough power to attack Austria-Hungary from the east. Greeks attacked Troy, I believe, not to avenge the kidnapping of a Spartan queen but for the same reason Churchill did: to win control of the strait. These campaigns, fought more than three thousand years apart, reflect the patterns, symmetries and repetitions in which history delights. Nowhere does history delight in them as fully as in the land now called Turkey.

· THREE ·

CALL TO PRAYER

☪

A distinguished-looking Turkish gentleman sat beside me on a flight I once took from Frankfurt to Ankara. No dinner was served, but soon after takeoff the German flight attendants brought each passenger a cellophane-covered platter of cheese and cold cuts. My companion eyed his suspiciously.

"What kind of meat is this?" he asked the attendant. She seemed taken aback, and after a moment's hesitation replied that she didn't know for sure.

"So it's possible there could be pork on this plate?" Again she hesitated, evidently not wanting to give a wrong answer.

"Yes, I suppose it's possible," she admitted.

"Take it away immediately," he demanded with a shudder. "Not just the plate but the whole tray."

The attendant, eager to please, quickly did as he wished and then asked, "Could I at least offer you something to drink?"

His face brightened and he said, "Yes, I'd love some red wine."

That day I was on my way to Ankara to cover a national election campaign in which an Islamic-oriented political party was looking surprisingly strong. The prospect of religious fundamentalism descending on this most secular of Muslim countries had terrified many Turks and more than a few foreign leaders. But I had just been given a reassuring lesson about Turkish Islam. The gentleman sitting next to me was a believer, else he would not have been repelled by the idea of pork. But the same Koran that forbids pork also forbids wine, so he obviously felt free to interpret his faith as he saw fit.

The zealous officers who conceived and built the Turkish Republic believed that religion could be domesticated by fiat. Their official history asserts that Turks "adopted and rapidly assimilated" Atatürk's sweeping secular reforms. Today, however, that conclusion looks dubious. In much of the country's heartland, religious belief remains strong. Mosques are full, women wear head scarves and imams command great moral authority.

This religious conservatism does not in itself threaten the secular basis of the Republic. Certainly there are those who want to restore the dominant role that Islam once had in Turkish life. Kemalist leaders are determined to defeat them, and rightly so. But their campaign has been disastrously unsophisticated. It has led many pious Muslims to conclude that the state despises religion and all who practice it, a conviction that feeds the fire of religious extremism rather than quenching it.

No fear at all, not even the fear of their country being torn apart by foreign enemies or ethnic separatists, grips the ruling Turkish elite so profoundly as the fear of Islamic fundamentalism. This is not hard to understand. Turks lived under a form of religious rule for centuries and did not emerge from it until Atatürk's revolution in the 1920s. One of their neighbors, Iran, is ruled by repressive mullahs, and sheiks who run the nearby Persian Gulf states are in some ways even more radically Islamic. Afghanistan is farther away geographically, but not far enough. Powerful figures in these countries consider Turkey a heretical state that has betrayed its Islamic roots and must somehow be brought back into the fold. So it is reasonable and indeed essential that Turkey be on guard against fundamentalism.

The state maintains this vigilance in a hundred ways. No mosque may be built without the permission of a powerful and well-financed state agency called the Religious Affairs Directorate. This same agency pays the salary of most imams, closely monitors what they say in their sermons and often even sends them texts that they must read to their congregations. It works closely with the ministry of education, which regulates religious schools and provides all texts from which religion is taught; it is a crime to publish others. If a dozen friends begin meeting regularly to discuss religious topics, they can expect a police raid and prosecution for operating an "illegal Koran school." Prosecutors also jump to indict anyone who publicly suggests that religion should play a greater role in national life. When Muslims slaughter sheep during the annual Feast of Sacrifice and follow tradition by donating the sheepskins to charity, they are required to donate every skin to a specific government-sponsored charity. Otherwise, it is feared, they would donate the skins to religious groups that would sell them to raise money for suspicious projects.

Turkey's government will have to abandon or adjust these practices as the country moves toward true democracy. That they violate modern concepts of free choice and the privacy of religious belief is bad enough. Far worse, they feed religious fervor because they seek to defy or overrule one of the deepest human instincts.

In every culture that has existed over the entire course of human civilization, people have sought answers to the great mysteries of existence, and invariably they turn to religion. Governments often seek ways to separate religion from state policy, but they cannot ever hope to crush it. Wise leaders, even the most atheistic among them, know they must balance the secular and sacred impulses in their societies. Those who govern Turkey have not yet been able to strike that balance. They have given many Muslims the sense that they must choose between their religious faith and allegiance to the state. No state has ever prevailed in such a confrontation.

Atatürk's scorched-earth campaign against religious power set the stage for this conflict. He had bitter memories of his years at a Muslim primary school, where pupils were made to memorize long passages from the Koran and robed imams cudgeled those who faltered. Many of the European writers he discovered in his teenage years were militantly anti-clerical, as were the positivist Turkish thinkers whose works he devoured. The Young Turk circles to which he gravitated as a cadet included some who drank alcohol and ate ham to show their modernity.

The sultan's meek subservience to foreign powers after World War I, not to mention his proclamation that independence fighters were apostates and that killing them was a religious duty of all true Muslims, led Atatürk to conclude that traditional Islam was the enemy of both reason and national dignity. "Can a civilized nation tolerate a crowd of people who let themselves be led by the nose by sheiks, dervishes and the like," he demanded, "and who entrust their faith and their lives to fortune-tellers, magicians, witch doctors and amulet-makers?"

When Atatürk declared soon after taking power that he intended to lead Turkey along "the path of civilization," he certainly wanted that path to lead away from state-sponsored religion. He was not reckless or foolish enough to break publicly with Islam, and during the War of Liberation he was even photographed praying in public. But as president he banned mystic religious sects, forbade the wearing of religious garb and denounced "superstitions dwelling in people's minds." In an assault on religious authority comparable to Luther's, he ordered the Koran translated into Turkish so that ordinary people could read it for themselves rather than relying on the interpretations of Islamic teachers. When a British correspondent asked him about his own beliefs, he replied: "I have no religion, and at times I wish all religions at the bottom of the sea."

As Turkey moved toward democracy in the years after Atatürk's death, it was inevitable that some of his draconian sanctions on organized religion would be eased. Leaders of his own Republican People's Party began the process by authorizing Koran courses, opening schools for training imams and establishing a theology department at Ankara University. The process accelerated after the party suffered a crushing defeat in Turkey's first free election in 1950. Adnan Menderes, who was elected prime minister in that year, was a secularist, but he did not detest or fear religious practice, as many Kemalists did. Soon after his election, religious schools and academies were opened in many cities. Islamic books and periodicals began appearing. The law requiring that the Muslim call to prayer be chanted in Turkish was repealed, and mosques were equipped with loudspeakers so that everyone could hear it in the original Arabic. Throngs turned out to protest whenever religious figures were brought to trial for violating one or another restriction on their practice. The number of people making pilgrimages to Mecca grew steadily.

Within a few years the new regime began to lose popularity, and sought to regain it by identifying even more fully with Islam. To a certain degree it succeeded, especially in rural areas, where the pull of tradition remained strong. But military commanders, disturbed by growing political and economic troubles as well as by what they saw as the regime's infidelity to Kemalist principles, grew increasingly unhappy. In 1960 they staged a coup, overthrew Menderes and imposed a regime of young officers. There was jubilation in the streets, but joy turned to horror when Menderes and two of the cabinet ministers ousted with him were arrested, hauled before a military tribunal, convicted of treason and hanged. More than a few Turks considered them martyrs to their faith.

Menderes's success at mobilizing pious Muslims made it inevitable that budding politicians would now recognize Islam as a powerful political force. One of the first to do so was a young engineer named Necmettin Erbakan. The son of an enthusiastically Kemalist judge, Erbakan had been educated in Germany, and after returning home had sought unsuccessfully to be named as a parliamentary candidate by an established center-right party. Stung by his rejection, he established his own party, National Order, in 1970. Soon he was barnstorming across Turkey, rousing the faithful with calls for a return to religious values. When the army staged a second coup in 1971, Erbakan and other National Order leaders were not arrested, as were leaders of leftist parties. A court later banned the party for fomenting fundamentalism, however, and Erbakan moved temporarily to Switzerland.

After a while there, Erbakan received word from Ankara that conservative politicians and perhaps even some military officers wanted him back. The student unrest that had already shaken the United States and many European countries had arrived in Turkey. Marxist ideologies were spreading. Generals feared that leftist parties would do well in the election they had called for 1973, and they hoped that Erbakan, with his appeal to conservative believers, could siphon votes away from them.

By cooperating with Erbakan, Kemalists were not only deciding to embrace religious politics but quite consciously choosing Sunni Islam, the branch to which most Turks belong and of which Erbakan was a leading symbol, over the more tolerant, heterodox Alevi tradition. They decreed that all religious education was to be in the Sunni doctrine, as it remains to this day, and in a variety of ways made clear that they favored Sunnis over Alevis. This angered and still angers the Alevis, who make up about one-fourth of the Turkish population, because they consider themselves Turkey's true democrats. Their tolerance of alcohol, their belief that Muslims need not pray in mosques, their refusal to fast during Ramadan, their conviction that pilgrimages to Mecca are less important than the pilgrimage into one's own heart—all of these are beliefs that Atatürk certainly would have favored over those of the Sunnis. In fact, Alevis suffered for centuries because of their resistance to the sultans, and they rallied enthusiastically to Atatürk's side when he rose in rebellion. Today's Kemalists are not sure what to make of them. They see Alevis as guarantors of the secular state but fear them because many of them resist authority and are by nature skeptics, individualists and freethinkers.

As part of their blind refusal to recognize that their country is made up of communities with coherent identities, Turkish leaders have for decades sought to deny the Alevi reality. That has pushed Alevis steadily away from the political mainstream and toward leftist political movements. It has also led Sunnis to attack them, sometimes with terrible violence. Many of the massacres during the late 1970s that were officially portrayed as clashes between rightists and leftists were actually cases of Sunnis massacring Alevis, most horribly during a spasm of violence in 1978 around Kahramanmaraş in southern Turkey, where scores were killed. In 1993 a mob of Sunni fundamentalists set fire to a hotel in Sivas where pro-Alevi intellectuals were holding a conference, killing thirty-five of those inside as police officers stood by.

Necmettin Erbakan, the politician who Kemalists once hoped would seduce Turks away from leftism, was an orthodox Sunni. His more than thirty years in public life established him as a truly historic figure, and the story of religious politics in Turkey is also his story. Fate and his own hard work gave him a historic chance to reshape Turkey by forging a synthesis between modernity and conservative religious values. He failed miserably, and his country is still paying the price.

After his return from exile in Switzerland, Erbakan became increasingly popular. His new party, called National Salvation, never won broad support but was successful enough at the polls to make him a kingmaker. During the 1970s he joined two coalition governments as deputy prime minister. In a remarkably short time he had risen from a position as an outsider and virtual fugitive to the citadel of state power.

Over the years that followed, National Salvation grew steadily more radical. The 1979 Islamic revolution in Iran inspired its members, and at rallies they began chanting "Khoumeni in Iran, in Turkey Erbakan!" In September 1980, one of its rallies in Konya degenerated into violence as militants smashed the windows of tourist hotels and ransacked shops where alcohol was being sold. They shouted slogans calling for Islamic law, and when a band struck up the national anthem, they drowned it out with chants of "We want the Koran!"

That was too much for the authorities. Several dozen of the rioters were arrested, and Erbakan was warned to curb his rhetoric. But the episode was quickly overshadowed by a much more profound event, the military coup of September 12, 1980, whose leaders immediately issued a decree dissolving all political parties. By then, however, Erbakan had become the unchallenged leader of the Islamic political movement. He knew that whatever else happened in Turkey, an army of believers was awaiting his command.

The dour generals who seized power in September 1980 hoped to use Islam as a counterweight to secular liberal and radical ideologies that were gaining strength in Turkey. They authorized the training of more imams and opened scores of religious academies. It was neither the first nor the last time that shortsighted Kemalists adopted policies toward religion that in the end encouraged rather than weakened fundamentalism.

Military officers held power for three years, and the ban they imposed on political leaders active before the coup remained in force until 1987. When it was lifted Erbakan plunged back into politics by forming his third party, Welfare. Muslims who had come to view him as a religious warrior jumped fervently back into the fray. Soon they were electing mayors around the country, capping their campaign with astonishing victories in Ankara and Istanbul. Most Welfare mayors performed exceptionally well, setting new standards for honesty and seriously addressing chronic problems like public transit, garbage collection and others that confront communities around the world.

Welfare also became the first party in Turkey to emphasize grass-roots political organizing. Passionately committed party volunteers, many of them women, did not simply arrive on doorsteps to ask for votes at election time. They made it their business to know the needs of their neighbors all year long, and to ensure that no one who sought the party's aid went unsatisfied. Through their efforts thousands of hungry Turks were fed, the homeless sheltered and the sick given medicine. In big cities, party workers waited at bus stations to greet migrants who had abandoned their bleak lives in rural provinces to search for work and prosperity. Many arrived without a clue of how to begin, so Welfare found them places to sleep and, in many cases, jobs at factories owned by pious businessmen. Naturally, their gratitude was limitless; many became not simply Welfare voters but enthusiastic organizers.

Erbakan brought to Turkey the same campaign techniques that have worked for political bosses from the Peróns in Argentina to the Daleys in Chicago. He also alarmed the establishment by showing how effectively he could turn the religious zeal of his followers into victory at the polls. The core of his support remained among political Muslims, but by most estimates these Islamists comprised only seven or eight percent of the Turkish electorate. Erbakan's party was winning far more votes than that. Obviously he was attracting voters who were not especially religious. All they shared was disgust for the self-serving political establishment.

The day I flew to Ankara together with the gentleman who would eat no pork but did drink wine, I was covering the 1995 election campaign. Erbakan was then sixty-nine years old and master of an avuncular, didactic political style that resembled that of a religious teacher. In fact, he was universally known as "Hoca," a title usually reserved for such teachers.

In Ankara I stopped by a small antiques store, and while bargaining for a silver-framed mirror that struck my fancy I learned a little about the proprietor. He was in his mid-twenties, full of ambition and obviously bright. His girlfriend was Austrian, and he flew to Vienna to see her whenever he could scrape together the plane fare. Other than dreaming of her, his favorite pastimes were drinking *rakı* and disco dancing until the wee hours. When I asked him which party he was voting for, he immediately replied, "Welfare."

I was astonished, and told him so. Here was a budding capitalist with a Christian girlfriend who spent his free time drinking and dancing. He was about to cast his ballot for a party that preached religious chauvinism, considered alcohol a tool of the devil and wanted to turn Turkey away from the West and toward a new brotherhood of Islamic states. How could this be? The answer came in a tirade that shocked me with its intensity.

"Politics in this country is totally corrupt," my new friend began, shaking his finger in my face. "Politicians only care about their privileges and keeping themselves in power. Everyone knows the problems this country faces, but no one does anything to solve them because that would mean shaking up the power structure. I tried to start a shop in my village, but so many people wanted bribes that I finally had to give up. No one expects this place to run like Switzerland, but things have gone too far. I've had it! Welfare is the only honest party. They aren't in politics for what they can steal. They really want to serve. I'm ready for them."

Much of Turkey was at that moment arguing over the true nature of Welfare and the extent of the threat it posed to Turkish secularism. Certainly its record in city halls across the country was impressive, and some of its leaders seemed reassuring. But others were true fundamentalists who harbored not-so-secret dreams of tearing down the edifice of Kemalism. What if, I asked this shopkeeper, the alarmists were right? What if Welfare were to come to power and begin to assault people like him, attack the Western style of life that he enjoyed and turn Turkey into another Middle Eastern backwater?

"Don't worry, that could never happen," he quickly assured me. "If they try to do anything like that, the army will throw them out."

Many Turks shared these views. Thoroughly disgusted with mainstream parties, they were willing to take a chance with Welfare. There wasn't any real risk, they believed, because the military would prevent things from going bad.

In a sense this is a reassuring system because it guarantees that if voters make a mistake, generals will step in and set things right. But it also encourages Turkish voters to remain permanently immature, like children who know they can keep throwing plates of food on the floor because their parents will always clean up the mess. It allows them to avoid ultimate responsibility for the consequences of their votes. Most perniciously, it creates an escape valve that keeps pressure for reform from growing too intense. As long as the army is around to do the system's dirty work, voters can avoid confronting the urgency of political change. This system serves the political class by allowing it to keep its privileges, including its right to divert public funds to cronies; serves religious parties by giving them the image of heroic crusaders; and serves the army by preserving its role as the repository of ultimate political power. It does not, however, serve the cause of democracy.

Erbakan campaigned far more effectively than his secular rivals, who arrived at rallies in helicopters as if descending from Olympus, deigning to allow their supporters to see and hear them for a few minutes and then rising again into the clouds. For Erbakan a city rally was a half-day event involving visits to nearby villages, tea with respected elders, a speech laced with intoxicating promises of the "just order" to come and then a couple of hours of baby-kissing and earnest hearing of private grievances. Erbakan was the only candidate who gave the impression of caring for ordinary Turks. More important, he was the only one who stood for an idea. In that sense he was a refreshing reaction to the end of ideology in Turkey, to a system in which politicians no longer believed much of anything and competed simply for personal power. Unfortunately, his idea, depending on the day, sounded unrealistic, silly or downright terrifying.

"We will create an Islamic currency," Erbakan promised in one fiery speech a few weeks before the election. In another he went further, pledging "an Islamic United Nations, an Islamic NATO and an Islamic version of the European Union." In a third he vowed to launch a jihad to recapture Jerusalem, rescue Turkey from "the unbelievers of Europe" and finally seize the reins of world power now held by "imperialism and Zionism, as well as Israel and a handful of champagne-drinking collaborators in the conglomerates that feed it." Rapturous crowds cheered wildly.

The 1995 election turned out to be the closest in Turkish history, with less than two percentage points separating the top three parties, but that was not the big story. To the astonishment of almost everyone, Welfare finished first, taking slightly more than twenty-one percent of the vote. It owed its victory to a split between the country's two ethically bankrupt center-right leaders, former prime ministers Tansu Çiller and Mesut Yılmaz, whose parties took twenty percent each. Secular Turks were in shock. "This was the worst-case scenario," one newspaper columnist told me despondently after the results were announced.

Military commanders and other pillars of the Kemalist elite looked frantically for a way to keep Erbakan from the prime minister's job. They managed to push Çiller and Yılmaz into a coalition, but from their first day in power the titular partners fought like scorpions, and their government soon collapsed. Erbakan was back at center stage.

Although Welfare had finished first in the election, its twenty-one percent entitled it to less than a third of the seats in Parliament. To win the job of prime minister, Erbakan needed an ally. No secular leader wanted to join him, but he guessed there was one he could persuade: the utterly amoral Tansu Çiller. On the surface it seemed an odd if not impossible marriage. Çiller had run the most militantly anti-Islamist campaign of any candidate, warning that a Welfare government would "bury Turkey in darkness." She had even publicly revived an old charge that Erbakan was financing his movement by heroin smuggling. But under the circumstances, these two cynics needed each other. Erbakan was prepared to make any deal that would bring him to power; Çiller needed protection from a wave of corruption charges. Bring me your votes in Parliament, he told her, and we'll form a coalition that will make those nasty charges go away.

Çiller jumped at the offer, and the malodorous deal was struck. On a June afternoon six months after his victory at the polls, a beaming Erbakan emerged from President Süleyman Demirel's official residence in Ankara. "I have very good news for you," he told waiting reporters. "A new government has been formed."

All eyes were now on Erbakan. If he could reassure Turks of his commitment to the nation's hallowed secular principles, he might strengthen civilian authority, diminish the army's influence in politics and prove that politicians of all stripes could compete under the broad Kemalist umbrella. Even if in his heart he believed Turkey needed to change course to embrace the "just order" of which he so often spoke, he had to realize that his first step must be to win his people's trust.

Nearly eighty percent of Turkish voters had cast their ballots for secular parties, and many feared and detested him. Now he had a chance to show that he embodied not religious fanaticism but simple Anatolian conservatism. By doing so he would be carrying out a mission of profound importance to Islam, Turkey and the cause of democracy.

The first sign that Erbakan would fail in this mission came the very day that President Demirel accepted his new government. Instead of reassuring the nation, Erbakan began dispensing utopian wisdom. He had not simply formed a government, he told reporters outside Demirel's residence, but reinvented Turkey.

"The other parties are finished," he declared. "In the first place, they have no identity, no character. They only want to imitate the West. That is a sickness. Their second mistake is their strongly capitalistic economic program, which helps a very small elite and leaves the rest of our people in misery. And their third mistake is that they are against religion. These parties have been hostile to religion for fifty years. They act as if there is no such thing as religion."

Turkey was now in a state of almost unbearable suspense. The entire nation was waiting for a signal that would show which way their new leader wanted to take the country. They did not have to wait long. Only a few weeks after taking office, Erbakan announced that he was departing on a foreign trip that would include a stop in Iran, then ruled by oppressive and fanatically anti-Western mullahs. When he got there they welcomed him like a long-lost brother.

Upon returning home, Erbakan declared that his trip to Iran was only the beginning of a campaign for worldwide Muslim solidarity, which, he vowed, would return Turkey to the position of Islamic leadership that it had held during the centuries when Istanbul was the seat of the Muslim caliphate. Evidently he had convinced himself that he was free to pull Turkey away from its Western mooring. That was a wild miscalculation.

"A party that won only twenty-one percent of the vote has no right to change Turkish foreign policy," Mesut Yılmaz, leader of the center-right Motherland party, protested. "There is no consensus in Turkey for such a change." Instead of heeding this and other similar warnings, Erbakan pressed on.

Soon after returning from Tehran he set off to embrace the Libyan tyrant Muammar el-Qaddafi, but he found Qaddafi in a foul mood. Far from showing gratitude to Erbakan for facing the wrath of Western powers by making this pilgrimage to his pariah state, the mercurial Bedouin used the visit as an opportunity to vent his hatred of every principle for which Turkey had come to stand. He received Erbakan and his party in a tent on the outskirts of Tripoli, and the moment they were seated he launched into a bitter tirade. "Turkey's foreign policy is wrong from A to Z," he shouted at the beginning of his harangue. "Turkey, a country under American control, has opened up its soil to American bases. As if that was not enough, it has concluded an accord with Israel, the enemy of Islam, and entered into military cooperation with it." He heaped scorn on Turkey for coming "under occupation" by Western powers, denounced its membership in NATO and issued a heretical call for cutting the country apart to give Kurds their own state. "Turkey has lost its will. Turkey's future lies not in NATO, U.S. bases and repressing the Kurds, but in its nobility and its past. Kurdistan should be established. I am talking about the Kurdish nation. This nation should have its place under the Middle Eastern sun."

The monologue was shocking enough, but Erbakan's response, or lack of it, infuriated even many of his friends. Rather than protest, he stared quietly upward as he listened, a beatific smile on his face. It was as if he loved the sound of words he wished to speak himself but dared not.

Turks, who have traditionally looked down on Arabs as ignorant and uncivilized, were enraged. Mass-circulation newspapers carried banner headlines like CATASTROPHE IN LIBYA, NIGHT OF SHAME and QADDAFI'S RAVINGS. A report in the secularist paper *Sabah* began, "A barefoot Bedouin stood in front of Erbakan and the Turkish delegation last night and hurled insults at Turkey." Even the Islamic-oriented *Zaman* was scandalized, with its correspondent writing: "Qaddafi's bitter words had the effect of a machine gun being fired at Erbakan. It was as if an atom bomb had fallen on the tent." One of Erbakan's own cabinet ministers described Qaddafi's words as "lunatic nonsense."

Erbakan gave not the slightest indication that he disapproved of anything his host had said. Floating blissfully above the drumbeat of criticism, he embarked on a series of domestic projects that seemed calculated to drive Kemalists crazy. First he proposed that female civil servants be allowed to wear head scarves, raising the specter of judges and city hall clerks dressed in clothing that Atatürk had banned decades earlier. Then he began making speeches encouraging young people to attend religious academies instead of public schools and urging that graduates of such academies be made eligible for placement in the officer corps. He started appearing in public surrounded by uniformed bodyguards from his Welfare party, seeming to trust them more than the government's official security agents. Almost every day, he removed some Kemalist or other from a post in the bureaucracy and appointed a Welfare follower to fill the vacancy. On one religious holiday he received leaders of Islamic sects, several of them dressed in traditional robes, at his official residence. And in his most powerfully symbolic assault on Kemalism, he announced that he would build a grand new mosque overlooking Istiklal, the bustling pedestrian boulevard that runs through the center of Istanbul, and another in Çankaya, the neighborhood in Ankara that is dominated by the president's official residence. He could not have been more offensive had he proposed building one next to Atatürk's mausoleum.

Islamist mayors in cities and towns throughout Turkey were encouraged by the eagerness with which Erbakan was thumbing his nose at long-established conventions of Turkish life, and many launched their own local campaigns. One closed cinemas on the grounds that they were places where unholy ideas were propagated. Another banned the selling of turkeys, saying they were being eaten at dinners whose purpose was to celebrate Christian holidays. A third shut down a lingerie market because he found its display offensive. Several began to fill their administrations with men who had been cashiered from the army for fundamentalist leanings. Others terrorized merchants into shutting their doors at prayer time and ordered restaurants to close every day during Ramadan.

Soon after Erbakan took office I applied for an interview with him. My application and those of other Western journalists were politely ignored, leading us to conclude that Turkey's leader had no interest in meeting with representatives of Christian imperialism. Increasingly frustrated as months passed, I began telephoning people close to Erbakan to ask for their help. Finally I found one who said he could arrange a meeting. Then, one day in December, I received an extraordinary message. Erbakan would deign to see me, but only if I came on Christmas Day.

This was a deliberate insult and a reflection of Erbakan's own intolerance, but although I found it tasteless, I accepted. At the appointed hour I arrived at the ugly cement building that serves as the prime minister's residence in Ankara. Inside the door I literally bumped into Erbakan as he emerged from a small elevator. We bent down to remove our shoes together.

Erbakan was a white-haired, grandfatherly figure, surprisingly elegant in appearance. He moved delicately, gestured calmly and spoke softly. For most of our two hours together, he smiled indulgently as he drifted from cliché to cliché, not showing much in the way of analytical power or concentrated intelligence. His discourse was an odd combination of conservative Islam and leftist anti-imperialism. All he wanted, he seemed to be insisting, was to change the world.

"At the end of World War II, the Western powers and Russia met at Yalta and set rules for the coming era," he told me as he sipped from a small coffee cup. "But the West and Russia can't make the rules by themselves anymore. They have to sit down with the developing countries to establish a new order. The world needs a second Yalta conference. The first Yalta did its job, but its time is now past. Now the world must again be reshaped."

I didn't need to ask which country would lead this great realignment. "Turkey is at the center of the world," Erbakan told me. "Turkey is going to take the first step toward ending this double standard and injustice in the world."

Erbakan's dream of worldwide Muslim solidarity was wildly unrealistic. He was pursuing a phantom in a way that seemed calculated to outrage the Kemalist establishment. He even felt free to disparage Europe and its ideals, thereby challenging Atatürk's most basic precept. "Turkey has been a European country for centuries, and it is a European country today," Erbakan told me that evening. "Five hundred years ago our territory stretched to the outskirts of Vienna, and Constantinople was the largest city in Europe. Today part of our territory is geographically in Europe. But, unfortunately, for a long time European policy toward Turkey has been very wrong. Turkey has been in NATO for more than forty years, but the West is constantly pushing us away. They treat us unjustly, and then they blame us."

Erbakan's profoundly subversive message was clear: Europe doesn't want us, so we have to look elsewhere for friends and allies. But on other issues Erbakan embraced the nationalist consensus, showing himself to be no true radical. He fiercely defended the army's conduct of the campaign against Kurdish guerrillas in eastern provinces, echoing the army's view that it was "not a war but a fight against terrorism." When I asked how he would deal with human-rights abuses, he shook his head sadly. "There is no particular human-rights problem in Turkey," he said with an indulgent smile, as if correcting a student who had come up with a wrong answer. "Western countries shouldn't talk to us about human rights. It's like an old record. When Western diplomats or cabinet members come to visit us, they take out this old record and play it. It has no meaning."

This interview showed me what already seemed clear from Erbakan's actions and public statements: that he was not only nutty but nutty in a highly provocative way. Where he might have dissented from established dogma and embraced the cause of democracy, he did not do so, choosing instead to fall back on the pat answers he had mouthed for years as a pillar of the establishment. None of this mattered to the Anatolian masses and urban poor, who viewed him as a holy warrior and didn't care about his position on issues that were merely political. But in facing the great challenge of modern Turkey, that of balancing Kemalism with the clamor for more democracy, he chose a course that managed to alienate both sides. To Kemalists he was a treasonous fundamentalist, to democrats a dreary apostle of the old order. I stepped out into the Christmas darkness convinced that he was too poor a political juggler to remain in power for long.

A few weeks later one of Erbakan's acolytes, who was the mayor of Sincan, a gritty town near Ankara, called an evening rally to celebrate "Jerusalem Day," a holiday that Iran's Ayatollah Khoumeni had proclaimed in Iran during the 1980s. Several hundred people jammed a local theater to watch a skit depicting Islam's victory in the forthcoming ji-had. They cheered wildly when the guest of honor, Mohammed Reza Bagheri, the Iranian ambassador in Ankara, arrived at the door. "Down with Israel!" they shouted. "Down with Arafat!"

Ambassador Bagheri sent the crowd into ecstasy with a fiery speech demanding that Turkey submit to *sharia*, the law of the Koran. "On behalf of Muslims all over the world, I say that we can wait no longer!" he cried, shouting to be heard above the delirious cheers. "Do not be afraid to call yourselves fundamentalists! Fundamentalists are those who follow the words and actions of the Prophet. God has promised them the final victory!"

For Turkish generals, this was the last straw. A couple of days later they ordered a phalanx of tanks to roll through Sincan's streets, and although they claimed afterward that the tanks had simply "taken a wrong turn," their message was clear. The mayor went into hiding but was soon found, arrested, charged with violating laws that forbid attacks on the secular state, tried and imprisoned. Ambassador Bagheri was sent packing.

The next weekend, feminist groups led a mass protest on the streets of Ankara. Thousands of women turned out to protest Erbakan's rule and proclaim their refusal to accept the social position he and his followers envisioned for them. As I circulated through the crowd, I found many women in a state of near-panic. Erbakan's proposal to encourage the wearing of head scarves, they said, was not a step toward free choice but the beginning of a pressure campaign that would ultimately force all women to cover themselves. I saw an older woman draped in a Turkish flag to which she had pinned a portrait of Atatürk, and asked her why she had joined the march. "I don't want to live under a black sheet," she replied. "We are the real Muslims, not those who want to turn back the clock."

With the atmosphere now so highly charged, every aspect of daily life became politicized. Newspapers and television news programs were filled with reports about the intensifying political conflict. Culture became a major battleground. When the Ankara Symphony Orchestra announced plans to play Beethoven's Fifth Symphony at an outdoor amphitheater, the city's Islamist mayor ordered nearby streets dug up to create obstructions for those heretics who would presume to listen to such an expression of European decadence. Sensing a challenge, enormous crowds turned out, some picking their way through piles of torn-up asphalt. Inside the stadium they shouted insults at Erbakan's culture minister, who had made a series of speeches proclaiming the superiority of Muslim culture over that of the West. They cheered wildly at the sight of President Demirel, who as prime minister had opened scores of religious schools but like the rest of the Kemalist elite, had changed with the wind and begun denouncing the spread of Islamic militance. Visibly moved by the response, Demirel leaned into a microphone and shouted, "This magnificent picture is the picture of contemporary Turkey!" The crowd responded by chanting, "Turkey is secular and will remain so!"

A dangerous chasm had opened within Turkish society. In tea houses and *meyhane* people spoke of little else. Although Erbakan was neither violent nor a religious fanatic, his effort to exploit religious feeling for political ends seemed highly dangerous. Sentiment had clearly swung against him, but what could be done? The answer was lamentably obvious. The army had to step in, and step in it did.

This time the generals did not launch an old-fashioned coup, which, they realized, was no longer possible in a country that belonged to NATO and claimed to live within the rules of democracy. Besides, they had no desire to run the country themselves. Their goal was to depose Erbakan and return power to traditional politicians who respected the rules of Kemalism.

The generals, through their National Security Council, had already officially directed Erbakan to change course, but he had ignored them. So in the spring of 1997 they began issuing "memoranda" listing his sins. Then they invited various groups—judges, civil servants, journalists and others—to "briefings" in Ankara at which they issued vivid warnings about the peril at hand. They never openly demanded Erbakan's resignation, but their pressure soon became irresistible. He surrendered after exactly twelve months in office, victim of Turkey's first post-modern coup.

This coup would have been unthinkable in any true democracy. Most Turks, however, breathed a palpable sigh of relief. The generals had acted on behalf of the Turkish nation, crushing a force that most people had come to fear but none could stop. Once again they had proven their indispensability. Erbakan's year in power had been a disaster. For a man who had spent so long in Turkish politics, he showed astonishing naïveté in believing that he would be allowed to pull Turkey away from the West. More important, he squandered a great opportunity to show a skeptical nation and its ruling elite that devoutly Muslim politicians could accept the ideals of republican Turkey. In fact, he did the opposite, fixing in the public mind the image of his movement as a threat to dearly held principles.

Being pushed from power was only the beginning of Erbakan's punishment. Later his Welfare party was outlawed (making it the twenty-first party since the 1980 coup to be dissolved by judicial order) and he himself was banned from politics. Then, in an act of unseemly vengeance, a prosecutor dredged up a speech he had made long before becoming prime minister and persuaded a judge that it was subversive. Erbakan was sentenced to one year in prison, although a subsequent amnesty allowed him to avoid actually serving time.

Triumphant Kemalists, often acting through prosecutors like the redoubtable Vural Savaş, who swore to seek bans on parties he didn't like even if they won ninety-nine percent of the vote, did not stop by punishing Erbakan. They began systematically targeting his followers, most of whom had stuck together after Welfare was banned and formed a new Islamic-oriented party called Virtue. Their first victim was Mayor Şükrü Karatepe of Kayseri, a flourishing city of six hundred thousand in central Turkey. Karatepe was one of the party's most moderate figures and one of the few whose wife did not wear a head scarf, but after he allegedly complained that he was tired of attending celebrations in honor of Atatürk—a remark he denied making—he was convicted of spreading subversion and sent to jail for five months. Later an even bigger fish was snared, Mayor Recep Tayyip Erdoğan of Istanbul. He was convicted of subversion and jailed for four months after reading an old poem that contained this verse: "The mosques are our barracks / The domes are our helmets / The minarets are our spears / The faithful are our army."

Erbakan had a clever bit of revenge after he was thrown out of politics. In quietly helping to prepare the list of Virtue candidates to run for

Parliament in the 1999 election, he slipped in the name of Merve Kavakcı, an unknown thirty-one-year-old computer engineer. She won a seat, and when she arrived at the Parliament building it suddenly became clear why Erbakan picked her: she was not only a practicing Muslim but one who wore a head scarf, which she refused to take off during the swearing-in ceremony. Pandemonium erupted in the parliamentary chamber. No woman had ever entered this Kemalist citadel with her head covered, and Kavakcı's decision to do so was considered an intolerable provocation. Newspapers denounced her as an agent of fundamentalism, politicians heaped abuse on her and the ever-vigilant Vural Savaş opened a case against her for "inciting hatred," later even demanding the death penalty. Ultimately the establishment found a way to exclude her from Parliament, invoking a rarely used law that allows the government to strip Turks of their citizenship if they take citizenship in another country without first asking permission. Kavakcı held an American passport, and after being stripped of her Turkish citizenship and with it her seat in Parliament, she quietly returned to Texas, where she had gone to college and where head scarves were among the less exotic forms of apparel. Erbakan must have had a good laugh. Kavakcı was his time bomb, and she had exploded as planned in full public view. As he had hoped, the episode conveyed his subversive message to the faithful: whatever Kemalists might say, the truth is that they hate everything that smacks of Islam.

Although Kavakcı went away, however, the head-scarf issue did not. On the contrary, it took on such symbolic importance that the Kemalist elite dragged out a forgotten rule banning scarves on university campuses and demanded that it be strictly enforced. Once again it plunged into battle against believers rather than looking for a way to embrace them.

The head scarf is tolerated in the Turkish heartland because it is part of the traditional female costume and does not necessarily symbolize religious orthodoxy. In the 1990s, a new generation of young women, assertive and liberated but still religiously conservative, began pursuing opportunities that had never been available to their mothers and grandmothers but that, thanks to Kemalism, were available to them. They enrolled by the thousands at universities across the country, eagerly grasping the chance for education offered to them by the Turkish state. At the same time they insisted on wearing their scarves. Certainly some of them were being manipulated, consciously or otherwise, by fundamentalists looking for ways to upset the established order. But public universities are supported by taxpayers, and the young women who enrolled believed they had a right to attend regardless of how they dressed. They were wrong.

Istanbul University was built on the grounds of what was once the Ottoman defense ministry but is today a bastion of Kemalism. One day I met two aspiring doctors at the McDonald's across the street. Both had been expelled from medical school for refusing to remove their head scarves.

"Hello, I'm Stephen," I said as I greeted them, extending my hand. They only smiled and nodded in reply. These women considered even shaking a man's hand sinful. I hated that, but still I found myself sympathizing with them.

One of the two, Tülay Erdoğan (no relation to Istanbul's deposed mayor), was twenty-three years old and had dreamed since childhood of becoming a doctor. But a few days earlier she had arrived to take an examination and was told that she could enter the room only if she removed her scarf. Suddenly she and several hundred of her classmates found themselves unexpectedly challenged. Nearly all of them refused to remove their scarves, choosing to quit school rather than uncover themselves.

"We love God, we read our Koran, we believe in our religion and we want to apply this religion in our lives," Ms. Erdoğan told me over a burger and fries. "What has happened in the last few weeks makes me very angry. I am protesting as much as possible because I really want to become a doctor. It's bad to become a fanatic, but they are pushing us toward fanaticism."

This young woman impressed me as highly intelligent and, although perhaps not exactly what Atatürk had in mind, a product of the Kemalist revolution. The triumph of Turkish secularism had made it possible for her to aspire to a career beyond the wildest dreams of girls in Saudi Arabia or Kuwait or Afghanistan. I admired her courage and would have liked to bid her good-bye in the traditional Turkish manner, with a kiss on each cheek, but under the circumstances that was of course impossible.

The arrival of the head scarf in such a citadel of secularism as Istanbul University was a challenge that Atatürk probably had not considered. Perhaps it would have outraged him. I prefer to believe, however, that the idea of women clamoring to become doctors would have seemed to him like a fulfillment of his dream. Turkish secularism no doubt requires that doctors in public hospitals be forbidden to wear head scarves, and along with them judges, lawyers, civil servants, diplomats and flight attendants on the national airline. But why college students?

"The head scarf is a symbol that represents an ideology," one member of Istanbul University's governing board, an economist named Toker Dereli, told me when I posed this question to him. "Many people who like to see scarves would also like to see a regime like the one in Iran. That suggests a totalitarian approach."

Dereli seemed uncomfortable when I asked him if the university had been pressured to take this stand. "If the military has certain targets, unlike civilian sectors they follow to the end until the targets are reached," he told me. "I personally find it odd for someone to be banned from classes because of what she wears on her head. But you have to have been raised in Turkey in the 1930s and 1940s, when we were torn by so many ideological battles, to understand the fear we have of being pulled back to absolutism and religious rule."

The conflict over head scarves, along with the state's relentless campaign to harass, prosecute and jail Islamic-oriented politicians, produced a remarkable transformation in the minds of Islamic politicians. Under Erbakan's leadership they had shared the elite's suspicion of democracy, voting, for example, to strip several outspoken Kurdish deputies of their immunity so they could be expelled from Parliament and jailed in 1994. By the end of the century, however, as prosecutors began sending Islamist leaders to jail for saying forbidden things, they began to break away from this consensus, adopting the rhetoric of human rights and demanding repeal of laws that limit freedom of expression. This presented the odd spectacle of a party campaigning for greater democracy while fending off charges from its enemies that it harbored a secret plan to impose fundamentalist rule and destroy democracy.

"When my wife went to MIT in Boston, she wore her head scarf to class every day and nobody said a word," Abdullah Gül, the most sophisticated of the young Virtue leaders, told me once. "If an exam was scheduled on a Muslim holy day, she would ask the professor if she could take it on another day, and every professor agreed immediately. The United States is a secular country that doesn't allow religion to influence government but doesn't suppress it either. That's all we want for Turkey."

I took a liking to Gül, and one day when a provincial prosecutor opened another case against an Islamist politician judged to have said something subversive, I called him for a comment. He said something very bland, and I pressed him. He replied: "Please don't ask me to say any more. If I say what I think, they'll open a case against *me*."

Kemalists may think they have won a victory by striking such fear into the hearts of observant Muslims, but in the long run that is no victory at all. They could oppose fundamentalism far more effectively by reaching an accommodation with the Islamic political movement, a historic compromise under which believers would be allowed to practice, study and debate their religion freely in exchange for their explicit acceptance of secular rule. Turkish Islamists have matured considerably since the Erbakan debacle, and their emerging young leaders are eager for such an accommodation. It would serve Turkey's interests because it would pull the Islamic movement toward moderation instead of demonizing it, forcing it into a corner and allowing it to fester dangerously. Kemalists must recognize that religious belief is a strong force in Turkey and that they cannot hope ever to suppress it.

Frozen into immobility, unable to accept the evolution of their society and long accustomed to seeing enemies under every leaf, guardians of the official ideology are not yet able to make that leap. Instead they relentlessly pressure even the most benign of Islamist politicians, retarding their country's progress toward democracy, alienating themselves from the conservative masses and feeding the polarization of Turkish society. Their clumsy campaign has turned them into models of the very intolerance they claim to detest.

On one of my first visits to a nargile salon, where Turks gather to smoke water pipes, I met a seventy-one-year-old pensioner named Ismet Ertep. He and the men who gather every afternoon at this salon beside the Bosphorus, along with the few women who join them, are heirs to a centuries-old tradition. Their worlds revolve around the soft sound of bubbling water, the sensation of drawing filtered tobacco smoke through long curled tubes and the love of contemplation and understated camaraderie.

"Smoking a nargile is nothing like smoking a cigarette," my new friend told me when I asked him to explain the attraction of this vice. "Cigarettes are for nervous people, competitive people, people on the run. When you smoke a nargile you have time to think. It teaches you patience and tolerance, and gives you an appreciation of good company. Nargile smokers have a much more balanced approach to life than cigarette smokers."

My travels in Turkey confirm these observations. Every time I arrive in a new town, I seek out the nargile salon. It is the ideal place, even better than the barbershop, to discover what is happening and what local people are thinking. The pace in these salons is slow, and time is plentiful. Usually there is not much noise. Conversation is only occasional, al-

ways soft and punctuated by long pauses. The sound of dominoes being played or backgammon tokens being moved is often all that competes with the pipes' gurgling. Some patrons work absently on crossword puzzles and others seem lost in reverie. No alcohol is served, only tea and sometimes coffee. Open windows keep the air fresh.

After a while I realized that I enjoy nargile salons not just because they are good places to take the local pulse but because the sensation of smoking a water pipe is so seductive and satisfying. It starts when the elaborate hookah is placed before you, its bowl cleaned with a soft cloth and then filled with damp tobacco. Some patrons choose strong Turkish tobacco grown on plantations near the Syrian border, but I prefer aromatic apple or cherry blends imported from Egypt and Bahrain. After an attendant fills your pipe with the weed of your choice, he comes by carrying a copper tray piled with burning coals. He picks up a couple of them with a pair of metal pincers and sets them atop the tobacco plug. With a few puffs, you are under way.

It takes at least half an hour to smoke a pipeful of fruit tobacco, even longer for the more potent stuff. The smoke is noticeably cooler than cigarette smoke, and lightly intoxicating. Before long the water begins to turn brown; smokers say it is filtering out many of the harmful substances they would normally be inhaling.

Perhaps no habit is associated more closely with Turks than smoking tobacco. Herman Melville reported walking along Istanbul streets lined with cafés where "Turks sit smoking like conjurers." By the nineteenth century, when he visited, nargiles had become important status symbols. Offering one to a guest was an important sign of trust, and withholding it could be taken as a serious insult. In 1841 a diplomatic crisis broke out with France when the French ambassador demanded a formal apology for not having been offered a chance to smoke with the sultan during a visit to the royal palace.

Today smoking is not only acceptable but almost mandatory in Turkey, especially for men. "A 'manly man' is one who is brave, loud, virile, does not hesitate to fight for what he believes in, does not show his emotions or cry, and knows no fear," the social historian Arın Bayraktaroğlu wrote in a treatise on the Turkish psyche. "He usually has a mustache, and drinks and smokes a lot."

Nargiles were first used in India, but they were primitive ones made from coconut shells. From India the custom spread to Iran and then to Turkey, where it flowered. A separate guild of craftsmen was established to make each of the nargile's pieces. The mouthpiece is traditionally made of amber, the tube of fine leather dyed in different colors, and the sphere that holds the water of glass, crystal or silver, sometimes decorated with floral motifs or other designs. In olden days the water itself used to be scented with perfume or herbs, but that custom has faded.

Turks took to smoking nargiles almost immediately after the first tobacco leaves arrived from America in 1601. Smoking quickly became a craze. People indulged at home, at work and in cafés. "Puffing in each other's faces, they made the streets and markets stink," wrote the contemporary historian Ibrahim Pecevi.

The authorities were not pleased by this development. At nargile cafés, then as now, people do not just smoke. They talk. In a society where the sultan's political power was supposed to be absolute and submission to it unquestioning, the specter of leisurely social gatherings where the topics of the day would inevitably be discussed and debated was unsettling. Ottoman rulers did not like being unsettled, and in 1633 Sultan Murad IV issued a decree that banned smoking on pain of death. An underground immediately took shape. Those afraid of being traced by smoke resorted to inhaling the aroma of chopped leaves. After fourteen years the ban was finally lifted. Tobacco soon became one of the empire's main exports, and Pecevi concluded that it had joined coffee, wine and opium as one of the four "cushions on the sofa of pleasure."

No one believes the nargile will ever regain its supremacy in the tobacco world. Indeed, logic suggests that the nargile salon should be a dying tradition in Turkey. The atmosphere inside is distinctly Oriental, the pace leisurely to the point of torpor. With Turks now turning ever more decisively toward Europe and modernity, they might be expected to shun such places. But although the number of salons is slowly declining, the tradition will not die. Every year brings a new crop of pensioners who have the time and often the desire to spend hours in quiet reflection. On some evenings I even see college students and other young people sitting and puffing. They embrace an experience that is at once solitary and convivial, that evokes nostalgia but also inculcates the values of peace, dialogue and tolerance that today's Turks must absorb if their nation is to fulfill its destiny.

In days gone by, some smokers used to fill their nargiles with illicit drugs. Some still do. I know a small hotel in Istanbul where there is a secret back room that the owner opens for friends and special customers. There they don rich Ottoman costumes, sit on embroidered velvet cushions and smoke a blend of fruit tobacco and hashish. The pleasure of such an interlude approaches that enjoyed by the sultans, who smoked a special mixture of opium, incense and crushed pearls.

"The important thing is not what you put in the pipe but who's with you when you're smoking," a sailor I met in one salon told me. "It's a complete experience. In a café like this one you find the good people, the old people, the interesting people. As long as there's a need for company and friendship, as long as people want to stop and think, there will be nargile cafés."

· FOUR ·

GHOSTS

☪

The shore of majestic Lake Van, eight hundred miles east of Istanbul and even further away culturally and psychologically, is a fine place to sit and reflect on the vicissitudes of history. This is Turkey's largest lake, covering a larger area than Luxembourg or Rhode Island. Around it lies magnificent scenery, with rugged peaks sloping down to wide, fragrant meadows that blaze with wildflowers during spring and summer. Crumbling ruins of ancient castles and fortresses give the region an exotic, almost spiritual aura. The lake itself is disturbingly beautiful, a great sea set incongruously amid a vast expanse of mountains and rocky prairie. Close by are Turkey's borders with Iran, Iraq and Armenia.

Cave paintings, inscriptions carved in rock and countless ancient artifacts testify to this region's rich history. Over the millennia dozens of peoples, some of them now lost to human memory, have lived in or passed through it. In 840 B.C. the town of Van, which sits on the eastern shore of the lake, became the capital of the kingdom of Urartu, a confederation formed to resist rampaging Assyrians. It remained so for more than two hundred years, until it was overrun by the Medes, said to be ancestors of today's Kurds. Later it was an Armenian capital under the governance of the Medes, but today it is almost entirely Kurdish. Among the most popular spots is an island just off the lakeshore that is dominated by the stately ruin of an ancient church. On warm days, families row to the island in small boats and enjoy picnics in its shady groves.

During my first visit to Van, I bought a copy of the only guidebook available in local shops. It says the island church was "built during the reign of King Gagik, under Byzantine sovereignty, between the years of 915 and 921 by architect Manuel, who was a monk." There are descriptions of the intricate friezes that decorate the interior, but that is all. Readers seek in vain for explanations of who King Gagik was and what became of his people. This is no accident, because Gagik was Armenian, and by the time his church was built Van had been Armenian for centuries. It remained so until 1915, the year of apocalypse for Armenians in eastern Turkey. But the words "Armenia" and "Armenian" do not appear in the guidebook I bought. A historical atlas produced by one of Turkey's principal newspapers also makes no reference to the fact that Armenians were once the majority there. History is not always a pleasant subject for Turks. They revel in the glories of their past, as well they should, but choose to ignore what seems dark and dangerous. Their celebration of history is selective. Often they shy away from it rather than confronting its painful lessons.

In the spring of 1915, Armenians in this region made common cause with their Orthodox cousins in Russia, who hoped to seize eastern Anatolia and turn it into a Russian-Armenian province. The Ottoman authorities, understandably alarmed, ordered the deportation of populations "suspected of being guilty of treason or espionage." Soon bands of Ottoman soldiers and Kurdish tribesmen were storming through Armenian towns, forcing their citizens to flee the land of their forefathers and killing hundreds of thousands of them in an orgy of ethnic violence. In one of many eyewitness testimonies, an American diplomat posted in Van reported that these bands were "sweeping the countryside, massacring men, women and children and burning their homes. Babies were shot in their mothers' arms, small children were horribly mutilated, women were stripped and beaten."

Officially sanctioned textbooks in Turkey barely allude to this tragedy, so Turks who learned their history in school may be forgiven for not comprehending its scope. At the small museum in Van, which is devoted principally to Urartian treasures, a few sets of bones and relics are said to be of Muslims who were killed by Armenians in 1915. This exhibit is part of an effort to portray the events of that year as an armed conflict in which both sides suffered regrettable civilian casualties. Most Turks quite earnestly believe that to be true.

Armenians may bear some blame for the tragedy of 1915, and some undoubtedly killed Turks during that tragic year. But this is far from the whole truth. Huge numbers of innocent Armenians were horribly victimized by armed bands operating with the sanction of the Ottoman authorities, and no individual or nation who denies it can honorably claim the mantle of truth.

One glorious summer afternoon, with Lake Van spread out before us like a glistening turquoise carpet, I sat at a lakeside café with a few local Kurds. They were educated professionals born at mid-century, among them a doctor, a poet and an engineer. The waiter had long since cleared away what remained of our kebabs, and we were working our way through a second bottle of *rakı*. For several hours we had been talking about Kurdish history, Kurdish identity, Kurdish frustrations and Kurdish hopes, topics that have dominated conversation in eastern Turkey for many years. As the sun began to set and the mood mellowed, I was struck by an impulse to change the subject. These were friends, and this was as good a time as any to bring up an unpleasant matter.

"Let me ask you guys something," I began, choosing my words carefully to avoid offense. "There used to be a lot of Armenians living here. After 1915, they were gone. People have different explanations for what happened to them. Some say a lot of them were killed. Did you guys ever hear about that?"

After a moment of silence, my friends began to look at each other with embarrassed smirks. Given the fact that these were Kurds and therefore outsiders in their own homeland, I assumed they would be skeptical of official Turkish versions of anything. Still, for a few seconds I feared I was about to hear another mendacious or ill-informed harangue about the events of 1915 that are staples of Turkish discourse. I need not have worried.

"We didn't just hear about it, we *know* about it," my engineer friend began. "Our grandfathers were the ones who did the killing. They told us everything. My grandfather said soldiers gave him a coin for every head of an Armenian that he brought to the command post. He told me there were bodies along the roadside everywhere you went. Kurds were promised that if they could get rid of the Armenians, they could have this land for themselves. In the end it didn't work out that way, but at that time our grandfathers were happy to help with the killing. Don't ever believe that this never happened, or that it was just a minor thing, or that both sides suffered equally. It did happen. Turks and Kurds did it, and Armenians were the victims. Many of them. Many, many, many."

The mood had turned somber, and although the sun had not yet sunk into the lake, I felt a chill. The other guests at my table nodded in agreement as the engineer spoke. "My family has a farm out in the hills east of here," another man said. "One day a couple of years ago my father was out plowing and he turned up some bones. We called the police, and the next day a truck full of soldiers came out to see what we'd found. They started digging, and they came up with five or six skeletons. Some of the skulls were crushed. One had a bullet hole in it. There were Armenian crosses and emblems in the hole. They loaded the bones and everything else into their truck and drove it away. We never heard anything more about it. You can be sure that if those had been bodies of Muslims, the newspapers would have been full of stories about new proof that Armenians had massacred Turks. The bones would be in a glass case at the museum. But what we found didn't fit the Turkish version of history, so it had to be ignored. It's very important for us to ignore things like this. There's a lot we have to pretend didn't happen."

Successive Turkish governments have resisted the campaign aimed at forcing them to acknowledge Ottoman atrocities against Armenians, which is waged not from Armenia itself but from Armenian communities abroad. In Armenia I have found that most ordinary people want to rebuild their country's relationship with Turkey, which is fated to be their neighbor forever, and look toward a better future for both peoples. In the Armenian diaspora, however, anti-Turkish feeling burns with passionate intensity. Some leaders of Armenian communities in the United States and elsewhere have become more nationalistic than most Armenians in Armenia. More than a few are driven by a desire not to shed light on the truth of 1915 but to bring modern Turkey to its knees as a form of long-delayed revenge. Once Turkey is forced to acknowledge the slaughter of 1915, these radicals say, Armenians must demand compensation for their losses and, ultimately, return of their lands and all of eastern Anatolia to Armenian rule.

In the 1970s and 1980s, terrorists calling themselves Commandos of the Armenian Genocide set out to murder Turkish diplomats in the United States and Europe and bomb targets like the Turkish Airlines counter at Orly Airport in Paris. The killing of diplomats in particular—thirty-four of them, a huge number in such a small, close-knit foreign service—embittered and outraged many Turks. Even now, decades later, the foreign ministry, which might otherwise be supporting overtures toward Armenia, remains deeply scarred by the trauma. Its anger is understandable, as is its frustration over the efforts of some Armenians, mostly in the diaspora, to take the events of 1915 out of their historical context and portray them as no more than unprovoked genocide. But Turkey has not set out to refute one set of historical arguments with another. It simply refuses to confront this tragic episode.

Despite what both Turks and Armenians say, much of what happened in 1915 is still unclear. Fair-minded historians might be able to answer many of the remaining questions, but the Turkish authorities, apparently fearing what could emerge from such research, have done all they can to discourage it, including limiting access to Ottoman archives. This is frustrating not for the parties themselves—they are already convinced of their respective versions of the truth—but for the rest of the world.

Armenians have built a Genocide Museum in their nation's capital, Yerevan, and all state visitors are expected to visit it just as they must lay a wreath at Atatürk's mausoleum when they come to Turkey. In one glass case at the museum is a copy of a 1915 telegram in which Ottoman leaders ordered their commanders in eastern provinces to kill as many Armenians as possible and expel the rest. Turks claim that this document is a forgery and that no such telegram ever existed. An even better-known debate is over a quotation from Hitler, who is said to have assured his confederates that they could get away with genocide against Jews by asking, "Who today remembers the extermination of the Armenians?" Armenian historians say they have contemporaneous notes to prove Hitler uttered those words, but Turks say this is yet another clumsy fabrication. It should be relatively easy for historians to determine the authenticity of a key order issued by a national government or a remark made by a major historical figure, but in this case it is not. Emotion and the demands of national chauvinism on both sides overwhelm such pursuits, which, although they may seem merely scholarly, are in fact pregnant with meaning for the future as well as the past.

As Turkey matures, its leaders, and hence its people, will have to face their history more honestly. In the case of the Armenian massacres, they would certainly be right to assert that whatever happened in 1915 was not their doing but that of distant ancestors, since the Ottoman regime then in power has long since passed into history. But to be sincere, such an assertion would have to be accompanied by a recognition of the boundless pain that these events inflicted on the Armenian soul and a pledge to encourage fair-minded historical research. If Armenians can persuade Turks that they mean no ill to the Turkish Republic, Turks should be able to break away from their years of denial and look more dispassionately at their past.

Other nations, including some in Turkey's neighborhood, have already begun to do that. Soon after Bulgaria elected Philip Dimitrov as its first post-Communist prime minister, for example, he came to Turkey and displayed a remarkable willingness to confront unpleasant aspects of his country's history. During the Communist era, thousands of Bulgarian Muslims had been brutalized, robbed of their property and forced to flee to Turkey. When Dimitrov convened a press conference in Istanbul, the first question came from one of these refugees, who had become a reporter for a nationalist newspaper. The question was more of a tirade, not unlike those that Turkish diplomats sometimes hear from Armenians. Dimitrov's answer was startling.

"You are right," he said. "I apologize in the name of Bulgaria. This was not our fault, but the fault of the Communists. And I add that any of our citizens who wish to come back may do so and will receive all possible help from the state." With those few words, Dimitrov set Bulgaria and Turkey on a path toward friendship.

It would be naïve to suggest that a similar statement from a Turkish leader would pacify Armenians, especially rabid Turkey-haters in the diaspora. But the reason Turkey must face its history is not to please Armenians but to become a complete nation, to emerge from its cocoon of insecurity and accept what is bad as well as what is good in that history. More and more Turks realize this, and despite their upbringing they are becoming steadily more interested in learning about the massacres. Between 1999 and 2001 no less than ten new books touching on this subject were published in Turkey, bearing titles like *Armenians in Our Neighborhood* and *The Armenian Taboo*. They bear witness to a new generation's thirst for truth.

Facing the facts of what happened in 1915 will not be enough to quench this thirst. As it becomes possible for Turks to research and discuss and debate the 1915 killings without restriction, it must also become possible to turn over many other rocks, pull back many carpets and look into many dark corners. This process is never easy. Many Europeans are just beginning to face the truth of their parents' and grandparents' collaboration with Nazi occupiers. Others barely acknowledge the brutality with which their forefathers oppressed people in overseas colonies. Even in the United States, efforts to come to grips with the monumental crimes of slavery and the extermination of native peoples are far from complete. But countries, like individuals, cannot become whole until they confront the truth of who they are and what they have been.

No country has been brave enough to look at its own history without illusion. Many, however, have sought to purge themselves of at least some of their historical sin. The example of Argentina may be typical. Once an eminently civilized nation, it fell into barbarism under the rule of fanatic military officers during the 1970s. Argentines shamefully averted their eyes as military squads abducted thousands of law-abiding citizens and tortured them to death on military bases. But after the dictatorship was toppled, elected leaders appointed Argentina's most renowned novelist to head a commission of inquiry. Its report left many questions unanswered, and the government went so far as to give blanket pardons to both generals and torturers. Yet the report documented much about the machinery of military repression, and made it possible for Argentina to begin reclaiming its moral position in the world. Turkey must do the same if it hopes to grow into true maturity.

Confronting the truth of 1915 might actually be an easy way to begin this process, because the massacres of that year were directed and tolerated by a regime that was overthrown by modern Turkey's greatest hero. Since Atatürk himself condemned the Ottomans so harshly, it should not be impossible for his successors to condemn them for their crimes against Armenians. It will be much harder for them to face up to more recent history.

When the Turkish army staged its 1980 coup, many citizens breathed an enormous sigh of relief. Most realized that their country was sliding toward chaos. Leftist groups, some of them frighteningly radical, were gaining strength, and rightists banded together to stop them, usually by the simple expedient of murder. People cowered fearfully in their homes as terrorists and counter-terrorists roamed the streets. Not a day passed without bombings and killings. But immediately after the government was overthrown and military officers began to rule by fiat, the violence ended. Once again the army had saved Turkey from itself.

It is still unclear how Turkey descended into such violent upheaval during the late 1970s. There is much debate over who supported the militant left and who encouraged and armed the rightist gangs that reacted so violently to the left's rising power. Even more painful are questions raised by the wave of arrests and torture after the coup. Thousands of Turks were taken into custody, stripped of their rights and held in appalling conditions for months or years. Many were never told what crimes they were supposed to have committed, much less given a chance to defend themselves. Today it is quite normal to find a journalist, politician, artist, businessman or university professor who turns out to have been one of the victims.

Several of my Turkish friends suffered this abuse. One of them is Orhan Taylan, a gifted painter who during the 1970s joined a leftist group opposed to military intervention in politics. After his arrest he was taken to a police station in Ankara for twelve days of beatings and torture by electric shock, then transferred to the nearby Mamak Military Prison, where a squad of soldiers welcomed him with a thirty-six-hour beating. Over the months that followed he and other prisoners were beaten regularly, deprived of sleep and forced to spend hours in a freezing courtyard while wearing only prison-issue trousers. Orhan believes this regimen was designed not to kill the prisoners, although two of his cell mates did die, but to ruin their health so they would not live long after being released. He spent more than three years in military custody, and when he was released he was so emaciated that friends did not recognize him, so broken that he could not speak at his trial. Ten years later, he and the other members of his Turkish Peace Committee were acquitted of all charges.

In 1999 a provincial prosecutor announced that he was investigating the general who led the 1980 coup, Kenan Evren, with the intention of indicting him for treason. A few days later the prosecutor mysteriously announced his retirement. Soon afterward the justice ministry not only quashed the investigation of Evren but threatened to indict the prosecutor himself for abusing his office.

Turkey's refusal to confront events surrounding the 1980 coup cannot continue forever. Criminal investigations may not be the best way to determine what actually happened during that period, but some way must be found. Turks need to know how their country fell into near-anarchy during the late 1970s and who ordered the imprisonment and abuse of Orhan Taylan and so many other citizens after the coup. They need answers not so they can seek revenge but so they can learn lessons to help them build a stable and peaceful future.

Turks must one day try to answer other, equally urgent questions. Most obvious are those surrounding the violent antagonism between partisans of Turkish and Kurdish nationalism. The war between these partisans was the dominant fact of Turkish life during the 1980s and 1990s, but it still cannot be freely discussed. In few countries has it been so difficult for so long to speak frankly about such an overwhelming issue. Kurds pass down stories of their sufferings from one generation to the next, but even the most sophisticated Turks know almost nothing about them.

"I was absolutely amazed when I started my research," the political scientist Kemal Kırışçı told me after he finished coauthoring a highly perceptive study of the Kurds. "When I began, I thought Kurdish violence had come more or less out of nowhere. That's what most Turks believe. But as I got deeper into my work, I realized that for the whole period from the founding of the Republic up to World War II there were Kurdish rebellions, one after another. I had to ask myself: How come I never knew any of this? Why wasn't it taught to us in school? Why are people in Turkey denied access to our history?"

War between Kurdish insurgents and the Turkish army raged for almost fifteen years, but journalists were forbidden to cover it and few outsiders know much about how it was fought. Certainly both sides committed gross crimes. Establishing the truth about these crimes is vital simply because such a seminal event in any nation's history cannot remain unexamined.

There have been many skirmishes in the Turkish government's campaign to deny or cover up what happened in the Kurdish war, but I have a favorite. One of my Turkish friends, a journalist named Nadire Mater, spent two years tracking down army veterans who had fought in frontline units. She gave each one she found the rare chance to tell his story. It was the first time that Mehmet, as the Turkish recruit is affectionately known, had ever been given such a voice. Nadire took pains not to insert herself into her work; she only turned on her tape recorder and sat back to listen. The stories she gathered were like those told by Americans who fought in Vietnam, Russians who returned from Afghanistan or, for that matter, soldiers who lived through any counter-insurgency campaign. Like most soldiers, they came to fear death, but they also mistrusted their officers, sometimes sympathized with their enemies and rejected the simplistic platitudes that sent them off to war in the first place.

Nadire published her interviews in a volume called *Mehmet's Book*. In many countries it would have been received as an authentic cry of pain from boys sent out as cannon fodder in a war they did not understand. In Turkey, however, its publication was considered a subversive act. Although it contained not a word of commentary, only the verbatim testimony of young men who had served their country in uniform, it was too much for the army to bear. Prosecutors could not find the veterans themselves—Nadire had promised them anonymity in exchange for their candor—so they vented their outrage on her. Her book was banned and she was indicted for slandering the army, a crime punishable by up to twelve years' imprisonment. Only after more than a year of legal maneuvering, with the political climate easing as the war wound down, was she finally acquitted.

It had been hard for Nadire to find ex-soldiers who had fought Kurdish rebels and to persuade them to speak. Like many unhappy veterans, they had melted back into civilian life, closely guarding their memories and emotions. But finding civilian victims of the war is no trouble at all. The towns of southeastern Turkey are overflowing with them. To hear a heartrending tale of forced exile, torture or some other form of brutality, one need only stop a pedestrian or walk into a living room there. Each of these stories represents both a personal tragedy and a piece of modern Turkish history.

Because Turks were denied the right to read or write about this war as it was being fought, most perceive it today as a jumble of violence and terror. Those who lived through it, however, remember each day, each bullet, each torture session. Their dead brethren cry out from the tomb, not necessarily for revenge but for recognition. Who killed them? Who gave the killers their orders? Why, and by what authority? No war is as cruel as a civil war, and even atrocities must be seen in their proper context. Yet questions like these cannot go unanswered forever.

Some of the challenges that history poses to Turkey seep slowly into the public consciousness. Others shock the nation by bursting suddenly onto the front pages. That was what happened one rainy night in the autumn of 1996, when a Mercedes speeding through the western town of Susurluk crashed into a truck that was slowly pulling out of a filling station. The effect of that crash is still reverberating through Turkish society. It has turned Susurluk into an instantly recognizable code word, standing for an obscure and chilling web of conspiracies that weave together the interests of politicians, gangsters and commanders of Turkey's most important military and security agencies.

Three men were riding in the Mercedes that night. One was a top-ranking police commander named Hüseyin Kocadağ, who had once run counter-guerrilla operations against Kurdish rebels and later became a director of Turkey's main police academy. The second was Sedat Bucak, hereditary chief of a feudal Kurdish clan who had gotten himself elected to Parliament and raked in millions of dollars by renting his private army to the Turkish authorities for use in their war against Kurdish nationalists. In the backseat, accompanied by his mistress, a glossy-lipped former beauty queen, was none other than Abdullah Çatlı, one of the country's most famous gangsters, a convicted heroin smuggler who had escaped from a prison in Switzerland and was being sought by Interpol. Çatlı was revered by ultra-rightists who credited him with murdering many "enemies of the state."

What was this odd trio doing together? That question was and is the heart of the Susurluk scandal. No one inside the car could answer it. Çatlı and his mistress were killed instantly. So was the police commander, Hüseyin Kocadağ. The only survivor, Bucak, did not shed any light on the affair because, he claimed, the impact gave him a severe and evidently incurable case of amnesia.

Traffic police who arrived at the scene of the crash found a small arsenal of pistols and silencers in the trunk, together with a diplomatic passport made out in Çatlı's name. Soon it was discovered that Çatlı had held not one but half a dozen diplomatic passports, each with a different name; several identity cards, each also with a different name; and a folder full of gun permits signed by top interior ministry officials. Evidence leaked from police files suggested that he had masterminded crimes ranging from the 1978 massacre of seven leftist students in Ankara to the jailbreak a year later that freed Mehmet Ali Ağca, the contract gunman who went on to shoot Pope John Paul II in Rome.

Çatlı, it turned out, had been far from a freelance killer. Together with an unknown number of other thugs, he had been recruited by government security agents as an assassin. As payment for his services they allowed him to run his lucrative heroin-smuggling operation, launder his money through crooked casinos and kill his rivals whenever he chose, all without interference. To their credit, Turkish newspapers reported these facts as quickly as their reporters could confirm them. Soon every Turk understood why police commanders had protected Çatlı rather than arresting him and turning him over to Interpol.

A thorough investigation of the Susurluk scandal would stain the reputations of many important politicians and military commanders. Some Turks clamor for it, hoping that it would not only reveal ugly truths but also set Turkey on a new path toward political morality. Others fear the political devastation that would certainly follow. Bad as it may be to ignore and thus effectively pardon such crimes, they reason, it would be even worse to bring them to light. One newspaper columnist wrote:

It is now obvious that the state has from time to time engaged in secret operations to commit illegal acts. Undemocratic-minded people, concocting their own brand of "patriotism," decided to use gunmen to eliminate people they saw as a threat. Most of the public believes that the truth about these gangs will never be fully exposed. Is it really an insoluble problem? No. But unraveling the tangle would upset so many powerful individuals and organizations that one tends to think maybe it is better kept as it is.

Susurluk was a key turning point in Turkey's modern history. For generations Turks had clung to a childlike belief that however confusing things seemed, the state probably knew best. Susurluk, meaning not only the facts of the scandal but also the state's refusal to allow it to be fully investigated, shook and began to destroy that faith. It stripped away the myth that security agencies exist to enforce law and that a clear line separates police from criminals. In the process it sobered many Turks and forced them to accept new truths about the society in which they live.

With their consciousness raised so dramatically by Susurluk, Turks were well equipped to grasp the essence of another scandal that rocked the country four years later. Like Susurluk, it exploded with an act of violence, in this case a police raid on a house in an outlying section of Istanbul. Those inside the house shot back, and the resulting gun battle, which lasted several hours, was broadcast live on national television. When it was over, two men emerged unhurt and were led away by police. A third was found dead, more than thirty bullet holes in his body.

What came next was far more horrifying. In a mass grave beside the house, detectives found the nude bodies of ten Kurdish businessmen, all bearing signs of gruesome torture. Some were without arms and legs, and others had nails driven into their skulls. It turned out that this house had been used by a fanatical terrorist group called Hizbullah, which claimed to be fighting to cleanse Turkey of unbelievers and make it safe for Islamic rule. (It is not related to the similarly named group that opposes Israel's role in Lebanon.) Later other Hizbullah hideouts were found in Ankara, Konya and Diyarbakır. Each had its own cemetery full of cruelly disfigured bodies. One contained the body of the feminist campaigner Konca Kuriş, who had written many articles describing Islam as a gentle, tolerant faith that demanded equality for women. The unspeakable tortures to which she and the other victims had been subjected were recorded on videocassettes that were recovered from the hideouts and later played for members of Parliament.

At first the authorities tried to present Hizbullah's savagery as an example of the depths to which religious fundamentalism can sink. But it soon became clear that the true lesson was even more sinister. Hizbullah had been not a band of outlaws but an arm of the Turkish state. Security agencies in southeastern provinces had made common cause with these terrorists. Based on their shared hatred of Kurdish nationalism, most of whose advocates are secular leftists, they had made a terrifyingly simple deal: Hizbullah thugs were turned loose to kidnap and kill their enemies, secure in the knowledge that the police would not investigate them.

There is no other plausible explanation for the hundreds of "mystery killings" that drenched southeastern Turkey in blood during the 1990s. The region was under such tight military control that a sparrow could not have flown across the sky unnoticed. Yet detectives failed to solve even a single one of these killings. That could only be because they did not want to. If they were not themselves the killers, they must have known who were.

When newspapers reported that weapons found at Hizbullah hideouts had come from a military arsenal in the southeast, Tansu Çiller, who had been prime minister when most of the "mystery killings" were committed, proudly admitted her responsibility. "Yes, it was my signature on the order to deliver those weapons," she said. "We met and made a decision. We decided that terror was the main issue and that whatever was necessary to stop it would be done." To the suggestion that she might have exceeded her authority by hiring one terror gang to fight another, she replied simply and no doubt accurately: "The military chief of staff, the governors, the police—everyone worked together on it."

Inevitably, the alliance between the Turkish state and Hizbullah collapsed when the war in the southeast began to subside. Hizbullah, no longer needed to do the state's dirty work, returned to its original agenda, which was to cleanse Turkey of infidels in preparation for Islamic revolution. Then the state recognized it as an enemy and crushed it.

A culture of impunity has protected security agencies in Turkey for many years. Questioning their actions, their commitment to democracy or their patriotism is considered a form of treason. The police and army have staged coups, ordered torture and murder and established criminal gangs to do their bidding. It is difficult for anyone, perhaps especially military officers, to confess such sins in public. Even more difficult is to accept the premise that such confessions are actually beneficial in the long run. Calls for openness, candor and full disclosure fill Turkish commanders with fear.

"You can't get them to look at this in a new way," an American intelligence agent with long experience in Turkey once told me. "Around the time that we were having sexual harassment scandals in our army, I was sitting around drinking *rakı* with a few of them. They were horrified that we were letting these women soldiers tell their stories in the press, and that we were disgracing and punishing our generals. They were saying, 'How can you allow this? How can you let your army be dragged through the mud?' I told them that in the long run this strengthens people's confidence in us, because it shows that we admit our mistakes and don't keep secrets. They didn't buy that at all. One guy said, 'When we punish soldiers for mistreating civilians, we never publicize it.' I was shocked, because I'd never heard of any cases like that. I said, 'You punish soldiers for abusing civilians?' They told me absolutely, they do it all the time. I tried to tell them they should spread these cases all over the newspapers, because they show that the army maintains discipline and doesn't tolerate abuses. No, they said. It wouldn't show that. It would give people the impression that we have an abusive army, and that would play into the hands of our enemies. When something goes wrong you can try to fix it, but you can't ever let outsiders know there was anything wrong."

Every nation makes use of historical myths, and Turkey is no exception. None of these myths, however, can live forever. Ultimately they dissolve or collapse, usually when the societies that created them mature to the point at which they prefer painful truth to pleasant fiction. Turkey is approaching that level of maturity. By rejecting official versions of what lay behind the Susurluk crash and Hizbullah's terror, Turks showed that they are ready to meet history on its own terms. This marks a profound break with the past. If Turks can accept the fact that the men and women who have governed them in recent years have sponsored death squads and turned a blind eye to drug smuggling and other crimes, they must also be ready to face truths about the Kurdish war and the slaughter of Armenians. When they do so they will feel a surge of liberation, and their country will rise to a political and moral standing it has never before enjoyed.

Thetis, the sea nymph who was Achilles' mother, stared up at me one hot day as I walked near the banks of the Euphrates River in southern Turkey. Her face was at the center of an exquisite Roman mosaic that archaeologists had just uncovered, surrounded by a host of dolphins, crabs and other sea creatures. Around me the archaeologists were still digging in the sandy earth. They had found ancient columns, remains of walls and artifacts ranging from pottery shards to a magnificent bronze statue of Mars.

This had once been Zeugma, a city of seventy thousand people at the eastern edge of the Roman Empire. It sat astride some of the world's most important trading routes, and its merchants became very rich. They spent much of their money paying the most accomplished artists of the age to create elaborate mosaics on the floors of their villas, competing with each other to see who could commission the most elaborate and original ones.

In the third century Zeugma fell to invaders from the east and then was struck by an earthquake. Its people drifted away and nature slowly reclaimed and buried the city. Archaeologists pinpointed its location in the mid-1970s and began sporadic excavations, but it was not until a dam was built across the Euphrates half a mile away that anyone felt the need to begin intensive digging there. Zeugma, or at least what were its lower-lying neighborhoods, was about to be flooded by the waters of an artificial lake. The archaeologists wanted to save whatever they could, and soon after they began their work they realized they had stumbled onto one of the most important collections of Roman mosaics ever discovered. They hauled a dozen of them to the nearest museum, but an unknown number were lost to the advancing water without ever being seen.

Publicity about the find at Zeugma led an American foundation to launch a multimillion-dollar project there. Its directors believe that most of the ancient city lies beneath nearby hills that are above the new water level. They hope to spend several years excavating the site, and if their hunch is correct they want to turn it into an open-air museum.

The discovery of these mosaics reflected an aspect of Turkey that foreigners do not always understand. This country's land has been populated since the beginning of human history by an amazing number of civilizations—pagan, Christian and Islamic, coming from Greece, Rome, Egypt, Arabia, Persia and places even farther away. King Midas and King Croesus, Saint Paul and Saint Nicholas, Homer and Herodotus—all came from the land that is now Turkey. This is where Aristotle taught philosophy, where Diogenes searched for an honest man and where Florence Nightingale treated the sick and wounded. Many of history's greatest conquerors have won or lost wars here, among them Alexander, Darius, Tamerlane, Hannibal and Saladin. No other piece of geography on earth has been home to so many different peoples over so many centuries.

Before I began traveling in Turkey, I thought ancient Greece was in Greece as we know it today. Much of it was, of course, including Athens, Sparta and the city-states of the Peloponnese. But many of its greatest, richest and most imposing cities arose in what is now Turkey. Pergamon, whose astonishing temple to Zeus was excavated and carried intact to Berlin in the nineteenth century, is in Turkey. So are Ephesus, which housed one of the greatest libraries of antiquity, and Halicarnassus, once a crossroads of the world known for its towering lighthouse. Traveling along Turkey's Aegean and Mediterranean coasts, one is overwhelmed by the density of Hellenic ruins there.

My favorite of these ruins is Phaselis, once a thriving capital and now a quiet, stately and abandoned monument facing an implausibly gorgeous Mediterranean cove not far from Antalya, the region's main city. It is well enough preserved to convey a vivid sense of what it must have been like to live in antiquity. Founded by colonists from Rhodes in the seventh century B.C., it quickly became a trading center rich enough to have its own mint, which not surprisingly produced coins depicting nautical scenes. Alexander spent several months there, choosing it over other towns in the region partly because he was deeply moved at the sight of its most impressive artifact, a broken spear supposedly used by Achilles. "The extraordinarily beautiful town had three harbors, straight avenues, a theater and plazas," he wrote. "Although it was winter, roses were in bloom everywhere."

Phaselis's broad main street, paved with cut stones, is lined with the ruins of many Roman structures, including a gymnasium that opens onto a public bath, a long aqueduct, a gate dedicated to Hadrian and a classically proportioned theater with twenty rows of stone seats. When I was there a large tortoise was all that moved on what had been the stage, but when I closed my eyes I thought I heard a toga-clad poet chanting tales of seafaring heroes. Cleopatra is said to have visited Phaselis, and it takes only a bit of imagination to picture her in one of the seats.

What is most remarkable about Phaselis is that for all its splendor, it is little known and rarely visited. If it were the only ancient site in Turkey it would be jammed with tourists every day, but it is one of thousands. Turkey has so many places like this that it cannot even catalog them, much less excavate and protect them. It is hard to turn a shovel without discovering something ancient. Even in Istanbul, the long-planned subway system cannot be extended to serve some of the most densely populated neighborhoods because any tunnel there would have to be drilled through priceless ruins.

One summer I spent a week sailing around the peninsula west of Phaselis. Two thousand years ago this was the heart of an ancient confederation called the Lycian League, which at various times was under the control of Greeks, Romans, Persians, Egyptians and even bands of pirates. Near one seaside village I explored a necropolis where the Lycians buried their dead in above-ground tombs, some of them freestanding and others carved into the sides of cliffs. Atop a nearby hill was a well-preserved Byzantine fortress built on the ruins of one from Lycian times. On my way down I stopped to admire the smallest ancient amphitheater I have ever seen, carved from rock in a neat semicircle and only large enough to hold about two hundred fifty people.

On that trip I spent one day inland. After driving about thirty-five miles in a rented car, I parked at the foot of a deep canyon in the Taurus range, which runs along much of Turkey's Mediterranean coast. Guided by a friend who had been there before, I walked for an hour along a Roman road and then across a farmer's yard where goats were grazing. Suddenly, emerging from a poplar grove, I found myself facing the ruined towers and walls of an ornate Byzantine church with two octagonal chambers in opposite corners. This church is not mentioned in any guidebook, and probably very few outsiders have laid eyes on it in recent centuries. How many undiscovered places like this there are across Turkey's vast territory!

Even the discovered sites are so remote and widely scattered that many are rarely visited. In Turkey I have followed routes taken by Julius Caesar and Saint Peter, walked among weird monoliths carved by Hittite sculptors three thousand years ago, crawled into caves used as churches by early Christians and climbed rocky hills up to crusaders' castles. Once I took a drive through eastern Turkey that in the space of just four days took me to unforgettable ruins from half a dozen great cultures.

My first stop was the huge fifteenth-century Ottoman cemetery at Ahlat, on the shore of Lake Van. It is filled with tall headstones carved with intricate Arabic inscriptions, mute messengers from times now only barely remembered, and at the same time objects of powerful beauty. From Ahlat I drove north along the Iranian border to the spectacular Ishak Pasha castle, built atop a mountain crag in the eighteenth century by a clan called the Çıldıroğlu, who, depending on which expert one believes, were either Georgians, Turks, Armenians or Kurds. I continued past snowcapped Mount Ararat to Kars, formerly a Russian garrison town, and then to the abandoned Armenian capital of Ani, which around the year 1000 was the seat of kings, bishops and one hundred thousand prosperous citizens; today it is surreal and abandoned, the

shells of its great churches and palaces conveying a deep sense of the im-
permanence of grandeur. My last stops were in the verdant hills around
Artvin, near the border with Georgia, which are dotted with awe-
inspiring Georgian churches more than a thousand years old.

Nowhere else in the world can one possibly have a tour like this.
Turks are rightly proud of what their land has to offer, but in one sense
not proud enough. Their culture ministry is pitifully poor, barely able to
pay its employees and maintain the country's most famous monuments,
much less preserve the lesser-known ones or begin new excavations. The
sheer number of ancient sites in their country has jaded them. Even
some people at the highest ranks of the government don't seem to under-
stand what lies on and beneath Turkish soil. All too many of their trea-
sures are slowly disintegrating.

Some Turks are less than comfortable with their land's pre-Islamic
history. They worry that if they celebrate their Arabian, Kurdish, Greek,
Armenian and Georgian pasts, Turkey will seem less theirs. Taught from
childhood that they are descended from Turkic tribes that followed the
legendary gray wolf out of Central Asia in the tenth century, many of
them have an insular Turkocentric view of the world, reinforced by the
government's having changed hundreds of place-names to make them
sound more Turkish. The mayor of Ankara (formerly Angora) has gone
so far as to launch a campaign to change the city's symbol from one
based on a Hittite design to one including a mosque; he says the Hittites
were "not Turkish."

In fact, Turks are heir to every culture that ever existed in Anatolia.
Their heritage is vigorous, cosmopolitan, diverse and unimaginably rich.
They should embrace it wholeheartedly and become caretakers of all the
glittering riches of Anatolian history.

FIVE

THE KURDISH PUZZLE

☪

An old man who is among the most respected denizens of the twisting Diyarbakır bazaar sat on a tattered sofa one afternoon and spun out his memories of Kurdish struggle. Speaking with a precision and energy that belied his years, he began his tale in the 1930s. There were patterns over the decades: rebellions crushed, villages burned, relatives arrested, friends lost to unknown assassins.

"Even though it's dangerous for me to say this, I have been greatly oppressed in my lifetime," he told me as he leaned his chin on his wooden cane. "I have been tortured many times. One of my sons died after forty days of torture by the police. All of this has happened to me and to so many of us because we claim our rights. Kurds don't even have minority rights in a region where we are the majority. But we have to keep demanding them. We can't stop. This war is our third since the great uprising in 1938. All have been fought for the same reason. Each generation produces a leader who fights for our rights."

Sitting silently nearby, taking it all in, were a handful of earnest-looking teenagers. They are the new generation of Kurds, eagerly absorbing stories that fire their political commitment. Watching this scene, I had the sense of a torch being passed. As long as Kurdish consciousness is nourished this way, no amount of military or political pressure applied by the Turkish authorities will be able to pacify these people.

Despite its poverty and the sense of intimidation that hangs in its air, Diyarbakır, with its winding streets, hidden courtyards and ancient city wall, became one of my favorite cities in Turkey. What truly enthralled me about the Kurdish region, though, was not its cities but the grandeur of its countryside. Much of western Turkey is either coastal lowland or rolling hills covered by farms and orchards. Central provinces are rugged and barren. The Black Sea region is cool, verdant and alpine. But no part of this country is as overwhelming as the east. Jagged peaks and precipices soar above gorges and lakes. In the warm months, dazzling colors and sweet fragrances assault the senses. When the snow falls it falls without pity, blanketing huge areas in deep drifts, cutting some villages off from the outside world and all but burying others. The landscape here is oversize, like the passions of the tribesmen who have lived amid it for millennia. It is not a geography that encourages moderation. Not coincidentally, it is also ideal guerrilla territory.

The Kurdish conflict is Turkey's festering wound, and to travel to Diyarbakır and from there through eastern provinces where Kurds constitute the large majority is to see the country's ugliest face. Caught in the grip of irrelevant experience, convinced that they are fighting to defend their nation's very existence and desperately resisting the worldwide trend toward regionalism and local self-rule, successive Turkish leaders have willingly done whatever was necessary to crush Kurdish nationalism. Despite or perhaps because of their refusal to compromise, Kurdish consciousness is stronger today than it has ever been.

For thousands of years Kurds have lived in what used to be called Mesopotamia and what some now call Kurdistan, a name the Turkish government rejects because of its supposed political taint. Today they are estimated to number about thirty million, with half in Turkey, another quarter in Iraq, about fifteen percent in Iran, five percent in Syria and the rest scattered in the region and beyond. Until recently most thought of themselves not as Kurds but as members of one clan or another. Only during the last decades of the twentieth century did they come to consider themselves part of a single nation or people. Governments of all countries in which they live view them with suspicion.

In the fourth century B.C. the Greek commander Xenophon came across tribesmen who may have been ancestors of today's Kurds, and later wrote: "They lived among the mountains, were very warlike and did not obey the king." That is the best one-sentence description of Kurds ever written, as true today as it was then. Although they have never had a country of their own, Kurds have no tradition of submitting to anyone.

In modern Turkey no one is discriminated against for being Kurdish. Many Kurds have reached the pinnacle of success in business, entertainment and even politics. Others could share this success by acknowledging that first and foremost they are Turks, but millions refuse to do so, and largely as a result of their stubbornness they are among Turkey's poorest citizens. Some live in muddy ghettos on the edges of prosperous, lovely towns like Safranbolu, far from their ancestral homeland. Most remain in the east, unemployed and unhappy.

"The Government has long denied the Kurdish population, located largely in the southeast, basic political, cultural and linguistic rights," the United States State Department asserted in one human-rights report. "As part of its fight against the PKK, the Government forcibly displaced noncombatants, failed to resolve extra-judicial killings, tortured civilians and abridged freedom of expression."

The revolutionary PKK, or Kurdistan Workers Party, was born not in the hardscrabble villages of Turkey's southeast but in Ankara. It was there that a Marxist firebrand named Abdullah Öcalan and a handful of his comrades met during the mid-1970s to begin building what would become the most effective rebel force ever to take up arms against the Turkish state. Kurds are poor, share a collective memory of rebellion and have used guns to solve their problems for as long as there have been guns. This, Öcalan concluded, made them the ideal base for a revolutionary movement in Turkey. He and his brothers in arms were infected by the same curses that have driven politics in this part of the world for too long: ethnic chauvinism, dictatorial arrogance and the impulse to mindless violence.

In 1978 this core of radicals, together with a handful of non-Marxist Kurds, formally established the PKK. After the 1980 military coup they moved their headquarters to Syria, where President Hafez al-Assad quickly recognized them as a useful tool in his country's long-running feud with Turkey. Encouraged by his patrons in Moscow, who were also looking for ways to undermine Turkish power, Assad gave the PKK training bases, weapons and generous financial support. Soon the guerrillas were ready to fight. On August 15, 1984, they launched their war with rocket and machine-gun attacks on Turkish government outposts in two villages near the Syrian border.

Within a few years the guerrilla force had attracted thousands of militants, and war had spread across eastern Turkey. The government responded by placing the region under "emergency rule," a form of martial law that permits censorship, detention without trial and the use of summary tribunals to try suspected subversives. But these efforts proved inadequate, and within a few years PKK units were moving freely through Turkey's eastern provinces, even naming their own mayors, judges and tax collectors. Energized by their success, Öcalan's men began assassinating Turkish schoolteachers who by the luck of a draw had been assigned to the southeast, newspaper vendors who dared to distribute Turkish newspapers and villagers they considered too friendly to the army.

In the early 1990s the government realized that what it officially described as a band of cutthroat terrorists was actually a disciplined military force that had won at least nightime control of huge swaths of territory, enjoyed growing popular support in the combat zone and counted on backing not just from Syria but also from powerful groups in Russia, Iraq, Armenia and Greece. Its treasury was swollen by profits from heroin smuggling and by contributions, voluntary and otherwise, from Kurdish exiles in Europe. The PKK had come to embody the most terrifying Kemalist nightmare: a conspiracy of foreign powers and renegade locals aimed at dismembering the Turkish motherland. Military commanders told Prime Minister Tansu Çiller they could crush this threat only if they were allowed to wage war without quarter. Lacking the imagination to come up with an alternative, she eagerly agreed. Soon hundreds of thousands of Turkish soldiers were flooding eastward to launch one of the century's great counter-insurgency campaigns.

The army began by identifying hundreds of villages and hamlets suspected of being pro-PKK. Squads marched systematically from one to the next, calling residents together and announcing that the village was to be burned in an hour. Distraught villagers would try to gather what they could of their possessions while soldiers machine-gunned their cattle and set their fields and crop stores ablaze.

At the same time, security agencies enlisted gangs of nationalist gunmen and sent them off to assassinate civilians suspected of sympathizing with Kurdish nationalism. Police "special teams" and rural gendarmes were encouraged to use whatever techniques of torture they considered necessary, either to extract information or simply to intimidate perceived enemies into silence. The Kurdish political party was banned and its representatives in Parliament dragged from their offices, summarily convicted of treason and sentenced to draconian prison terms.

The brutality of these tactics is indisputable, as is the brutality of the PKK's rebellion. Yet the eagerness with which some foreign governments have condemned Turkey, justified as condemnation may be, is more than a little disingenuous. Turkey was facing a threat to its very existence as a unified state, and it responded the way other countries in the post-war world have responded when peoples under their sovereignty rose in rebellion. The Turkish campaign against the PKK was comparable in various ways to those waged by the Dutch in Indonesia, the British in Malaya, the French in Algeria, the Americans in Vietnam, the Serbs in Bosnia and the Russians in Chechnya. Turks understandably react unpleasantly when those former imperial powers condemn them for using tactics they themselves perfected not so long ago.

Most Turks, eager to believe the best about their army and knowing only what the pro-government press told them about the war, perceived it as a heroic struggle against terrorism. Young soldiers by the hundreds were coming home in flag-draped coffins, and Turks began to view the PKK as a font of unspeakable evil. But in the southeast everything looked different. There people used the word "martyr" to describe not soldiers ceremoniously buried with military honors but guerrillas dumped into unmarked graves. During my trips through the vast war zone, which covered an area the size of New England, I never found a Kurd who did not consider the security forces guilty of repression, torture and murder. Everyone there either has suffered at the hands of men in uniform or knows someone who has.

This campaign naturally led many Kurds to hate the Turkish army and the state it represents. It also led many to view Abdullah Öcalan and his PKK as beacons of hope. By banning almost every kind of Kurdish organization, the government made it impossible for moderate Kurdish leaders to emerge. This policy allowed Öcalan, a figure of marginal intelligence and great political immaturity, to became the sole embodiment of Kurdishness. Even today he could easily be elected mayor of any town or city in southeastern Turkey.

Security officers carrying poorly concealed pistols shadowed me whenever I walked through the streets of Diyarbakır, the unofficial capital of the Kurdish region, but sometimes I managed to sneak out alone. Wandering through the dusty alleyways that spread back from main streets, I would stop to chat at grocery stores, shops and tea houses. Everywhere, even in the midst of this poverty, I found a remarkable sense of ethnic identity, a stubborn belief that as long as people hold on to their Kurdish consciousness they cannot be truly defeated.

"People say this is a new problem, but I'm forty-four years old and it's been going on ever since I can remember," a soccer coach sitting in a nargile salon told me one day. "Europeans would see this as something that has to be discussed and negotiated so that people can stop hating and dying and killing. But Turkey is different. Here the impulse is to fight, not to talk. In 1915 it was the Armenians who had to be killed; now it's us. We're living under a regime that doesn't see human life as something sacred. They don't care how many people have to die. What's important is keeping power."

I puffed for a while and finally ventured to ask my fellow smokers what they thought of the PKK. There was a long silence. Either the men around me were enjoying one of the breaks in conversation that make nargile salons centers of reflection, or I had crossed into forbidden territory. Finally one man spoke up. "How can you ask us that question?" he said. "You can imagine how we feel."

Journalists had to apply for permission to travel in the war zone, and most of the time my applications were ignored. Once in the spring of 1998, for reasons I never understood, one was approved, and immediately I flew to Diyarbakır and set off by car toward the mountains. At the first military checkpoint outside town I was invited to sit at a picnic table while my credentials were checked. I found three officers there sipping tea. They were curious about my impressions, but rather than sharing them, I began asking questions. If the guerrillas had no support, I wondered, how had they survived and waged war for so long? Might there not be some ordinary Kurds who support them?

The officers looked incredulous. Obviously they found the very idea absurd. "There is no political or social basis to this conflict," said a major who told me he was serving his third tour of duty in the southeast. "It is all fomented by foreign countries. You say it is a war, but I have to correct you. This is not a war. It's a peace operation. We're defending the country from terrorism, just as armies do all over the world. The only difference here is that it's taking a little longer."

I spent half an hour chatting with these officers. They seemed genuinely convinced that the PKK was implacably evil, that it had not a shred of popular support and that the only option for the Turkish state was to fight on until it had wiped away every vestige of Kurdish nationalism. Amazingly, they believed this could actually be accomplished.

Word finally came that I should be allowed to pass. Perhaps I would be allowed to reach my destination, Lice, a remote town in the heart of the war zone, after all. This was a thrilling prospect, because Lice (pronounced LEE-jeh) had been closed to outsiders for years. Even members of Parliament had been refused permission to visit. Lice is not just a hotbed of Kurdish nationalism but a legend, a rumor, a place few have ever visited but many believe they know.

For years the area around Lice was controlled by the PKK, and when the army began its scorched-earth campaign in the early 1990s, the town was among the first targets. Soldiers first razed the outlying villages, then set fire to nearby forests in which guerrillas had found refuge and finally, one day in 1993, burned down the town itself. Ninety percent of its ten thousand suddenly homeless residents fled to Istanbul or other cities, carrying identity cards that listed Lice as their birthplace and thus marked them instantly as suspicious or worse. They have been replaced by refugees from destroyed villages who were herded into town and allowed to build new homes on the rubble.

The checkpoint at the edge of Lice was manned by plainclothes officers from "special teams," men whose job it was either to ferret out terrorists or to repress and torture Kurds, depending on one's perspective. They were tough-looking guys, beefy and with no necks. Unlike their counterparts in Diyarbakır, they made no effort to cover the pistols on their hips. After a few minutes, several of them climbed into an unmarked car and told me to follow them. As I drove into Lice I turned to my Kurdish translator, who had doubted we would ever be allowed in. He was smiling nervously and shaking his head in disbelief.

We were led to the local police station, and as I crossed the threshold I felt an involuntary shudder. Who knew how many unfortunates, guilty or otherwise, had been brought through this door for rough, perhaps very rough, interrogation sessions? Inside, a thickset fellow named Hasrettin Bayraktar introduced himself as the chief of security in Lice. He seemed friendly enough as he asked me what I wanted to do, who I wanted to see, what I knew about Lice and what I hoped to learn.

I told him I had no agenda and simply wanted to look around and chat with townspeople. He assured me I was free to do so, and told me Lice was all but pacified. "Things are much better than when I got here three years ago. We lost a lot of people to migration, but not many are leaving now. We have a factory here. People are free to farm their land. When people don't work they get bad ideas in their heads, but now that there are more jobs, fewer people think like that."

Most people in Lice know better than to talk to strangers, but I was able to discover a few of the town's secrets. A strict eight o'clock curfew had been in force for years. Food distribution was controlled by the police, who feared that if free sale were allowed, people would buy extra and smuggle it to the guerrillas. A female suicide bomber had killed herself and wounded a few soldiers at a grocery store a couple of months before.

In one overgrown lot I picked up a piece of glass that had melted into a strange shape during the great fire that destroyed the town. I asked a man passing nearby who had set that fire. He shrugged and said he didn't know. When I asked if the fire might have been sparked by a bolt of lightning, a mischievous smile crept over his face. "Lightning," he mused, turning the idea over in his head. "That must have been it. Lightning."

I was torn between my curiosity and my desire not to cause trouble for the people I spoke to in Lice. Most would say only a sentence or two, always choosing their words carefully, and then hurry off. When I asked one man if the police considered everyone in Lice either a terrorist or a potential terrorist, he kept on walking as he nodded and answered, "That's the way it is." I found a refugee from a burned village and asked who burned it. He stared at me for a moment and then asked in reply, "Who burned *your* village?"

Lice has only one main street, dotted by cafés where unemployed men spend much of the day drinking tea and smoking. Across from an enormous statue of Atatürk, standing on a base that bears the admonition "The Nation Is One and Cannot Be Divided," I found several men sitting on a sidewalk smoking nargiles. One of them looked to be well into his seventies but told me he was just fifty. Like most people in town, he had no work. Unlike most of them, he spoke freely.

"First the villages were torched, then it was our turn," he began. "They saw this place as some kind of temple, and they wanted to destroy it. It was a way of showing that they have the power to do whatever they want to us and we can't do anything back. Now the town is like an open prison. We can't talk and we can't move without being watched.

"But we still feel free," he went on. "Real freedom comes from inside you. I can still think what I want. I know I was born a Kurd and I'll die a Kurd. They can't take that away from me. So in spite of everything I'm a happy man. I'm winning my own personal war, because they haven't been able to crush my mind." He puffed his bubbling pipe and seemed absolutely tranquil.

I was deeply moved by his strength of character, but also worried. Wouldn't police agents come to bother him the moment I was gone?

"They will," he replied simply. "I'm ready for that too."

At that moment a new customer arrived and sat down. It was immediately clear that everyone knew him as a police informer, and with a quick hand gesture my friend signaled that our interview was over. I smoked for another couple of minutes, finished my tea and took my leave.

The Turkish army's vast numerical superiority in both men and weapons made its victory over the PKK only a matter of time. By the end of the

1990s the military tide had turned, with soldiers painstakingly winning control of one mountain after another. It was a costly victory, not just in blood and treasure but also because it deeply alienated the people of southeastern Turkey and blackened the country's image abroad. The generals probably realized that this would be the price of victory, but they saw no other option. In the early years of the conflict, the PKK had declared its intention of turning southeastern Turkey into an independent Marxist state. Later Öcalan claimed several times that he was ready to negotiate a cease-fire and accept political compromises, but by then it was too late. The army had taken too many casualties and was determined to destroy his rebel force regardless of political cost.

As the war wound down, the PKK could claim a curious legacy of abject failure mixed with astonishing triumph. Its fighting force had been reduced to ragged bands cowering in foreign hideouts and unable to launch anything more than hit-and-run attacks inside Turkey. Its popular support network had been broken by the government's savagely effective military campaign. Perhaps most important, it had utterly failed to evolve into a democratic movement embodying the aspirations of a long-suffering people. Instead, thanks to Öcalan's megalomania, it was a rigid Leninist force that not only used terror against its enemies but punished its own dissenting members with torture and summary execution.

Despite these failures, however, the PKK could claim what were from its perspective two great victories. First and most transcendently, Kurds emerged from the war with a greater sense of their own identity than ever before in their history. An entire generation of Kurds has grown up knowing that Kurds have been at war with Turks. Even those who did not support the rebellion have come to believe that there is such a thing as a Kurdish nation and that they belong to it. Whatever may be said about Öcalan's ruthlessness and corruption, he must be recognized, for better or worse, as the figure who lit the fire of Kurdish consciousness in countless souls.

Öcalan's second triumph was his success in luring the Turkish army into the brutality of counter-insurgency warfare. Armies fighting to defeat guerrilla uprisings use a classic set of tactics: they burn villages, shoot cattle, destroy food depots, displace populations and torture and execute suspected collaborators. Turkish security forces did all this and more. They won their war but, in doing so, earned worldwide opprobrium and polarized their own people. Öcalan wanted to inflict a deep wound on Turkey, and he succeeded.

For most of the war years Öcalan lived in Syria, supposedly a guest of the dictator Assad but in effect his prisoner. Like every other leader in the region, Assad had no use for Kurds and did not hesitate to repress his own Kurdish population whenever necessary. His support for Öcalan had nothing to do with the Kurdish cause and everything to do with his fear of Turkey's rising power. He knew that by encouraging Öcalan's rebellion he could tie down huge numbers of Turkish troops and bleed the Turkish economy.

Since the early 1980s Turkey had been diverting water from the Euphrates for large-scale irrigation and hydroelectric projects, ignoring Assad's bitter complaints that the diversions were turning the adjacent region of Syria into a desert. Assad calculated that if PKK guerrillas fought well, he might be able to force Turkish leaders to accept a deal in which he would end his support for their rebellion if Turkey would adopt a more generous water policy. In his dreams he may even have imagined that a PKK victory might help Syria regain Hatay, an ethnically Arab province of southern Turkey that sticks down like a thumb into Syria. Hatay was considered part of Syria from the Roman era until the early twentieth century. In 1939, however, departing French colonial rulers held a referendum asking local people whether they wanted to be left under Syrian or Turkish sovereignty. Most chose Turkey, and as a result France bequeathed Hatay to the Turks. To this day many Syrians believe Turkey stole it by rigging the referendum, and their official maps still show it as a Syrian province. Assad decided that sponsoring Öcalan was a fine way to punish Turks for their perfidy and perhaps extract valuable concessions from their government.

By the late 1990s the military balance between Turkey and Syria had shifted decisively. The Turkish army had bought hundreds of tanks and jet fighters, complemented by a host of high-tech weapons systems, and could claim to be the only modern fighting force in the Middle East other than Israel's. Syria was weak by comparison, friendless since the collapse of the Soviet Union and as backward militarily as it was politically. Turkish generals decided it was time to decapitate the PKK by demanding that Syria surrender Öcalan.

This campaign began the way all such campaigns begin in Turkey, with a speech by a general. In this case the messenger was General Atilla Ateş, chief of staff of the Turkish army. His threat, delivered in the autumn of 1998, was simple: Syria must expel Öcalan or risk war with Turkey. To underline his seriousness he sent ten thousand soldiers to mass along the Syrian border. Assad buckled almost immediately, and suddenly Öcalan was gone from Damascus. For a few days no one knew where he was, but intelligence agencies soon tracked him to a dacha outside Moscow. President Boris Yeltsin wanted him out of Russia, and a group of Italian leftists with connections to the Italian government, then led by ex-Communists, came to his aid. They brought him to Rome, and a couple of days after his arrival Prime Minister Massimo D'Alema said that extradition was out of the question since Italy's constitution forbids extraditing anyone who could face the death penalty in his home country. Turks were outraged, and their anger intensified as prominent Europeans began to suggest that since terrorists were turning to peacemakers in other places, maybe Öcalan could do the same.

"He calls himself a guerrilla, but what could he do when his people were being systematically killed?" asked Danielle Mitterrand, widow of the French president and a longtime supporter of the Kurdish cause. She suggested that if Öcalan was to be put on trial, Turkish generals should be in the dock with him.

Within hours of Öcalan's arrival in Rome, throngs of Kurds living in exile there converged in front of the hospital to which he had been admitted for a checkup, waving Kurdish flags and chanting pledges of eternal love for their leader. Soon they were joined by thousands of their compatriots who arrived in buses, trains and auto caravans from other parts of Europe. So passionate was their emotion that they even set upon and beat Turkish journalists who had come to cover the story.

"If so many Kurds are coming to support him, then it cannot simply be a terrorist issue," reasoned Cardinal Achille Silvestrini of Rome. "It is a European issue."

What had at first looked like a triumph for Turkey became, almost overnight, a public relations disaster. Öcalan took up residence at a seaside villa and started receiving visitors as if he were a head of state. European politicians focused on the Kurdish problem in ways they never had while Öcalan was living in remote obscurity in Damascus. Some suggested that instead of being tried he should be invited to an international forum where he could present his case to world opinion. Prime Minister D'Alema urged Turkey to "find a solution to this long and bloody conflict by following the examples of Northern Ireland and the Basque country." Hans-Ulrich Klose, chairman of the foreign affairs committee in Germany's parliament, called Öcalan's capture "a good opportunity for solving the country's problems with the PKK and making the necessary reforms in Turkey." The European Parliament called for an international conference on the Kurdish issue.

Turks furiously rejected these ideas as intolerable infringements on their sovereignty. Whipped into a nationalist frenzy by politicians and the press, they turned their anger from Öcalan to Italy. Wild-eyed demonstrators burned Italian flags and Versace neckties in street-corner bonfires. Some of them, carrying placards that showed Prime Minister D'Alema with long fangs as he consumed Turkish children, or maps of Italy drenched in blood, tried to storm Italian diplomatic missions. Others jammed rallies where they joined in impassioned chants of "Damn Italy! Damn Italy!" Fruit dealers offered customers the chance to stomp on imported Italian lemons. Leaflets signed "Turkish Youth" urged patriots to stop eating pizza and spaghetti. Television transmitted pictures of these excesses across Europe, where they naturally appalled everyone who watched. Turkey's case against Öcalan was forgotten, replaced in the popular mind by images of Turks as mindless fanatics bereft of the manners expected of those who would sit at the European table.

But Turkey's leaders had learned from their successful intimidation of Syria that flexing their considerable muscle could bring results. They turned up their pressure on Italy, not just on the streets but in the boardrooms. Turkish companies began to cancel contracts with their Italian partners, and the army announced it would no longer accept Italian bids on lucrative procurement contracts. Leading Italian politicians became uncomfortable with the position in which their country suddenly found itself, and Prime Minister D'Alema soon came to share their misgivings. One day, eight weeks after Öcalan had arrived in

Rome, he was suddenly gone. A few days later a private plane on which he was a passenger appeared in the air above Rotterdam, but air-traffic controllers there denied him permission to land. So did their counterparts in several other European cities. Frustrated in another attempt to find a home, the fugitive vanished again.

Exactly twelve days after that bizarre flying circus, on the morning of February 16, 1999, my telephone rang and a friend in Ankara told me excitedly that Öcalan had fallen into Turkish hands. At first I had trouble believing it. Quickly, like almost everyone else in Turkey, I switched on my television. A few minutes later Prime Minister Bülent Ecevit, who had taken office just a month before, appeared on the screen. He seemed to be struggling to contain his emotions as he read from a paper he held in his hands.

"Ladies and gentlemen, I have an announcement," he began. "The terrorist has been in Turkey since three o'clock this morning."

For a short while I was so confused and amazed that I could not focus on the details. When they emerged they made a wild story of betrayal and derring-do. It turned out that after his failed attempt to find a European government that would grant him asylum, Öcalan had secretly been taken under the protection of Greece. His plane refueled at a Greek airport, remained there for a few hours while senior officials made a series of frantic telephone calls, and then took off for, of all places, Kenya. Öcalan entered Nairobi with a false Cypriot passport and was whisked to the Greek embassy compound.

By offering one of their diplomatic missions as a clandestine shelter for a fugitive wanted not only in his homeland but also by Interpol, Greek officials broke both international law and the most elementary rules of diplomacy. They did not act out of any deep conviction that Öcalan was a wronged innocent, or even out of serious sympathy for the Kurdish cause. They simply believed in the age-old axiom that holds that the enemy of one's enemy is one's friend. Öcalan had greatly weakened Turkey, and, by their Machiavellian calculation, this made him a uniquely valuable asset.

Greek intelligence officers, however, made a terrible mistake in choosing to hide their man in Nairobi. The American embassy there had been bombed with horrific loss of life only a couple of months before, and more than one hundred agents from the CIA and other secret services were in town for the investigation. Öcalan himself was no cleverer. Once inside the Greek compound, he insisted on strolling around the grounds rather than remaining out of sight. He refused suggestions that he move out of Nairobi to a remote spot in the countryside. Most incredibly of all, he began using his cell phone to call people he thought might help him find a permanent base somewhere. He could hardly have made his presence more obvious if he had sent change-of-address cards to foreign embassies.

When Kenyan officials learned that Öcalan was illegally on their territory, they immediately demanded that the Greek ambassador remove him. No one other than a handful of intelligence agents is sure what happened next. According to the most widely disseminated version, Öcalan was hustled into a car one night and told that he was headed for the Nairobi airport. Probably he believed he was going back to Greece, or if not there then to some new sanctuary arranged by his Greek patrons. But before his car had driven far it was intercepted by a team of commandos. They pulled him out, threw him into their jeep, raced to the airport and hustled him onto a waiting Turkish plane.

How could this have happened? Greek diplomats angrily denied that they had given up hope of protecting Öcalan and knowingly led him into a trap. Kenyans denied that they had known about the operation in advance. Israel denied rumors that the Mossad had designed it. The United States denied that its agents had provided any "direct assistance." In the end, the truth or falsity of those denials was unimportant. What mattered was that "Operation Safari," as the Turks code-named it, had succeeded. After more than a decade as Turkey's most wanted fugitive, Öcalan came home a prisoner.

No Turkish film ever packed the emotional power of the three-minute video that showed commandos leading the blindfolded revolutionary onto a private plane at the Nairobi airport, handcuffing him to his seat and then unmasking him to show his sweat-drenched face. For two days and nights television stations broadcast it almost continuously, as if viewers needed to see it a dozen times in order to believe it, another dozen to unleash their jubilation and then a dozen more to focus their hatred.

Even more astonishing than the pictures was the soundtrack. This monumental figure, object of one of the world's last Stalinist personality cults, hero to thousands of Kurds and demon to millions of Turks, a man who could order executions between dinner courses without the slightest disturbance to his digestion, blubbered like a child.

"I really love Turkey and the Turkish people," he told his captors. "My mother was Turkish. Yes, if the truth needs to be told, I love Turkey and the Turkish nation and I want to serve it. If I have the chance, I would be pleased to serve. Let there be no torture or anything. I would be happy to serve."

Öcalan was groggy when he spoke, possibly under the influence of drugs. The video had obviously been heavily cut and edited. Nonetheless, there was no sign of the defiant revolutionary who had vowed for years to lead his people to liberation or death. It was a pitiful spectacle.

Much of the world was riveted by the Öcalan case, and the Turkish authorities might have won great good will had they bent over backward to observe every legal nicety. Instead they did the opposite. Prosecutors subjected the prisoner to ten days of intense interrogation without benefit of counsel, and then allowed two lawyers to see him for twenty minutes on condition that they discuss only his health. The next day one of the lawyers was arrested, ostensibly on an old charge of collaborating with the PKK, and the other quit for fear of his life.

Emotions were running very high in Turkey, as I was able to see in travels through the countryside during those weeks. One day I visited the conservative town of Kayseri and had lunch with a young engineer who lived there. As we sipped our lentil soup, I asked him if local people were debating a possible death penalty for Öcalan. Oh, yes, he replied, it was the hottest topic in town. So, did most favor an execution or not? My friend gazed at me, first blankly and then incredulously.

"Maybe I didn't understand your question," he said. "There isn't any debate about whether or not to hang him. The debate is over whether he should be hanged after a trial or right away, without a trial." As I was taking this in, he added offhandedly: "Personally, I favor hanging him without a trial. What has he done to earn a trial? What kind of trial did he give to all the people he killed?"

It was inevitable that the process of trying Öcalan, finding him guilty and sentencing him to hang would display all the peculiarities of the Turkish judicial system. The evidence against him was overwhelming, so perhaps it would have been best, as some dreamers suggested, for the government to have rid itself of the case altogether by sending it to an international tribunal. But Prime Minister Ecevit declared that Public Enemy Number One would be tried for treason by what he called "the completely independent Turkish judiciary, which no one can influence in the slightest."

Upon his arrival as a prisoner in Turkey, Öcalan was brought to an island called Imralı, a pleasant speck of earth in the Sea of Marmara, the small body of water south of the Bosphorus that separates Turkey's European and Asian provinces. Imralı had for years been used as a low-security prison where pickpockets and other minor criminals were allowed to stroll about freely, take the sea breeze and watch passing freighters as they served their sentences. They became the first victims of Öcalan's new status, because they were immediately packed off to more conventional jails to make way for him. Öcalan became the sole inmate, moved to a different cell each night.

A handful of brave or foolish lawyers, a couple of them veteran supporters of the Kurdish cause and the rest young idealists imbued with the odd notion that every defendant is entitled to good counsel, signed up to defend the prisoner. From the beginning they faced extreme obstacles. Gangs of rowdies pelted them with rocks as they waited for ferries to take them to Imralı, and when they arrived they were allowed only brief interviews with their client, always monitored by hooded officers. Several quit in disgust, unwilling to play their role in this scripted drama.

Hundreds of journalists and others with varying credentials applied to cover the trial, and I found myself among the lucky ones given a courtroom seat on the first day, May 31, 1999. I awoke before dawn and drove to the port of Mudanya, where we had been told to assemble. Photographers and television crews had gathered in droves near the dock to film us boarding our ferry. Crowds of angry mothers shouted curses at us, as if our interest in covering the trial somehow made us complicit in their sons' deaths.

A new courtroom, modern and air-conditioned, had been built on

Imralı especially for this trial. As is normal in Turkish security courts, the judges and prosecutors sat together on a raised dais; they are considered to represent both the state and the cause of justice. Below them sat defense lawyers and spectators. A booth made of bulletproof glass had been built for the defendant, like the one in which Adolf Eichmann had sat during his famous trial in Israel.

We spectators took our assigned seats and sat for a while, murmuring among ourselves. Then, without any warning or announcement, a side door opened and Öcalan shambled out, alone and seeming a bit disoriented. He looked around the room, opened the door to his booth and sat down inside. He wore a suit and blue shirt with no necktie. The paunch he had developed during his years as a pampered deity had disappeared. He looked thin, haggard and quite defeated.

I had expected the relatives of his victims, several dozen of whom had been invited to attend the trial, to explode in anger when they finally were able to see the man they blamed for their grief. They did not, obviously having been warned against it. Nonetheless everyone in the hall was riveted by the sight of this near-mythical figure in mortal form.

Prosecutors began with a monotonous reading of their case, which comprised an abbreviated history of the PKK interspersed with accounts of various battles, ambushes and killings. After several hours of this, the presiding member of the five-judge panel called for a lunch break. We expected the afternoon session to be equally boring, but soon after it began Öcalan unexpectedly rose to his feet and began to speak. The judges did not interrupt his extraordinary monologue.

Speaking at first tentatively and then more quickly, as if he feared the judges might silence him at any moment, Öcalan admitted that his guerrillas had committed all the acts attributed to them by the prosecution, and added: "I could list many more that you haven't mentioned." But he said he now realized that he had led the Kurds down "a dead-end street."

"Now is the time to end this conflict, or it will get much worse," he said. "I want to dedicate my life to bringing Kurds and Turks together."

For several years before his capture Öcalan had been declaring temporary cease-fires and making various overtures to Ankara, so perhaps we should not have been so surprised when he depicted himself as a would-be peacemaker. Yet there was something quite astonishing about this towering figure of resistance, this fearsome warrior who for years had held a great army at bay, transforming himself into a meek supplicant rather than thundering defiance, defending his people as oppressed victims and warning that thousands were waiting to pick up the banner of Kurdish resistance. I thought of the Wizard of Oz, a pipsqueak who hid behind a curtain and pulled levers that made him appear to be a terrifying giant, all the while dreading the moment when someone would be bold enough to peek behind the curtain.

"We want to give up the armed struggle and have full democracy," Öcalan told the court. "I will work with the Republic of Turkey toward the goal of peace and brotherhood. In the past I was the one to blame, the one responsible. But that is not the case today. I call on both sides to stop the bloodshed of armed conflict. Call it a cease-fire or whatever you want. Turkey's future is at stake."

What should the Turkish state do to placate angry Kurds? Öcalan's demands were suddenly quite moderate: "Barriers against the Kurdish language and culture should be removed. Today the best policy would be to give the Kurds linguistic and cultural freedom. Kurds should not hesitate to use this democratic chance in the best way possible. I call upon the state not to block the way."

Öcalan used the word *devlet* in this last sentence, which meant that he had chosen to appeal to something bigger than the judicial system, bigger than the Turkish government, bigger than the people. He was offering to collaborate with that incorporeal but holy entity that is at the center of Turkey's consciousness. This was truly astonishing, almost incomprehensible.

"I will serve the state, because I now see this is necessary," Öcalan continued. "These are my most important words. My service is important if it extinguishes the fire." Later on he said he wanted "to work for brotherhood and the state" and declared that the PKK was ready to "give up its stance against the state."

Then came his offer. "If I am given the means," he declared, "I can bring the fighters down from the mountains in three months. But the state cannot do it. Let us join together to end this danger. The PKK should see that the only solution is living together in a single country, together and without weapons. I realize that I am saying this too late, but what can I do now? Maybe I can help. The best shelter for Kurds would be a democratic Republic."

Öcalan spoke for forty minutes, interrupted occasionally by mothers of war victims who, unable to restrain themselves, had burst into tearful tirades, shouting curses and waving photos of their dead sons. After he sat back down, the chief judge began to question him. His answers came in jumbles of sentence fragments and disconnected words, betraying not only a lack of poise and intellect but also the effects of so many years living as a demi-god, with no one contradicting him, scorning him, speaking sharply to him or demanding that he justify himself. The judge did all those things, and for Öcalan the situation was so unfamiliar that he could not respond coherently.

From that point the trial moved quickly toward its inevitable denouement. Prosecutors elaborated their charges, but since the defendant had already in effect pleaded guilty, there was little left for them to say. After five days the prosecution rested and the judges called a fifteen-day recess. When the court reconvened, defense lawyers protested the legitimacy of the proceedings but were overruled. Öcalan spoke once more, repeating somewhat more coherently the themes he had struck on the opening day. There was another recess of several weeks, and when the court reconvened again it handed down the death sentence that had been a foregone conclusion from the day of his capture.

Just as there was never any doubt that Öcalan would be sentenced to die, there was never any real prospect that the sentence would be carried out. European leaders appealed for a stay of execution, and Prime Minister Ecevit calmed his people's emotions by assuring them that the state would find it "more useful" to keep the prisoner alive. The press was mobilized to reshape public opinion, and it managed to do so in a remarkably short time. Öcalan seemed likely to spend many years in his island cell.

With that decision, the matter was more or less laid to rest. Nearly all of the few thousand remaining PKK guerillas heeded their leader's call to stop fighting. Most withdrew to Kurdish bases in northern Iraq, and the rest simply melted back into the Kurdish population within Turkey. After so much blood and suffering, the war was over.

The greater question of how to resolve the conflict between Turkish and Kurdish nationalism, however, remains unanswered. The government is frozen into immobility, unwilling to produce or accept new ideas. Kurds and their supporters inside Turkey risk imprisonment if they speak too freely. The only place where people think creatively and openly about the Kurdish future is in the diaspora. Half a million Kurds live in Germany, part of a Turkish-speaking community there that numbers about two and a half million; perhaps another two hundred thousand are scattered in other European countries. They have spent years reflecting on the great dilemmas facing their people, so after Öcalan's trial I toured several of their communities in Europe to see what they were thinking.

My first stop was Haringey, a neighborhood in north London that has become that city's Kurdish quarter, with Kurdish restaurants, shops and businesses. The Kurds there live among Turks without any evident tension. On my first day I visited a community center and found a seminar under way. About fifty people were listening attentively as speakers discussed the eternal questions of Kurdish identity and how best to preserve it in the face of implacable hostility from Ankara. During a break, I invited one of them aside. We adjourned to a cafeteria where we were served kebabs with rice and salad, just as one would find in Istanbul or Diyarbakır.

The man across from me was Kamal Mirawdeli, a poet of some repute who for nearly twenty years in London had been active in Kurdish causes. That had often put him at the side of Öcalan's PKK. I sensed that for some time he had been looking for a way out, and that he saw one in the glimmer from Imralı.

"In the past I always believed that there should be an independent Kurdistan," he told me. "My concept has changed. National borders don't concern me anymore. I agree with Öcalan that our job now is to help Turkey evolve into a democratic and multicultural state. That isn't going to happen overnight, but maybe slow change is actually more lasting and stable. Of course symbols are important, and what we would love more than anything else is to see some Turkish general shaking hands with the PKK. But even though we're ready now to shake that hand that has been killing us, we know the other side isn't ready. So we have a different hope. We want to do what we can to help build a democratic Turkey where everyone can live peacefully.

"Technology and politics have changed so much that our old ideas don't make sense anymore. You can put up a satellite dish or make a Web page and connect with the whole world. We want personal freedom. We want to live in an environment that is democratic, multicultural and politically pluralist. If that environment is called Turkey, it's fine with me."

Here, at last, was the outline of a reasonable way out of this bloody conundrum. Most Kurds I spoke to in London told me they could accept a formula like this, and so it was at my next stop, Berlin, home to the world's largest community of Kurdish exiles. There too, Kurds seemed tired of war and excited about the prospects ahead. Shopkeepers and intellectuals alike were depressed that nothing positive had emanated from Ankara, but they seemed willing to wait.

One of the most impressive Kurds I met in Berlin was a twenty-nine-year-old woman named Songül Karabulut, who represents what I like to believe is her people's brighter future. Educated, articulate and thoughtful, she is the product of life in Western Europe, where she has lived since childhood. Kurds like her have no experience with either the brutally enforced regimentation of life inside the PKK or the political taboos that restrict public discourse in Turkey. If conditions change enough for them to return, they will bring with them an open, free-thinking approach to politics that will help democratize both the Kurdish movement and Turkey itself.

I met Songül at a Kurdish center, and as we sat earnestly discussing politics, something almost unbelievable happened. A young Kurdish man came into the room to ask if we wanted tea. We said we did, and a few minutes later he brought us two cups on a silver tray, along with a small plate of cookies. After making sure we were satisfied, he withdrew and left us to our conversation. This was a complete reversal of traditional gender roles in Turkish and Kurdish life, and it gave me at least as much hope as the content of our conversation. When I mentioned my amazement, Songül replied only with a contented smile.

I asked her how she and her friends had reacted to Öcalan's call for peace, and she confessed, "It took some time for us to adjust to it. We had to think it through. It wasn't that we thought he was betraying his cause, but we didn't understand it at first. Kurds are very emotional people. At first there was a sense that he was asking the Turks to pardon him, which people didn't like. But there's been a huge amount of discussion about it, and now almost everyone agrees that this is the way to go."

Many Kurds in Europe were for years enthusiastic PKK supporters. Allowed by law to express themselves as they never could in Turkey, they marched, held rallies, published newsletters, lobbied government officials and raised money for the rebel cause. But nearly all have now concluded that their best hope is to find some compromise between Turkish and Kurdish nationalism that would allow them to live in a liberalized and more tolerant Turkey. Even PKK leaders in Europe, where many had moved since being expelled from Syria, came to share that hope. They decided to show their good faith by sending groups of militants to surrender ceremoniously to Turkish army units. The response was predictable: all those who surrendered were immediately arrested. President Demirel dismissed the PKK's declaration that it was ceasing military operations as a "routine, seasonal tactical retreat." The military high command, traditionally the most uncompromising force in the fight against Kurdish nationalism, rejected Öcalan's calls for peace as "false and deceiving" and asserted: "It is out of the question that the general staff accept the PKK terror organization as an interlocutor, discuss its suggestions or make any concessions."

Yet the political thaw in Turkey is unmistakable. Fighting in eastern provinces has all but ended and conditions there are slowly improving. The unbearable tension that hung in the air for so long has begun to lift. Kurds may now speak their language in public, and cassettes of their music, long illegal, are widely available. The twice-banned Kurdish political party has reemerged under the name People's Democracy, and in the 1999 elections its candidates were elected overwhelmingly as mayors of every important city in southeastern Turkey. The country's two leading judges made unprecedented calls for sweeping political reform, including an end to the ban on teaching the Kurdish language, and one of them, Ahmet Necdet Sezer, was elected president of Turkey soon afterward. Five leading cultural figures, among them the much-admired novelists Yaşar Kemal and Orhan Pamuk, issued a statement calling the state's policy toward Kurds "a huge mistake" and urging that Kurds be given "their rights and dignity." And when President Clinton visited

Turkey in the autumn of 1999, he told Parliament that it was time "for Kurdish citizens of Turkey to reclaim that most basic of birthrights, a normal life." In another speech, not mentioning the Kurds by name but obviously encouraging Turkey to listen to their pleas, Clinton asserted: "In order to isolate and undermine the terrorists, there must be a political dialogue and a political settlement, not with terrorists but with those who are willing to seek a political solution."

To the Kemalist elite in Ankara, however, everything Kurdish remains suspicious. Although millions of Kurds speak little or no Turkish, Kurdish-language television remains illegal. Schools and universities are still forbidden to offer instruction in Kurdish, and academies where people may freely learn English, French, German and even Japanese may not teach Kurdish. It is still not possible to discuss what happened during the long war. Schoolchildren in Israel are sometimes asked to write essays about how they would have felt if they had been Palestinian villagers in 1949; I long for the day when Turks will be asked to reflect on how Kurds might have felt as they watched soldiers set fire to their villages.

The PKK and its supporters had long believed that no good could come from Turkey, certainly not from the Kemalist elite that holds power in Ankara. That too began to change. One day soon after the Öcalan trial ended, I was driving with a Kurdish friend outside the southeastern town of Cizre, which I had known in the bad old days of the early 1990s, when its streets were filled with tanks and tracer bullets lit up the night sky. My friend seethed with anger as he recounted the outrages he and his friends and relatives had suffered at the hands of marauding Turkish troops. But when I asked him what he would do if the Kurdish region were to become an independent country, he answered, "Move to Istanbul immediately!"

My closest friend in Diyarbakır is a sophisticated professional who feels personally oppressed by the law that forbids him to send his children to a Kurdish-language school. Why, I asked him one day, would he even want his kids to be educated in this esoteric language? "I wouldn't, of course," he answered. "It's bad enough to grow up in this modern world speaking only Turkish. I want my kids to learn German or English, not Kurdish. But I should have the option. All I want is the chance to decide for myself that my kids shouldn't go to a Kurdish school. I don't want someone in Ankara making the choice for me."

These answers reflect the Kurds' new realism. They have come to realize that a new state established in such an isolated and turbulent corner of the Middle East would have little chance to survive and even less chance to prosper. Far better to live in a renewed, democratic Turkey. But how, after so much blood has flowed, can they bring their erstwhile enemy, the Turkish state, to share this vision?

Despite all the years of conflict between Turkish and Kurdish nationalists, Turks and Kurds live together peacefully in cities and towns all over Turkey, often barely conscious of each other's backgrounds, and intermarry frequently. During the war it was considered treasonous for any Turk to express sympathy for Kurdish demands, but as the fighting died down, some in the Turkish establishment finally felt able to sympathize openly with their Kurdish cousins. Not simply university professors and other intellectuals but ordinary people have begun to view the Kurdish issue more dispassionately. Their common sense tells them that if modest cultural concessions to Kurds can end forever the stream of coffins coming back from the east, Turkey should jump to make the deal. It also tells them that if Kurds remain unhappy and frustrated, the war can start again.

But in Turkey, public opinion has only a slight effect on official policy. The will of the voters is not sovereign. Any substantial change in direction must be approved by the military-dominated elite. The great challenge for Kurds and their many friends, then, is to persuade this elite that they no longer threaten the Turkish Republic and indeed can strengthen and enrich it.

Since time immemorial, leaders in the Middle East have nurtured a culture of power and confrontation. Winners take all, losers are annihilated and compromise is considered a sign of weakness. As products of this culture, Turkish generals and their civilian supporters viscerally reject not only the idea of conciliation with possibly rehabilitated terrorists but also that of dialogue with peaceful defenders of Kurdish identity. Turkey, however, is not simply a Middle Eastern nation trapped in the mentality of desert tribes and nomadic warlords. It is also a European nation, and its central ambition, reiterated endlessly for more than a century, is to move ever closer to the West. In this respect it is like Israel, a country geographically in the Middle East but with democratic aspirations that are profoundly European. Kurdish demands, however, are far more moderate than Palestinian demands, and Kurds are infinitely more willing to compromise with the Turkish state than Palestinians are to compromise with Israel. Most want nothing more than to be productive and happy citizens of Turkey.

During the 1990s, the logic of national reconciliation spread across much of the world. It led to the election of a former guerilla spokesman as mayor of San Salvador; to a trip to North Korea by the president of South Korea; and to a declaration by the leader of Zapatista rebels in Mexico that his fighters want to lay down their weapons and join the political process. It brought at least temporary peace to Spain, where in a thirty-year campaign Basque extremists killed eight hundred people, among them mayors and city councillors whose only crime was defending the idea of democratic politics. In Northern Ireland, where three thousand two hundred people were killed during the same period and a whole generation grew up fearing death at the hands of cruel terrorists, calm was restored at a high price, including the release of prisoners convicted of bombing pubs and killing police officers. People on both sides of these murderous conflicts came to realize that even if they considered their struggle to have been entirely just, the cost of continuing it was too high to inflict on their children.

Compare the Spanish and Irish conflicts, then, to the one that wracked Turkey for fifteen years. It led to the destruction or abandonment of three thousand villages and hamlets, sent millions fleeing from their homes and shattered countless lives. It tore apart Turkey's social fabric, brought a plague of urban problems to cities into which refugees flooded, and crippled the economy by forcing the expenditure of tens of billions of dollars on armaments. It led the army and police to use tactics that undermined Turkey's moral standing in the world. Most awfully, it took a staggering toll in human life, by one count more than twenty-three thousand guerillas, five thousand Turkish soldiers and nearly nine thousand civil servants and other civilians. That toll was equivalent to eleven Northern Irelands or forty-five Spains in half the span of time.

A reasonable case can be made that the war was the fault of Kurdish fanatics who roused their people to pointless rebellion and massacred all who stood in their way. An equally credible case might hold that the Turkish state was responsible because it oppressed the Kurds for years and gave them no choice but revolution. But after so much bloodshed and the passage of so much time, what does it matter which of these arguments is right? Even definitively answering the question of guilt, which is of course impossible, would solve only the problems of the past. Turkey's challenge is to overthrow the tyranny of the past and begin to lay the foundation for a new future.

To an outsider this challenge seems almost ridiculously simple. Let Kurds pledge their loyalty to the Turkish state, let the state offer them more rights in the framework of broadened democracy for all citizens, let everyone agree to resolve disputes at the conference table and the polls, and peace will be achieved. But this is a political solution, and the reason Turkey is reluctant to grasp the chance for peace is not political but psychological.

The Kurdish conflict is mainly about fear. Turks who hold power in Ankara fear that granting Kurds more political or even cultural rights would begin a process that would ultimately lead to separatism and the death of the Republic. Many Kurds, for their part, fear that Turkey will never allow them to shape their own destiny and live freely with their culture and language.

To end this conflict, Kurdish nationalists must find ways to convince the ruling establishment, particularly the military, that they no longer harbor designs against the Turkish state. The state, in turn, must embrace the idea of unity in diversity as a guarantor of stability rather than a threat to the nation's survival. This is no mean task, because it requires millions of people to break away from paralyzing fears that have been inculcated in them since childhood. The fate of Turkey in the twenty-first century depends on their success.

I couldn't tell what time it was when three scary-looking cops appeared in front of the cell into which they had thrown me the night before. It must have been mid-morning. I had maintained a semblance of composure during an intense all-night interrogation and laid awake since, but at the sight of these men unlocking my cell door I unaccountably lost it.

"No!" I shouted, clutching my knees in my arms and bracing for a beating. "No! Don't! Don't do it!"

That was the worst moment of my worst day in Turkey. I had been arrested while engaged in the highly suspicious activity of driving aimlessly around the war zone. The army liked fighting its Kurdish campaign without anyone watching, so prying eyes were most unwelcome.

My adventure, like most adventures in what is never supposed to be called Kurdistan, began in Diyarbakır. I had arrived there by plane, checked in to a hotel that was built in the sixteenth century for Silk Road traders and telephoned trusty Hasan, a Kurdish college student who was bold or foolish or penniless enough to spend his spare time working as a translator for whatever outsiders turned up in town. We greeted each other warmly, and after a few glasses of rakı decided to visit a local lawyer who tried to keep up with events in the surrounding countryside. He told us he knew little more than we did but could pass along a few rumors. On a scrap of paper he wrote the names of three villages where people were supposedly unhappy. Had these villages been forcibly evacuated? Had their men refused to help the army? Had atrocities been committed there? No one knew.

The next morning Hasan and I began winding our way northwest from Diyarbakır. By asking villagers and farmers, we figured out more or less where we might find Gümüşsorgü, one of the hamlets our lawyer friend had mentioned. We were about to reach the top of the hill behind which it was hidden when we were stopped at an army roadblock. Obviously we were not going to be allowed to find out what sort of outrage, if any, had been perpetrated there. As we had done at several other roadblocks that day, we agreed to turn back. But this time the soldier in charge would not let us leave. Instead he brought us into his blockhouse and ordered us to sit.

We were held there for a couple of hours while radio calls were made, and finally were told that we would be escorted to the regional military headquarters. An armored personnel carrier drove along the dirt road ahead of us and a soldier rode in our backseat, his automatic rifle pointed at my back to discourage any thoughts of escape.

At the headquarters we were met by a very agitated lieutenant who was apparently the regional commander. For more than an hour he harangued us, jumping around the room and demanding to know why we had violated his security regulations. I showed my government-issued press card and told him he was making a mistake, but he would have none of it. Our transgression was too egregious for him to deal with, he said. We would be brought to the provincial capital, Batman, for interrogation.

"This is crazy," I told him, "but I'll tell you what. If the commander in Batman really wants to talk to us so badly, we'll show up there at nine o'clock tomorrow morning and answer his questions."

"Don't tell me what to do!" he shouted. "You're not getting away that easily. On your feet!"

Only then did it begin to dawn on me that this might develop into more than an inconvenience. Night was falling, and as Hasan and I stepped outside we saw not one but four armored personnel carriers waiting to escort us. Two rode ahead, the other two behind. Soldiers with machine guns at the ready scanned the roadside, perhaps waiting for my imagined confederates to spring an ambush and try to free me.

In about an hour we reached Batman, a miserable town fifty miles north of the Syrian border that, like many other towns in the region, was swollen with refugees. No one looked up as our caravan passed through the streets; evidently the sight of soldiers atop lumbering war machines was nothing new here. Finally we stopped at a gate and then passed under a large arch bearing the word JANDARMA.

Men in uniform are not widely loved in the Kurdish region, but local people perceive differences among them that are often lost on outsiders. Soldiers from the regular army often behave with a modicum of respect and act according to rules which may at times be harsh but are nonetheless predictable. The police, as in many parts of the world, are tougher. Worst of all is the gendarmerie, which is officially a military body but functions more as a rural police force. Ask a Kurd into whose hands he would least like to fall and the answer will probably be "Jandarma."

Despite my growing concern, I could not help smiling when I saw that two lines of soldiers, a total of twenty-four men, had been assembled to oversee my arrival. Never had any military body taken me so seriously.

Under the watchful eyes of these recruits, I was brought down a set of steps to the subterranean jail. I knew that because I was a foreigner, nothing too serious would happen to me. Nonetheless, while descending that concrete staircase I could not help thinking of the many unfortunate Kurds, guilty and innocent, who must have been dragged down here on their way to brutal abuse.

I was led into a small room that quickly filled with unshaven interrogators. There were eight in all, and soon the cell was ripe with their sweat and mine. One sat behind a small desk and pecked continually at a typewriter that was placed next to my ear. The others shouted questions.

Who was I? Why had I been prowling the back roads here? Where was I going? Who had sent me? What was I hoping to find? Who was I planning to meet? What messages was I carrying? What was I delivering or picking up?

Now the ordeal was beginning in earnest. Over and over I explained *that I was a journalist accredited by the Turkish government, but my hosts were not impressed. They took turns glowering at me and shaking their heads in disbelief. Finally one said, "We think you're a spy for the PKK."*

To be suspected of collaborating with Kurdish rebels is about the worst thing that can happen to a Turkish citizen, and it isn't taken kindly among foreigners either. I knew that no one in the world had the slightest idea where I was, and I asked to use a telephone. "Too bad," one of my hosts replied dryly. "All our phones are out of order."

Hours passed, and my interrogators kept shouting. One or two would leave the room for a time and then return. At one point they took me out to be photographed and fingerprinted. For a time they videotaped me, warning that if I did not agree to speak before the camera they would hold me "for a long time—a very long time." Slowly I began to realize why police everywhere in the world use the tactic of long, intensive and repetitive interrogation: it works. I was isolated from the world and completely in the hands of the men facing me. My resistance was weakening, and I felt a strong urge to confess my crimes. All that stopped me was that I had none to confess.

At one point the men ordered me to empty my pockets. With intense interest they scrutinized every card and paper. Suddenly one of them cried out, "Işte!" which means something like "Here it is!" The others quickly gathered around him and, one by one, nodded and smiled triumphantly. If I had been carrying a PKK membership card, I would know that it had been found. Since I was not, however, I wondered what could have provoked such a reaction.

"If you aren't working for the PKK," the chief interrogator asked, waving a slip of paper at me, "then what's this?"

I looked at it and couldn't fathom their excitement. "It's nothing," I said. "It's a receipt from the Pera Palace bar in Istanbul. Look, right here at the top: 'Pera Palace.'"

"Sure, but what's this you have written on it?"

"It says 'Jean-Paul Marthoz.' That's the name of the guy I had a drink with. I have to write the name for my expense account."

"But keep reading. What does it say under the name?"

Jean-Paul Marthoz worked at the Brussels office of Human Rights

Watch and had been in Istanbul to attend a political trial. He had called and asked to meet me, and I had bought him a drink at the Pera Palace.

"It says 'Human Rights Watch,' " I said, still not comprehending.

"İşte! PKK!"

"No, not PKK. Human rights."

"That's what I said. Human rights. PKK."

I stopped to absorb this. The men facing me obviously considered the phrase "human rights" to be a synonym for terror. To them, meeting with someone from a group that used that phrase in its name was the same as meeting with a PKK agent.

The interrogators next told me they were going to search my car. They took me outside to watch while they probed the radiator, tested the tires, opened the first-aid kit and ripped out the seats. Suddenly there was another cry of "İşte!" One of the searchers had found the scrap of paper on which my Diyarbakır friend had scrawled the names of three villages.

"These are PKK villages," one of the interrogators shouted at me. "What were you going to do there? Who were you going to meet?"

This was another revelation. According to the official version there was no such thing as a "PKK village," nor could there be, since the PKK was devoted only to mindless terror and had no civilian base. I had learned something in a basement prison that I could not otherwise have learned: just as there are friendly villages in the southeast, there are also hostile ones where people sympathize with the enemy.

At four o'clock in the morning, after seven hours of harsh though not physical interrogation, I was led to a cell and locked in. I'm not having any fun, I told myself, but I'm definitely in better shape than the last guy who was brought here and the next guy who will be brought here.

A few hours later the cops showed up at my cell door. They smiled at my terrified reaction, opened the door and asked me to step out. I followed them back to the room where I had spent such an unpleasant night. The interrogation began again, but this time each question was asked only once, and in a civil tone. I was made to sign many papers, and after an hour was told that a decision had been made to release me. Outside I was reunited with Hasan, who told me that the cops had threatened to come for him some night and punish him for "working with foreign motherfuckers who want to destroy this country." We were led to our car, which had been partly reassembled, and I was given the key. I turned the ignition and drove very slowly toward the gate, still not sure I would be allowed to leave. But the gate opened and we drove to freedom.

We passed through the streets of Batman in silence, breathing deeply and looking anxiously behind us. At a small shop we stopped for fruit juice and cigarettes.

"That was awful," I told Hasan after we got back into the car. "That was terrible. I can't believe that happened."

Hasan shook his head in disbelief. Then he broke into a broad smile. "Believe me, that was nothing," he said. "It could have been much worse. Much, much worse."

· SIX ·

FREEDOM RISING

☪

On a stroll along Istanbul's glorious Istiklal promenade one Saturday, I caught an unexpected glimpse into the retrograde aspect of Turkey's divided soul. In the midst of the delightful bustle, near music stores from which the latest hits blared and across the street from Burger King, about a hundred people, most of them women, were sitting on the pavement. Some were dressed in long patterned skirts and colorful head scarves, marking them as villagers and making them seem out of place in such cosmopolitan surroundings. Most carried homemade posters bearing enlarged photos of young men, each with a name and date. They had come to bear silent witness, but sometimes their emotions boiled over and one or another of them shouted, "Tell us where they are!" or "Mothers' rage will strangle the murderers!" Busloads of police officers hovered menacingly nearby.

These demonstrations were held every Saturday at noon for more than two years. They lasted just thirty minutes. When this one broke up, I tried to approach some of the departing women, but they seemed terrified and hurried away as I came near. Later I learned that police officers sometimes harassed or grabbed them as they tried to disperse, so they liked to slip away as quickly as possible. The few who were willing to talk had more or less the same story to tell. Their sons or husbands, most of them Kurds, had disappeared while in police custody. For months or years they had waited in vain for signs that their men were alive, or an acknowledgment that they were dead.

A middle-aged woman named Tosun told me that she, like several million other Kurds, had fled her native village in the southeast soon after 1990. The police there had suspected her husband of supporting Kurdish guerrillas, and to escape their pressure he moved the family to Istanbul. One evening in 1995, she kissed him good-bye as he left their apartment and then, as was her custom, watched from her window as he emerged onto the street below. She saw three men in civilian clothes jump from the shadows, surround him, throw him into a waiting car and drive off into the darkness. She wrote down the license-plate number, and with the help of human-rights activists later traced it to the police. Since then she has devoted her life to searching for her husband but has found nothing.

As Tosun and her partners in grief sat on the pavement that Saturday, people around them went about their business with absolute freedom. Vendors hawked newspapers full of anti-government venom. A handful of earnest young people handed out leaflets calling for Marxist revolution. At nearby offices, political rabble-rousers were planning all manner of campaigns.

This striking contrast between freedom and repression crystallizes Turkey's conundrum. In no other country does so much liberty coexist with such sustained violation of elemental human rights. Of all the countries with bad human-rights records, Turkey is the freest. To put it the other way, Turkey has the worst human-rights record of any free country. This is its deepest and most troubling contradiction.

Turkey's failure to keep pace with new and evolving global human-rights standards is the single greatest reason for its failure to integrate itself fully into the community of civilized nations. Turks must strive to wash away this stain not so they can improve their reputation abroad and be patted on the back by foreign leaders but because they themselves deserve better and wish fervently for better. The habits of Turkey's security forces and criminal-justice system place the Turkish government in awful company that shames the nation and its people. Turks, heir to a highly cultured tradition based on tolerance and mutual respect, desperately want to embrace—and be embraced by—the modern world. Few of them still believe that criticism of their government's human-rights record is part of a foreign conspiracy. More and more dream of a Turkey where levels of freedom match those anywhere in the world.

Underlying the official Turkish approach to individual rights is the abiding belief in *devlet*, the strong and sacred state, whose rights transcend those of individuals. Not so long ago this was also a guiding principle in many European countries, but it has fallen away as threats to those nations' security have faded. Here, Turkish leaders like to say, is Turkey's difference. Their argument goes something like this: Of course Norway and Portugal can afford to allow their citizens virtually unlimited freedoms. They are surrounded by friends and allies, all of whom understand that the rise of one nation helps all its neighbors. But where we live, the rules are very different. We are surrounded by vipers waiting to strike, enemies who plot against us day and night. How easy it is for our critics to denounce us! But give the Belgians or the Swedes borders with Iran, Iraq and Syria, and see how quickly their commitment to human rights evaporates. They would soon realize that predatory neighbors are constantly looking for ways to exploit our freedom, hoping to weaken us by sowing the seeds of division and hatred among our people. If those seeds bear fruit, not only Turkey but the cause of democracy around the world will lose. Freedom-loving nations devoted to that great cause should be grateful for the efforts we are making, praise us for our achievements rather than ostracize us for our shortcomings and understand that at this critical juncture, freedom in Turkey, already almost unique in the Middle East and the Islamic world, cannot be limitless.

"We are not going to allow debates in which the Turkish flag is called 'a piece of cloth,' the national anthem is called 'a piece of music' and the founder and leader of the Turkish Republic, Kemal Atatürk, is exposed to humiliation," Admiral Güven Erkaya asserted in 1997, when he was commander of the Turkish navy and scourge of political and religious dissidents. "Debates like these aim to create a vacuum that would be exploited by those who wish to replace the current regime with an outdated model."

This argument is powerful but no longer persuasive. To be sure, restrictions on public speech exist everywhere. Germans are forbidden to express admiration for the Third Reich, French citizens may not foment hatred of immigrants, and the Dutch are not allowed to question the authenticity of Anne Frank's diary. In the United States it is illegal to joke about killing the president. But in modern Turkey, even expressing provocative dissent is a crime.

During the early years of the Turkish Republic, restricting public discourse was probably necessary. Many citizens were shocked by Atatürk's radicalism, and some might have responded if they had been encouraged to rebel against his "sacrilegious" regime. That threat has now all but evaporated. Rather than lift restrictions on free speech, however, the Kemalist establishment searches ceaselessly for new excuses to maintain them.

In the 1960s and 1970s the pretext was the threat of Communism. Later it was the Kurdish war, and after the war wound down it was the supposed rise of Islamic fundamentalism. These arguments were strong. No state happily allows citizens to denounce its armed forces in time of national emergency, and none refuses to defend itself against those who detest its most cherished principles. But the restrictions Turkish leaders have imposed on free speech inhibit debate over vital issues the nation must confront if it is to keep pace with the rest of the world. As long as they remain in force, Turkey will be regarded, unfairly but quite understandably, as a primitive backwater ruled by repressive officers.

The patriots who run Turkey have the moral right and duty to safeguard their nation's remarkable achievements. Yet they still have not learned to assess their country's security needs broadly and profoundly. They must now realize that repressing beliefs and restricting free discussion drives undesirable ideas underground, where they can become truly dangerous, and stunts the growth of individual conscience, hence of Turkey itself. Nations that do not respect their citizen's physical and moral integrity are always unhappy nations. In Turkey, frantic rearguard campaigns aimed at preserving national unity produce the very bitterness they are designed to avoid.

The irony is that today, public discourse in Turkey is astonishingly free. Politicians attack each other virulently, newspapers campaign loudly against abuses of power and late-night television programs feature intense debates over national issues. For all its failings, the Turkish press is the great platform for its civil society, and there are some among Turkish journalists who would be heroes in any country. But all Turks who speak out in public understand the limits, explicit and implicit.

Laws that embody these prohibitions are vaguely worded and selectively enforced. A newspaper column judged inoffensive one year might lead to a jail sentence the next. Older and well-established commentators in mainstream papers are often allowed more leeway than brash newcomers working for smaller publications whose loyalty to the state is suspect. Yet everyone who writes, publishes, speaks in public or otherwise expresses opinions feels the chilling shadow of the law.

Turkey's constitution stipulates in its preamble: "No protection shall be given to thoughts or opinions that run counter to Turkish national interests, the fundamental principle of the existence and indivisibility of the Turkish state and territory, the historical and moral values of Turkishness, or the nationalism, principles, reforms and modernism of Atatürk." A handful of repressive laws have been written in the spirit of that preamble. They forbid the publication of "articles that threaten the internal or external security of the state"; "articles inciting people to break the law"; articles that "make people unwilling to serve in the military"; and articles or statements that "publicly insult or ridicule the moral personality of Turkishness, the Republic, the Parliament, the Government, ministers of state, the military or security forces or the judiciary." Also forbidden are radio or television broadcasts that undermine "the national and spiritual values of society"; political party platforms suggesting "that minorities exist in the Turkish Republic based on national, religious, confessional, racial or language differences"; and, of course, anything that "insults or curses the memory of Atatürk."

Two laws are used to prosecute most of the journalists, intellectuals and politicians whose imprisonment has been one of the most deplorable aspects of modern Turkish life. One, used frequently against those who propose new ways of dealing with Kurdish nationalism, is Article 8 of the 1991 Anti-Terror Law, which bans "written or oral propaganda, along with meetings, demonstrations and marches, that have the goal of destroying the indivisible unity of the state." The other, which has become the main prosecutorial weapon against Islamic-oriented politicians, is Article 312 of the penal code, which prohibits "praising an action that is considered criminal" and speech that "incites people to enmity and hatred by pointing to class, racial, religious, confessional or religious differences."

Most defendants charged with violating these laws are tried by one of the State Security courts, which operate in eight cities. These courts are five-member tribunals that for years consisted of two civilian judges, two prosecutors and a military judge; the provision requiring a military judge was excised during the trial of Abdullah Öcalan to give the trial an air of civil legitimacy. Like all courts in Turkey, State Security courts are formally independent, and higher authorities rarely if ever seek to pressure their judges to reach guilty verdicts. The judges are acutely aware of the political climate of the moment, however, and most consider it their duty to render whatever verdict that climate demands. Among the hundreds they have convicted for crimes of thought and speech are the playwright Mehmet Vahi Yazar, who wrote a play portraying the state as anti-Islamic; the leftist politician Doğu Perinçek, who charged on television that government agents were responsible for several high-profile acts of terrorism; the blind lawyer Esber Yağmurdereli, who asserted that Kurds in Turkey are an oppressed minority; the Muslim sect leader Mehmet Kutlular, who told his followers that the 1999 earthquake in northwestern Turkey was God's vengeance on the secular state; the publisher Ahmet Zeki Okçuoğlu, who wrote an article headlined THE TURK-ISH REPUBLIC DOES NOT WANT TO MAKE PEACE WITH KURDS; and the theologian Mustafa Islamoğlu, who claimed that "people of many races live in Anatolia" and that "unity could be achieved in an Islamic framework."

There is a small cadre of incorrigibles who are determined to work freely regardless of the consequences. One of my favorites among these repeat offenders is Ayşe Nur Zarakolu, who opened a small publishing house in 1976 and runs it from a cluttered basement in downtown Istanbul. She has published books that denounce the government's policy toward Kurds, accuse the security forces of sponsoring death squads and document massacres of Armenians in the early twentieth century. Among her many distinctions is having been convicted for a single word; she published a translation of a report by Human Rights Watch that quoted an unnamed American diplomat describing some Turkish soldiers as "thugs." In the 1980s and 1990s she served four prison terms, and at any given moment there are a good twenty cases pending against her. "If we are going to have real freedom in Turkey," she told me when I visited her subterranean bunker, "we have to break away from the official ideology."

Crusaders like these make life uncomfortable for authoritarian regimes around the world. They preach heresies that, if carried into practice, could change the course of their nations' histories. In secure and self-confident countries they are tolerated and even honored, but in unstable countries they are considered no better than traitors. Into which of these categories does Turkey fit? Its leaders see the country surrounded by belligerent enemies and with a population full of potential or actual subversives. They underestimate their own people. Turks are well aware of how much they have achieved since 1923, and are acutely sensitive to ideologies that would rob them of their freedom and prosperity. Many would like to see profound changes in the way their country is governed. Some of those changes might be disastrous, others badly needed. If they are to be sorted out and assessed, they must be discussed.

One night I joined a group of friends at a funky restaurant in Istanbul's artistic Asmalımescit quarter for a farewell dinner. We were bidding adieu to Ragıp Duran, a journalism professor at the French-language Galatasaray University who also worked as a correspondent for Agence France-Presse and wrote columns for various Turkish newspapers. Ragıp, then forty-three years old, wasn't leaving Istanbul for an extended vacation, nor had he taken a job or accepted a fellowship abroad. He was going to jail.

For years Ragıp had maintained a special interest in guerrilla movements. He closely followed the Kurdish conflict, and one of his columns included an interview with Abdullah Öcalan. He described Öcalan as a thoughtful figure who "cites Zarathustra or Freud" and "gives a lot of importance to equality and fraternity." This description was a criminal offense because it undermined the state's campaign to portray Öcalan as a ruthless terrorist without redeeming virtues.

I feared that the evening would have the pall of a wake, but it was just the opposite. Spirits were high, jokes and stories were told and much *rakı* was consumed. In Turkey, festive parties like this are traditionally held for people about to begin jail sentences, not just those convicted of political offenses but also common criminals. This one was a celebration and, because so many reporters were present, a chance to renew one's commitment to the practice of free journalism.

Before he had put away too much *rakı*, I asked Ragıp how he looked back over his life of crime. He shrugged and paused, perhaps wondering how to condense his thoughts into a few words.

"Since the founding of our Republic, four or five subjects have been established as taboos, and you can only write about them if you accept the official line," he said. "You are free to say that Kurds are Turks or that Kurds do not exist in Turkey, but if you try to understand the Kurdish problem and say that Kurds have rights, that is a problem. The second taboo is Islam, or any suggestion that the Republic has not been able to wipe away the influence of Islam in daily life. The third is the role and function of the army in the Turkish government and state. Free discussion of the Armenian problem and its history is also impossible, and the same is true about relations with Greece and Cyprus. The state tries to say that the press shouldn't be getting into these issues, but I think they're very complex problems that need to be examined and studied. That's what got me into trouble."

Many people might disagree with Ragıp's view of Abdullah Öcalan, but without open debate, without the presentation of various perspectives and alternatives, no one can reach an educated conclusion about anything. On matters of the greatest national import in Turkey, such debate is illegal. The state not only rejects certain opinions but forbids their expression. If it were to allow unfettered public speech, a cacophony of dissonant voices would certainly advocate all sorts of distasteful views. That is the music of democracy, and Turkish leaders should learn to appreciate it. It will not divide their country or lead to its collapse. On the contrary, it will strengthen, unify and invigorate a people who are quite mature enough to deal with the challenges of freedom.

Although there is no official censorship in Turkey, a corps of zealous civil servants across the country is charged with reviewing everything that is printed. Curious about their routines, I visited one of them, an earnest gentleman named Erol Canözkan. I found him in a sunlit Istanbul office near the Bosphorus, surrounded by copies of the newspapers he is assigned to monitor. On his desk were several pink folders. If you are a journalist in Turkey, you want to stay out of these pink folders; into them Canözkan places articles he thinks may have violated one or another of Turkey's laws. With the offending passages underlined, they are sent to prosecutors who decide whether to use them as the basis for criminal charges.

"We have special laws here because a war is being fought in this country," Canözkan told me. He meant not just the Kurdish conflict but also the broader debate over Turkey's future. "As part of their strategy, the terrorists have set up all kinds of little newspapers that openly advocate the violent destruction of Turkey. The people who write for these newspapers are not journalists, but spokesmen for terrorist groups." When I asked if he felt uncomfortable doing a job that led to putting people in jail for what they wrote, Canözkan looked at me quizzically, as if I had misunderstood his duties. "I get a very good feeling doing this work," he said with what I took to be great sincerity. "I'm defending the Turkish state and its unity. My only regret is that we have not been able to explain to our friends in the West why it is so urgent that we do this."

Laws that stifle public discourse are one of the main reasons Turkey has won a reputation for hostility to the principle of human rights. Another reason, equally intimidating and certainly more frightening, is the abuse to which criminal suspects are subjected. There is no tradition of conventional police work in Turkey. Detectives trying to solve crimes do not normally begin by looking for clues, as do their counterparts in other countries. Instead they rely on informers, whose motives are often mixed at best. Once the police have a suspect in custody they assume he is guilty and become angry if he does not confess. Often they apply physical pressure until he does, sometimes increasing it to the point of extreme brutality. It is common to read in Turkish newspapers that the police have found the culprit in a particular case and he has confessed; rarely are there articles about prisoners who deny the charges against them.

Every day in every country, police officers arrest people they believe have committed crimes but against whom they have no solid evidence. In countries governed by the rule of law, they use various nonviolent though often coercive interrogation techniques to provoke contradictions in the suspect's alibi or to find some other opening. When these techniques fail, and when no eyewitnesses or physical evidence can be found, they must release their prisoner even if they are convinced of his guilt. Police forces in Turkey do not work this way. Investigative techniques that are common in the United States and many other countries are all but unknown, and the moral bar against physical abuse is almost nonexistent. Torturing suspects until they confess, or even simply to establish the suspect's impotence and the absolute power of the state, is distressingly common.

One of Turkey's most experienced police reporters told me that after a few years of working at Istanbul's main lockup he was allowed to remain in the building after five o'clock, when visitors are supposed to leave. Soon after nightfall he would begin hearing the screams of torture victims. When he protested, one of his police-officer friends replied: "Don't worry. We only do that to the ones who are guilty."

Most Turks believe their government's restrictions on freedom of speech are excessive and undemocratic, and they are ashamed when writers, journalists and politicians are imprisoned for what they say or write. If a referendum were held on whether to repeal laws that ban certain phrases and opinions, it would probably win handily. But a similar consensus against jailhouse torture is only beginning to emerge. Especially in rural areas, where the inviolability of the human person is not a familiar concept, many people believe the state has a right and even a duty to use violence to protect public order. People like the image of the police officer as a tough guy whose job is to inspire fear and obedience rather than to meet abstract standards of compassion. A man who was beaten by police at a political rally told me: "When I was a kid my parents beat me. In school the teachers beat me. While I was doing military service my squad leader beat me. So I almost expect the police to beat me when they don't like what I'm doing."

In every country, test cases display the criminal justice system for all to see. In Turkey one of them centers around a journalist named Metin

Göktepe, who was little known during his life but in death became a symbol for human-rights crusaders across the country and beyond. In 1996 Metin Göktepe was working for the leftist newspaper *Evrensel*, which the government later shut down, when he was assigned to cover the funeral of two prison inmates who had died mysteriously in their cells. The funeral procession turned into an anti-police protest, and officers posted nearby reacted as they often do when they face groups they perceive as hostile. They charged repeatedly into the crowd with batons swinging, not caring who they hit. Göktepe was among the victims. Police officers smacked him a few times, then threw him and a few others into a van and took them to a detention center. The others were quickly released, but he was held, and the next day his body was found in a nearby park. Police officers at first denied having detained him, and after eyewitnesses asserted the truth they changed their story and said Göktepe had indeed been arrested but unfortunately had fallen from a wall. An autopsy left no doubt that he had been beaten to death.

Earlier in Turkish history the matter might have ended there. But Turkish society is changing, and Göktepe's murder sparked protest rallies in several cities. Members of Parliament denounced the cover-up and demanded an honest investigation. Finally, forty-eight police officers were named as suspects. As is common in Turkey, their trial stretched on for years, with the court convening for only a few days each year. Several of the judges who heard the case at various stages quit after complaining of pressure from obscure quarters. The authorities, hoping to discourage people from following the case, convened sessions in provincial towns far from Istanbul. When I read one day that the court would convene in the Anatolian town of Afyon, which is far from both Istanbul and Ankara and known only for the quality of its *kaymak*, a kind of whipped cream, I decided to go there.

Several busloads of Göktepe's supporters were already in Afyon when I arrived, but they were being kept several blocks from the courtroom by a veritable army of police. The entire downtown had been turned into a high-security zone, complete with sharpshooters posted on roofs near the courthouse. After half an hour of pushing and pleading, I fought my way into the jammed hall where the hearing was to be conducted. It was small, no bigger than a good-size living room, with space for only a few dozen spectators. The atmosphere was chaotic and did not improve after the three judges arrived. One ordered all journalists out, but his order was followed by several minutes of shouted protests and in the end forgotten. Lawyers then spent the better part of an hour screaming insults, calling each other filthy swine devoted to the ruination of Turkey. Those representing Göktepe's family finally presented a motion demanding that five of the most directly implicated officers be imprisoned. After a series of whispered conferences, the judges agreed and issued an arrest order. Lawyers for the officers declared they would not recognize it. After three tumultuous hours, during which the judges never won control of their courtroom, the session was mercifully adjourned and the accused officers walked away smiling. Many months later most of them were acquitted, and the trial of the others was postponed time and again. Their chief was ostentatiously promoted to a post in Ankara, a signal to police torturers that they were not only immune to punishment but favored candidates for advancement.

This same pattern of immunity for security officers saved the careers and freedom of sixty-five prison guards who beat ten Kurdish prisoners to death and seriously injured two dozen others in the Diyarbakır prison a few months after Metin Göktepe was murdered. It also protected the policemen who tortured a group of teenagers in Manisa around the same time and were brought to trial only because one of the victims' lawyers, a member of Parliament, was left alone in a waiting room and managed to sneak upstairs to the cell in which they were being violated. These cases sent the same message as the Göktepe trial: that there is no limit beyond which security officers may not go as they perform what they believe to be their duty.

At least as outrageous as these high-profile cases, and the hundreds like them that are less well known, is the sustained campaign the government wages against doctors who dare to tell the truth about torture. Turkish law allows prosecutors to investigate whether defendants in criminal cases have been tortured, but the police frustrate this law quite effectively, sometimes with help from the prosecutors themselves. They warn prisoners not to claim to have been tortured, threatening them with further abuse if they do, and also pressure doctors who examine the victims to file false reports. Those who refuse often find themselves facing criminal charges alleging that they are in league with terrorists and criminals.

The practice of granting informal immunity to torturers is, however, coming under increasing challenge. Highly publicized cases, like those of Metin Göktepe and the Manisa teenagers, have pushed the issue onto the front pages. Several popular films made during the late 1990s contain graphic scenes of police officers abusing prisoners in horrific ways. Leading politicians now admit publicly that torture is a lamentable fact of Turkish life. And as the population grows steadily younger and better educated, it naturally turns ever more strongly away from old ideas about how the police should treat citizens.

Good words from prominent political leaders have not, however, penetrated the local police stations where most of the abuse of prisoners takes place. Part of the reason is that Turkish interior ministers, who oversee the police, are often cops or ex-cops themselves. Products of a culture that condones torture, and having risen through a system in which it is common practice, they are themselves tainted by it.

Each recent Turkish prime minister has named a cabinet minister responsible for human rights. Pity the incumbent, who must investigate abuses and try to stop them while at the same time pretending they do not occur or are only occasional aberrations. For a time Parliament's human-rights committee gave more hope. It served notice of its seriousness by showing up one afternoon in the spring of 2000, completely unannounced, at an Istanbul police station known as a torture center. Members quickly found a series of torture implements, including a "Palestinian hanger," a device used to suspend prisoners above the floor; it is so named because the Israeli police are said to use it on their Palestinian prisoners. The committee chairman, Sema Pişkinsüt, turned the device over to prosecutors, but the local police chief was unrepentant. "They found a stick," he sniffed. "What's the big deal?" When Ms. Pişkinsüt refused to back off, powerful police officials and right-wing politicians realized that she was taking her job seriously. They complained to Prime Minister Ecevit, and to his eternal shame, Ecevit supported a move to oust her from her chairmanship. That sent another powerful signal to torturers.

Police officers continue their abuses despite appeals from the government in Ankara because they do not take those appeals seriously. Why should they? As long as prime ministers block human-rights investigations, as long as interior ministers are former police officers who themselves have directed or participated in torture sessions, and as long as doctors who challenge torturers are more likely to be prosecuted than the torturers themselves, the police can be forgiven for concluding that denunciations of torture are only for public consumption. They will continue believing that until those who commit or sanction torture are swiftly investigated, tried, convicted, sentenced and imprisoned. Half a dozen merciless prosecutions would do more than a mountain of pretty words to shock the police out of their old ways.

Repealing laws that limit freedom of speech and putting a decisive end to jailhouse torture—two steps that Turkey must take if it is to reach standards of human rights that the world expects a model nation to uphold—requires political will. Beyond that it requires a change in attitude, a definitive recognition of the inviolability of the human mind and person. Abuses like those that are still common in Turkey are possible only when citizens are considered subjects to be ruled rather than masters of their bodies, their ideas and their destinies. Turks must be free to organize, speak and write as they please, and their police officers must not only enforce the law but subject themselves to it. Then Turkey will be free of its shame, free to shine as an example to the turbulent Balkans; to the Caucasus and Central Asia, where democracy is fighting an uphill battle against tyranny; to all Muslim nations, many of whose leaders are terrified of the very idea of human rights; and to lovers of freedom around the world.

Everyone in the seaside village of Adrasan knows Ali Taşgan, but not by his real name. Nearly half a century ago he exchanged it for a one-word moniker that he shares with ten thousand of his countrymen: Koreli. The restaurant he owns, which sits directly on the Mediterranean sand, is also called Koreli. So are dozens of other restaurants in Turkey, along with all manner of businesses, including a grocery in the Black Sea town of Rize, a tea house in the bustling southern city of Adana and a tire dealership at a busy intersection in Istanbul. At many Turkish ports there is at least one vessel, usually a skiff or small fishing boat, called Koreli. I have seen the name painted on trucks, buses and automobiles, and also above doors in remote villages. Among Turks of a certain age it is a badge of honor and commands instant respect.

Koreli is the Turkish word for Korean, but neither Ali Taşgan nor any of the other Turks who bear that name has a drop of Korean blood. They are veterans of the Korean War, the first and only foreign war in which soldiers of the Turkish Republic have fought. The bravery they exhibited on Korean battlefields earned Turkey a permanent place in the grateful memories of South Koreans. It also deeply impressed countless soldiers who were part of the Allied force fighting North Korea and China on that remote Asian peninsula. "Whenever you had a real tough or dangerous mission, you'd call in the Turks," an American veteran once told me. "Didn't matter how freezing it was or how many bullets were flying through the air. They'd go anywhere."

Nearly eight hundred Turks were killed in combat during the Korean War and are buried in cold Korean soil. That is a sobering toll and, to those who appreciate the virtues of soldierly courage, proof that Turks still burn with the fire that once made them some of the world's most fearsome warriors. Time has shown, however, that the true legacy of the Korelis had nothing to do with their willingness to race across minefields or charge uphill toward machine-gun nests. They were the first large group of Turks since the founding of the Republic who left their country and saw the world beyond. With their return, Turkey changed forever.

Atatürk believed that his new nation's domestic challenges were so urgent and overwhelming that it could not afford to devote its energy to foreign affairs. The Ottomans had ruled a vast empire, but their limitless ambition, symbolized at the end by their mad alliance with Germany in World War I, was ultimately what destroyed them. Chastened by this history, Atatürk sought to avoid foreign entanglements at all costs. During his fifteen years as president he never set foot outside Turkey and never entertained a single one of the world's great statesmen. Pushing his people toward modernity was such a huge challenge, he realized, that it would be foolish for him to try to project power or influence abroad at the same time. He focused his attention on developing Turkey, and imposed rules that made foreign travel all but impossible for those few Turks who could afford it.

Atatürk's successors faithfully followed his isolationist precepts. Chastened by their disastrous experience in World War I and afraid of making another such blunder, they kept their country out of World War II until it was nearly over. But after the war ended they realized that they could not look inward forever. They sent a delegation to the conference at which the United Nations was formed, and Turkey went on to become a founding member of the world body. A few years later, when the Security Council approved the "police action" in Korea and appealed to all nations to join the American-led fighting force there, the Turks decided to respond. Over the course of the war fifteen thousand young men, almost none of whom had ever heard of Korea, left Turkey to fight there.

"I had no idea where Korea was," Ali Taşgan told me as we sat under the stars at his restaurant, listening to waves gently lapping onto the beach a few feet from our table. "No one is happy to go to war, but we had the feeling that we were on the side of freedom."

Like the other Korelis, Ali reached Korea after a long and eventful trip by land and sea. Just past his eighteenth birthday, he saw things he had never imagined and met people whose lives were astonishingly unlike his. When he arrived at Pusan, part of a force sent to replace a three-hundred-man Turkish unit that had taken two hundred twenty-five casualties, his world continued to expand beyond anything he could have imagined. For nearly two years he lived among Koreans, Americans and other foreigners, at first dumbfounded and then fascinated by how different they were from everyone he had ever met. When the war ended, he and his Turkish comrades in arms returned home worldly and restless. They brought a beautiful virus to Turkey, and it has been spreading ever since.

Each of the Korelis was welcomed home by awed neighbors. Almost no Turk had ever known people who had traveled so far. To them, what these veterans had done in the combat zone was secondary; more important was the simple and astonishing fact that they had seen and learned so much. As soon as they returned they became local wise men. "The village elders, men I had been brought up to respect, were coming to me for advice," Ali Taşgan told me. "I was twenty years old, but somehow it seemed right. They had never been more than a day's mule ride from home. I had been to the other side of the planet. It made sense that they should listen to me. I wasn't just Ali anymore. I was Koreli."

As is often the case with subtle movements that build quietly in many places, the Korelis' return was not at first recognized as a profound social phenomenon. Soon, however, this breach in the dam of Turkish isolationism widened. Turkey's appearance on the world stage drew the attention of powerful foreign governments, especially that of the United States, and after 1952, when Turkey became a member of the NATO alliance, thousands of foreign soldiers and sailors passed through Turkish cities and towns. Turkish leaders began to accept the responsibilities of their nation's partnership with powerful allies.

Less than a decade later, Turkey was drawn further beyond its bor-

ders as the economies of northern Europe, especially that of West Germany, started to boom. Factories destroyed in the war were being rebuilt, new businesses were emerging and old entrepreneurial classes were reasserting themselves. These resurgent economies needed more labor than their own countries could supply, and for that the West Germans and their neighbors turned to southern Europe, mainly to Turkey. By the late 1960s hundreds of thousands of Turks, most of them from small towns and villages, were providing the muscle that powered the "miracle" of Western Europe's economic rebirth. When they went back home for their annual vacations and described their experiences to their neighbors, they became a force for change, as the Korelis had been, but far greater in number and influence. The infidel, they told their friends back home, had built a society as free as it was prosperous. Turkey's way of doing things was not the only way, perhaps not even the best way.

For a time the Turkish elite did not hear this message, much less understand its far-reaching implications. The dominant politicians in that period, most notably Süleyman Demirel and Bülent Ecevit, believed they could keep Turks as far from the international mainstream as they had been before World War II. As late as 1980 a Turk could obtain a passport only with difficulty and could not take more than one hundred dollars out of the country. Possession of foreign currency or foreign goods, even a pack of American cigarettes, was a crime. Turkish companies produced only for the domestic market; import and export were almost unknown. There was only one television station, owned and operated by the state.

Those conditions could not survive, and after the iconoclastic Turgut Özal came to power in 1983, he threw open doors and windows that had been tightly shut for decades. Suddenly Turks began to travel wherever they pleased, as both tourists and traders, and foreigners flooded into Turkish cities and onto Turkish beaches. In an amazingly short time Turkey became an important factor in regional affairs, first economically and then politically and militarily. But although Özal deserves credit for recognizing that his country needed to break out of its self-imposed solitude, he only delivered the final blow to the old system. The first blow, the first assault on the wall that had imprisoned Turks within their borders, must be credited to Ali Taşgan and the other returning Korelis.

Their stories led their friends and neighbors to wonder why Turkey was still insisting on keeping itself apart from the world. Korelis paved the way for the masses of "guest workers" who took jobs in Western Europe and who, although not always welcomed there with open arms, came home with new ideas about freedom, democracy, social justice and human rights.

Perhaps inevitably, new generations of Turks feel no special kinship with the Korelis, and certainly little gratitude toward them. To them the Korean War belongs to a forgotten era, its veterans more like relics than heroes. There are still plenty of cafés and restaurants where a Koreli can count on a free meal, a bottle of rakı and a warm welcome, but they are places run by old people. Today, as the Korelis age, many feel forgotten by a state that sends them pensions worth no more than sixty dollars a month and by a nation that has no time to celebrate their sacrifices. Some have even been ridiculed, told they were crazy to have allowed faceless generals to ship them halfway around the world to fight in a war that meant nothing to them or their country.

"Young people don't respect what we went through," a veteran named Selahattin Sanlı complained as he showed me the scars he still bears from his war wounds. He lives in lonely retirement in Ankara. "Many aren't even aware of it. Nowadays they don't even give up their seat on the bus when they see the veteran's badge on my jacket."

What Ali Taşgan, Selahattin Sanlı and their compatriots have done for Turkey! Nearly all were born into peasant families for whom travel and social mobility were unimaginable concepts. They saw more as teenagers than their parents and grandparents and great-grandparents saw in their entire lives. When they returned, they used their experiences to fire the curiosity of their people. Every modern Turk, everyone who revels in the opportunities Turkey now offers its citizens, is deeply in their debt.

• SEVEN •

GUARDIANS

For some reason Turks shed their inhibitions when they board an inter-city bus. As the Anatolian landscape rolls by hour after hour, they spill intimate secrets to total strangers who happen to be seated next to them. After a time I found this forced intimacy too taxing, so when I boarded a bus for the three-hour trip from Konya, home of the whirling der-vishes, to Ankara one midsummer day, I chose to sit next to a young man in uniform. I thought a soldier would surely keep his own counsel, and this one did. He nodded to me as I sat down but spoke not a word.

Long-distance buses in Turkey are equipped with every conve-nience, including an attendant who brings passengers tea, cold drinks and even lemon-scented cologne. Soon after ours left Konya, however, it became clear that the air conditioning was out of order. Everyone be-gan to sweat, and much clothing was removed. But although the officer sitting next to me squirmed and wiped his brow like everyone else, he did not take off his beribboned jacket. After an hour, with evident un-certainty, he went so far as to loosen his tie just slightly. When we made a rest stop along the road, he pulled it tight again even though he was going no farther than the toilet.

This officer had been considerate enough not to bother me, but I found myself unable to return the favor. Why, I asked him when we were once again aboard, didn't he shuck the jacket, loosen the tie and relax along with everyone else? Why worry about appearances on a bus, or when walking a few steps to the bathroom and back?

"I'm an officer in the Turkish army," he told me quite seriously. "Other people can look sloppy, but not me. When I'm at the stadium and my team scores a goal, I can't jump up and scream like everyone else. I can't run after buses or elevators. I can't hang around in bars and make passes at women. That's the kind of thing civilians do. It's okay for them, but not for us. We're different. We're dignified. We have a mission. We discipline ourselves because we're responsible for the future of this country. Naturally we have higher standards." He stared out the window for a long time, then turned back and added, "Much higher."

One of the greatest achievements of the democratic ideal has been its success in subordinating military power to civilian control. Where democracy rules, army officers do not. They cannot even decide when, where or how to use their power in the field. Those decisions are left exclusively to the people, who through their elected civilian leaders hold a monopoly on political power. When a general in a democratic country speaks out on matters of public policy, he is reprimanded or fired and suffers the opprobrium of his people.

The process of asserting civilian control over armies has been under way for several centuries, and it has become normal for democrats around the world to view military involvement in politics as the antithesis of freedom. The long and horrific periods of military rule through which dozens of African, Asian and Latin American countries suffered during the second half of the twentieth century are taken as confirmation of this basic principle. Democracy is always assumed to suffer when military officers start trying to shape their country's destiny. Conversely, as generals become quieter and more submissive, nations become more democratic and their peoples happier and more free.

More than any country on earth, Turkey challenges this stereotype. Its revolution was led by army officers, and their breathtaking success in building a modern state on the ruins of the Ottoman Empire ranks among the century's most extraordinary achievements. Turks realize that, and many feel deep gratitude and a genuine connection to their army. They believe it exists and works for them.

But at the dawn of the twenty-first century, the Turkish army, like the Kemalist ideology it so fervently defends, risks losing the admiration of its people and hence its leading position in Turkish society. Its historical role has been to guard the achievements of Atatürk's revolution and to guide Turkey on a steady course toward social progress and the embrace of universal ideals. Today it is a victim of its own achievements. So successfully has it encouraged Turkey's integration in the world that ever more Turks want to escape from its political power, which has become intrusive and suffocating. They have learned the lessons of democracy and now want to live by them.

This leap of consciousness confronts the Turkish army with its greatest challenge. It must either resist the people's will by continuing to block the establishment of true democracy, or step voluntarily back from power and leave the country's fate to civilians whose ability and good faith it has never fully trusted.

Military conquest was the basis of Ottoman power. The greatest sultans were the greatest conquerors, and the empire's decline began with sultans who found military campaigns less appealing than the pleasures of hearth and harem. When the empire collapsed after World War I, the decadent ruling class virtually abandoned the idea of the Turkish nation and kept silent as foreign powers divided Anatolia among themselves. Thanks only to the valor of officers and the peasant soldiers they recruited, national honor was redeemed and the Turkish ideal salvaged.

Since then Turkish officers have defended their country against a host of foreign and domestic threats. They staged three military coups between 1960 and 1980, but each time they acted with considerable popular support and each time they withdrew voluntarily from power after a few years although there was no one to push them out. Although their record is not unblemished, it is one in which today's generals take justified pride. They see little reason to abandon ways that seem to them and to many Turks to have been remarkably successful.

Military commanders today are the ultimate arbiters of life and politics in Turkey, just as they were in the early years of the Republic. Elected officials can act without their consent but not over their objections. Prime ministers accept orders from the generals who dominate the National Security Council, Parliament retreats when officers warn

that this or that bill should not be passed and defense ministers unques-
tioningly endorse every project presented to them by men in uniform.
Military men do not run the government, and they intrude only into areas of public policy that they consider vital to national security. But since
they themselves define "national security," in practice theirs is the decisive voice whenever they want it to be.

Military intervention in civilian politics waxes and wanes in Turkey.
It peaked in the years after the coups of 1960, 1971 and 1980, but ebbed
each time after the officers returned to their barracks. Most striking was
its retreat when the generals left power in 1983. They wrote a new constitution that guaranteed their continuing influence in politics and then
explicitly warned voters that they must safeguard their newfound stability by electing the army's favored candidate, a retired general, as prime
minister. But after voters overwhelmingly rejected that advice and instead elected the civilian challenger, Turgut Özal, his vigor and broad
vision of Turkey's potential allowed him to dominate the army. When
generals told him who they wanted for chief of staff, he rejected their
choice and appointed someone else. When they told him Turkey must
not take an active role alongside the United States during the Gulf War,
he overruled them. Once he even reviewed a military parade wearing
shorts and a T-shirt; there could not have been a clearer signal that a
civilian was the nation's supreme leader and that generals should submit
themselves to him rather than the other way around.

The army's willingness to retreat from power during Özal's tenure
showed an important aspect of its role and its self-image. It does not
seek to rule for the sake of ruling, but believes it is there to fill whatever
vacuum is left by civilian leaders. During Özal's rule there was no such
vacuum. In the years after his death in 1993, however, there suddenly
seemed to be no steady hand on the tiller of government. Irresponsible
and corrupt party leaders spent their time bickering and amassing personal fortunes while the Kurdish rebellion reached a peak, the economy
collapsed and inflation skyrocketed. Prime Minister Tansu Çiller, a
young American-educated economist in whom the army had at first
placed limitless hope, turned out to be a scatterbrained rogue.

After the 1995 election, the supposedly secularist Çiller made a cyn-
ical backroom deal with the Islamist leader Necmettin Erbakan, giving

him the support he needed to become prime minister, and in exchange he used the power of his new office to quash corruption charges against her. When their new government veered dangerously away from principles shared by most Turks, not just generals but many civilians concluded that a disciplining force needed to step in and set the country back on course. That force could only be the army. The generals responded with gusto, forcing Erbakan and Çiller to resign after a year in office and then setting about to limit politics so that such figures would be prevented from ever again attaining power. The worst legacy of Erbakan's disastrous year in power was that it convinced the army that Turks were still not ready for democracy.

In the last years of the twentieth century, the Turkish army, acting always with the enthusiastic support of its friends in Parliament, the government bureaucracy and the judicial system, launched a new and vigorous offensive against what it considered dangerous trends in Turkish society. Acting in unison, this elite enthusiastically banned political parties, sent politicians and journalists to jail, harassed Kurdish activists and crushed efforts to repeal laws that limited personal freedom. These steps were not in themselves new, and in fact have been depressing aspects of Turkish life for as long as there has been a Turkey. What was new was the political climate. Most Turks have begun to chafe under the restrictive nature of their state. Many doubt that the threats facing their nation are really as dire as military men make them out to be. Turks today understand what democracy is, which means that they realize how far their country is from it. They believe they have reached the point at which they can be trusted to make their own decisions, even to make their own mistakes. Army commanders, however, remain unconvinced. They consider themselves Atatürk's heirs and justify everything they do by claiming to be the only ones who truly understand what he wanted for his country. But are they upholding his vision or preventing its realization? Their narrow view of what constitutes national security and their terror of free inquiry and debate contradict Turkey's needs now more than ever.

From the moment Turkish cadets enter military high school at the age of fourteen, they are inculcated with a sense of mission. Like the officer I met on the bus from Konya, they consider themselves purer than most civilians, less tainted by greed and dishonesty, more willing to make sacrifices for the good of the nation. They are a priesthood that lives and grows together, largely isolated from the rest of society. Most of the people they know are other cadets and officers. They live in their own neighborhoods and follow each other's careers intently. Many of the ambitious among them even choose their wives from military families.

Cadets are educated quite differently from other Turks. Like aspiring officers everywhere, they are taught the values of discipline, order and hard work. They also enjoy immeasurably better facilities than pupils in normal public schools. The buildings in which they study are modern and well maintained. Their computers are new, their science laboratories well equipped and their libraries full. Their teachers are wise and experienced, not like the ill-trained and poorly paid ones who must make the best of pitifully inadequate resources at many civilian schools. But the greatest difference lies in what they are taught. Cadets are told over and over that they are Atatürk's children, a selfless cadre set forth in a dissolute world. They learn the values of state and nation, not necessarily those of humanity and the individual. The most successful among them emerge with a deep sense of mission, an almost mystical conviction that Turkey's fate, not just militarily but also politically and spiritually, depends on their superior wisdom.

At the academy, cadets are taught strategic doctrine that presents a world fraught with danger. Threats are everywhere. Foreign powers plot endlessly to subvert, divide and weaken Turkey. Bad Turks, the enemies of Atatürk, lend themselves to these plots. To defend the nation in the face of such dire challenges, the army not only must have masses of tanks, helicopters and artillery but also must reconcile itself to the thankless task of regulating society, of suppressing dangerous ideas and individuals who seek to lead the nation astray. With this message drilled into them day after day and year after year, cadets naturally become officers who revere abstract ideals like "state" and "duty" more than humanistic values like individual rights and the supremacy of civilian power. They do not see the vibrant, self-confident and boldly ambitious Turkey that many civilians see. Rather they see a nation surrounded by enemies and populated by simpletons who are easily manipulated. The army and the army alone, they are taught, stands between this fragile nation and utter doom.

This outlandish perspective, like much of Kemalist doctrine, was once quite reasonable. In the 1920s and 1930s Turkey was indeed a fragile and besieged nation, and there was no social class or political force better than the army to defend it. The educated elite was small, and there was neither a middle class nor anything resembling civil society. All that has now changed. Turkey is bursting with energy and overflowing with people who can guide a nation at least as capably as military officers can. Army commanders do not seem to recognize that Turkey is racing past them and their stagnant worldview. Because their institution encourages the strictest orthodoxy and punishes creative thinking, it is drifting slowly away from its nation.

Each year about nine hundred Turkish cadets are commissioned as lieutenants. Only about thirty will ultimately become generals, or "pashas," as Turks still call them. Their progression through the ranks is determined partly by their command capacity and military expertise, but also according to their perceived fidelity to the rigid principles of Kemalism. An officer who prays, shuns alcohol or is married to a woman who wears a head scarf not only is an unlikely candidate for advancement but runs the risk of being cashiered. The same is true for any who question the accepted view of the army's role in Turkish society. As officers rise through the ranks and compete ever more intensely for the fewer and fewer available promotions, they naturally feel pressure to seem—and to be—more fiercely Kemalist than their rivals. The self-perpetuating elite this system has produced is highly resistant to change.

To portray Turkish generals as hopeless reactionaries, though, would be quite mistaken. The average general is better educated, more worldly and in some ways more liberal than the average politician. Hundreds of regional party bosses, mayors and members of Parliament are fanatic nationalists, ignorant demagogues or scheming crooks. Few generals fit into any of those categories. This truth is depressing because of what it says about the political class, but at the same time it is encouraging. It means that the military commanders of today and tomorrow know Turkey must change, even though they deeply fear that change. No one repeats more often than they do the old cliché about Turkey being a special case that cannot risk opening its society as completely as more comfortably located and traditionally democratic countries can. In their hearts, though, more than a few realize that the contradictions inherent in their self-image are sharper today than they have ever been.

Turkish officers command a huge force of more than half a million soldiers, bigger than any army in Europe and the second largest in NATO after that of the United States. Most are draftees, required by law to serve between one and two years in uniform. Over several generations the system of universal male conscription has effectively bound the citizenry to the army and led most Turks to view it as a part of their everyday lives. When they see a soldier they understand instinctively that he is Mehmet, the fellow from down the street or over in the next village.

Conscription was originally imposed not only to create a large army but also as a socialization tool. For generations it was invaluable in giving sons of peasants a glimpse of modernity, training in basic social skills and exposure to the ideals of patriotism and discipline. But today those functions are filled by education, travel and mass communication. Many Turkish youths have come to view their military service as a waste of time, almost a joke.

Partly in response to this mounting unhappiness, in 1999 the army instituted a system under which young men could buy their way out of military service for fifteen thousand German marks, the equivalent of about eight thousand dollars. Those who cannot afford such a sum naturally resent this system, but even many who take advantage of it slip into cynicism and frustration. After making their payment these men must spend twenty-eight days on a military base as a kind of token service. Many come home with stories that portray the army as an almost ridiculous institution.

"We never learned a thing about tactics or how to fight," a friend told me after returning from his twenty-eight days at Burdur, an army base near the Mediterranean coast. "In the morning we heard speeches about why Turks are the best soldiers in the world; it's because we are Turks. Then there were speeches about how joining the European Union is the strategic goal of Turkey. In the afternoon, four or five times a week, we had belly-dance and striptease shows. Everyone had to pay four million lira [then about seven dollars] for a ticket. At first some of the recruits from Anatolia didn't want to go because they didn't have enough money and didn't like the idea of seeing naked women. But any-one who didn't go had to march around the base in the hot sun all after-noon, so after the first few days everybody came. We had more than a thousand people in a huge hall. And during the shows, subofficers would go around selling Coke and ice cream. It was all a way to get money from us. After four weeks of this I came home. Do you think I came home respecting my military? Of course not. I came home thinking it's a stupid organization run by stupid people."

The Turkish army is able to get away with practices like this because it is not subject to outside control. Logic suggests that long ago officers should have begun to take advantage of this freedom not simply to ex-tort money from recruits but to enrich themselves. Quite remarkably, however, they have not. Unlike many civilian politicians, the generals do not take bribes or extort money from contractors. When they retire they do not live in mansions, and their children do not attend expensive schools or drive flashy cars. Instead they set an example of probity and expect everyone in uniform to follow it.

Not all do, especially those whose service has taken them to tradi-tionally lawless southeastern provinces. The war against Kurdish rebels led many people into crime, including some officers. When fighting was at its peak during the early 1990s, some used brutish tactics and collab-orated with terror groups in ways that deeply alienated millions of Kurds. Others succumbed to temptation and made lucrative arrange-ments with the smugglers who for decades have been moving huge quantities of Iranian and Afghan heroin to Europe across well-worn paths in eastern Turkey. One captain who retired from the army and re-turned home to my neighborhood in Istanbul after serving for six years at posts near the Iranian border bought himself a twelve-villa vacation complex overlooking the Sea of Marmara, an unimaginable luxury for someone with no income other than a soldier's salary. Some of his old friends were so disgusted that they refused to speak to him again, but he didn't seem to mind.

Turks know these cases are exceptions and rightly consider their army to be fundamentally honest. Many also consider it decent and hu-mane, although they have never heard the full story of how the Kurdish rebellion was suppressed. The Turkish army does not risk losing its prestige or its position in national life by being brutal, repressive and rapacious, like armies that became despised in countries from Indonesia to Chile to Zaire. But it is finding for the first time that a gap has developed between it and the Turkish people.

In one sense the Turkish army is beginning to resemble the elite Janissary corps that guarded Ottoman sultans and formed the backbone of military power during much of the imperial period. Originally Janissaries were servants of the state, but gradually they accumulated so much power that they became its masters. "The sultan trembles at a Janissary's frown," went an old Turkish proverb. Ultimately the Janissaries degenerated into brigandage and cruelty, and their corps was destroyed by Sultan Mahmut II in 1826—an episode known in Turkish history as the "auspicious event." Today's Turkish officers have never approached the lawlessness into which the Janissaries degenerated, but freethinking civilians tremble at a general's frown, and many Turks believe that the officers' withdrawal from politics would be an "auspicious event" every bit as crucial for republican Turkey as the first one was for the Ottomans.

Not long ago, nearly all Turks viewed their army as a valiant force of selfless patriots dedicated to defending the nation against its many enemies. Today growing numbers of young people view universal conscription as outmoded and harmful to the cause of national development, forcing them to waste time they might otherwise use studying or working. Among the citizenry at large, doubts run even deeper. More and more Turks are concluding that their army has failed to keep pace with their aspirations, that despite its stated commitment to Europe and European values it has become an obstacle, perhaps even the main obstacle, to modernization and democracy.

Some Turkish generals believe that foreign powers have never given up their secret desire to carve up Turkey for themselves, as they tried to do at Sèvres in 1920. They suspect that the European Union in particular uses human-rights issues and the status of Kurds as wedges in a campaign to destroy Turkey's unitary state and ultimately its nation. Closer to home, the generals see even more dire threats. In their view, Iran is directing a massive destabilization campaign designed to bring Turkey under the rule of reactionary mullahs; Syria plots to capture the ethnically Arab province of Hatay and adjacent regions rich with water and other resources; Iraq harbors Kurdish guerrillas waiting for the right time to launch a new offensive; Armenia directs a worldwide defamation campaign aimed at blackening Turkey's name and ultimately seizing its eastern provinces; even Greece cannot be trusted, its relatively recent desire for cooperation across the Aegean only a feint that may hide nefarious intentions. Worst of all are the threats from within Turkey itself. Bad children of the Turkish nation are cooperating with Turkey's foreign enemies, the generals believe, cynically disguising themselves as democrats, human-rights advocates, peaceful religious believers and defenders of cultural pluralism.

For a long time Turks were inclined to accept these views, mainly because they have great confidence in their military officers and assume they must know best. That changed during the 1990s. Turks are hearing more voices, younger and newer voices, and are inclined to doubt what their leaders tell them. They see a world very different from the one their generals see—a world where foreign powers do not necessarily wish Turkey ill and, on the contrary, want to see it become prosperous and free. The European Union has extended a friendly hand by declaring Turkey a qualified applicant like any other. As for Turkey's supposed enemies, Iran is in the midst of an all-encompassing domestic political conflict, Syria is pitifully weak and Iraq is divided and an outcast in the world. The Kurdish rebellion within Turkey is over and its leader imprisoned. Many devout Muslims, including those who are active in politics, learned important lessons during the 1990s and want to cooperate with secularists in building an open, tolerant nation. Civil society, more vibrant than ever, holds the promise of empowering ordinary people in ways that can only be positive.

This world view is profoundly subversive to the army's place in society. If a country is surrounded by snarling enemies, it must naturally turn to its army for protection and give that army whatever it claims to need. But if a country is peaceful and secure, with urgent social and political challenges but not military ones, then the army is not so crucial. Some Turks believe their generals relentlessly exaggerate and even invent threats in order to maintain their exalted role in national life. This is ungenerous. The generals naturally want to preserve their enormous institutional power, but their fears are also sincere responses to years of training and immersion in a strategic doctrine that no longer fits the time.

For many years the Turkish army was a more or less typical third-world force, wielding much political power and using conscription to swell its ranks but not a serious fighting machine. But Turkish soldiers impressed many foreign military commanders with their bravery in Korea, and after Turkey joined NATO in 1952, Western powers, especially the United States, gave it new importance as a frontline state in their confrontation with the Soviet Union. They trained Turkish officers, equipped Turkish units with modern weaponry and stationed their own soldiers, ships, planes and even nuclear weapons on Turkish soil. This transformed the mentality of the Turkish officer corps. As it was drawn ever closer into the bosom of NATO, it became militantly anti-Communist, reveling in the new importance NATO assigned it. But in the 1980s, when Kurdish nationalists launched their rebellion, the army suddenly realized that although it was well equipped to resist a Warsaw Pact invasion, it had no clue how to suppress domestic insurrection. The generals began to reorient their army, slowly building it into a tough combat-trained force well armed with modern weapons. Many of these weapons are American-made and highly sophisticated, including multiple-launch rocket systems, F-16 jet fighters and M-60 tanks. After learning how to use them and slowly mastering counter-insurgency tactics, field commanders were able to defeat the Kurdish rebels.

Now Turkish generals are masters of a truly modern army. Flushed with success on the battlefield and presuming that the Turks have no choice but to give them whatever they want, they announced plans to spend more than fifty billion dollars on new weaponry in the first decades of the twenty-first century, beginning with seven billion to buy a thousand battle tanks and another four billion for a fleet of high-tech American helicopter gunships. For the first time, they found quiet resistance. Turks could not help asking themselves how many schools and hospitals could be built with that money, how much urban and economic development it could buy. And for the first time, the generals responded to public discontent, agreeing after the country suffered an economic shock in 2001 to postpone their purchases. They were following Atatürk's dictum: "A nation must be strong in spirit, knowledge, science and morals. Military strength comes last."

When Turkish commanders staged their "post-modern coup" to depose Necmettin Erbakan in 1997, they were reacting not simply against his brand of religious politics but also against his lack of enthusiasm for the West, against his belief that Turkey should look to the Islamic world for ideas and allies, which was an affront to the very essence of Kemalism. Atatürk had declared over and over that European values were those of "universal civilization" and that the nation's supreme goal should be to embrace them. When the European Union, at its December 1999 summit in Helsinki, named Turkey as an official candidate for membership, a wave of ecstatic self-congratulation washed over the country, accompanied by solemn newspaper commentaries declaring it the most important event in the history of the Republic.

But the European Union then laid out the conditions under which Turkey could become a member, and the military and its civilian allies balked. To repeal limits on free speech, grant every citizen the right to cultural expression, subject the military to civilian control, resolve social conflicts by conciliation, allow citizens to practice their religion as they see fit—suggestions like these froze the generals into immobility. Six months after the momentous decision at Helsinki, an American student arrived in Ankara to conduct research for her doctoral thesis. She spent ten days there asking politicians, journalists and university professors how quickly they thought Turkey might complete its long march toward democracy. "Every one of them wanted to talk about the military," she told me. "They made me shut off my tape recorder, and then they said the military is the main obstacle to democracy."

It has come to this! Pillars of the Turkish establishment fear military power so much that they dare not urge their generals toward democracy unless they are assured that their sentiments will be kept secret. If the army ignores these warning signals, it risks losing the popular support it has enjoyed through so many crises.

Turkish officers begin their military career with a solemn oath: "I will remain loyal to Atatürk's principles and reforms, and I will defend them." Never have they been more urgently called upon to live by that oath. To do so they, like the rest of the encrusted Kemalist establishment, must trust the wisdom of the Turkish nation. If they want their people to believe in them, they must believe in their people. As soon as they do, the army will again become Turkey's great unifying force. There are of course other Kemalists in Turkey who fear democracy, but their fears are exceeded by their reverence for their uniformed commanders. That makes the army the indispensable element in the grand national coalition that can bring true democracy to Turkey. It must lead the crusade toward "universal civilization," not try to block it.

Many senior officers, and even more in the middle ranks, are acutely aware of this challenge and understand what the army must do to remain true to this essence of its modernizing mission. They hesitate, for the step they are being asked to take entails risk, and military officers detest risk. But it is unthinkable that the army will choose to go down in history as the force that turned Turkey away from the course on which Atatürk set it.

I knew Hamza Akmeşe was a real man when I noticed that he doesn't care how much camel saliva drips onto his shoulders. He loves his beast and would probably take it to bed with him if he could. A little spit, even a lot of spit, doesn't bother him.

The day I met Hamza he was furtively surveying the competition before a big camel-fighting match in Selçuk, a town near the Aegean coast that is known to foreigners only because it is on the road to the ancient ruins of Ephesus. He quickly realized he had nothing to worry about. "My camel is strong," he told me. "He has a good body, good technique, and he knows how to use his front legs for tripping."

Turks are becoming steadily more European and that is good, because it means they are embracing ideas and perspectives that will make their lives richer and more fulfilling. But they will never be completely European, and that is also good. They have a different heritage, a different psychology. Like many Europeans they love soccer, but they also have more exotic sporting tastes, and camel fighting is one of them. Hamza Akmeşe, who has been in the game for forty years, compares its hold on Turks to the hold bullfighting has on Spaniards. "It's our tradition," he told me as he led his hulking creature toward the ring, bells on its humps, a mirrored blanket covering its back and colorful pom-poms woven into its tail. "It's very big, very important."

Turks migrated from the steppes of Central Asia a thousand years ago, but something of their past remains within them. It must be a kind of collective imagination; it cannot be a personal gene, since most people in Turkey today have no Central Asian ancestry at all. As they hurtle toward modernity, they are also looking back. The prospect of becoming European thrills them, as well it should, but they also find it vaguely disturbing. They do not want to lose what makes them different and special, which is why so many thousands of them turn out every Sunday during the three-month winter season to watch camels fight.

The owner of a fighting camel is invariably a celebrity in his village. Children admire him, men defer to him, women compete for his attention. He may shine shoes, sell vegetables or work in an office, but when he is with his camel he is an incarnation of Turkishness. Fighting camels have names that express valor and fearlessness, like Thunderbolt, Falcon, Destiny, Black Ali and Jackal. They are not to be trifled with, and neither are their owners.

Fans of camel fighting can discourse endlessly about the sport's finer points. They compare bloodlines, assess technique and trade rumors about young camels that seem to be developing into future champions. To the untrained eye, however, the game's subtleties are not immediately visible.

A match resembles an outsize version of sumo wrestling. It begins with two camels, the largest of which can weigh well over a ton, being led toward each other. Sometimes one bolts and runs away, thereby forfeiting the match. More often, they crash into each other and begin shoulder-to-shoulder pushing. For a minute or more, there is little movement as the contestants strain against each other. Their owners urge them on, spectators cheer and an announcer breathlessly calls the play-by-play. Finally one of the animals collapses onto the ground. The winner's owner is awarded a carpet.

"I have piles of them at home," one successful owner told me the day I was in Selçuk. "They're all machine-made and not so good. I give them away. But this isn't about money or carpets. It's about keeping something alive that was given to us by our grandfathers and great-grandfathers."

Yet camels are not and never were the animals most central to the

Turkish identity. As long as there have been Turks they have been known for their horsemanship, and watching men on horseback is still one of the Turk's great pleasures. There are of course country clubs where the privileged practice the stylized delicacy of dressage and the tightly controlled ritual of show jumping. But in the Turkish heartland, especially on the plains of wild provinces like Erzincan and Bayburt, once home to ancient cultures and still places where tradition is strong, it is the wild sport of cirit *that captivates and thrills.*

Cirit matches are lightning-fast, played by riders who gallop toward each other in clouds of dust, hurling wooden javelins. They win points by striking an opponent or forcing his horse to veer off course. Like the owners of fighting camels, they are heroic figures, at least in their own minds. Many seem as if they might be more at home in untamed, horse-crazy places like Afghanistan or Kyrgyzstan than in Turkey. The growing popularity of their sport, which is now played even in Ankara and Istanbul, reflects the resolve of Turks not to lose their old identity as they embrace a new one.

People are thought to have begun riding horses more than four thousand years ago in Central Asia, and the first to do so were probably ancestors of today's Turks. So were the first mounted archers, who began roaming the rugged highlands north of the Caspian and Black seas in the eighth century B.C. Turkic tribesmen spent much of their lives on horseback. Children were put on sheeps' backs before they could walk so that they would become accustomed to the feel of riding. Adults ate, drank, conducted business, held meetings and even slept on horseback. The ancient Chinese knew them as "horse barbarians."

Mounted cavalrymen called sipahi *were the backbone of the Ottoman army that spent centuries winning victory after victory. They were considered almost helpless when on foot but invincible when mounted. To gallop at full speed, turn backward and shoot a deadly arrow at a distant foe was only their most famous skill.*

The sipahi *rode off to war almost every spring, and their commanders devised* cirit *as a form of off-season training and exercise. In those days competitors had to hurl spears through rings while galloping and shoot arrows at suspended brass spheres. Their sport declined in the early twentieth century as new forms of warfare replaced mounted cav-*

alry and machines weakened the tie between rural people and their horses. But in the 1990s it became popular again. Rules were codified, an official federation was established and the University of Erzincan, many of whose students grew up in isolated villages on the surrounding prairie, began offering formal training courses for aspiring players. For a time Turks seemed to have forgotten how to ride toward conquest, but they are learning again.

The third of Turkey's great sporting traditions, oil wrestling, was born in the town of Kırkpınar, a few miles from the present-day border with Greece, at the beginning of the fifteenth century. Almost every year since then, boys and men have traveled there from across the country to test their strength and skill. This is the only wrestling tournament in the world at which contestants use three tons of olive oil.

Rules for these matches have changed only slightly over the centuries. In olden times they could go on for hours or even days, since the only way to win was to pin one's opponent to the ground. Some contestants expended so much energy that they died on the field. Now it is also possible to win on points, and matches are limited to forty-five minutes. But wrestlers still fight stripped to the waist, wear specially designed leather trousers and enjoy the boundless admiration of their countrymen. Most important, they begin fighting only after being drenched with olive oil from head to toe.

Once oiled, the competitors skip across the field in lines, slapping their knees and jumping as they move forward. Drummers in Ottoman costume keep a steady beat, and as matches are about to start announcers sing the praises of "Ye, oh great wrestlers" and recite verses like this one:

You cannot get wood from a willow branch.
Every girl cannot be a woman.
Every woman can give birth,
But not every boy can be a wrestler.

Lovers of this sport say it is psychological as well as physical. Because matches go on for so long, combatants cannot fight without interruption. They spend much time circling, grunting, feinting and trying to intimidate each other. When they sense an opening they charge, grab their opponent, often between the legs, and try to smash him to the ground. Pinning an opponent's shoulders to the ground for three seconds, or throwing him down more often than he can throw you down, is what it takes to win.

The undisputed king of modern oil wrestling is a former factory worker named Ahmet Taşçi. He is an eight-time champion in the heavyweight division, considered a superman because he continues to win even though he is more than forty years old. The only man to have defeated him since he rose to greatness in the 1980s is a whippersnapper in his mid-thirties named Cengiz Elbiye. On the day I saw them face off I realized I was seeing not just a match but the classic confrontation of aging champion versus rising challenger.

The match had been under way for more than half an hour when suddenly, so fast I am not sure I actually saw it, the veteran Taşçi smashed his younger opponent to the ground, pinned his shoulders and was pronounced the winner yet again. Elbiye, his defeated rival, remained on his knees with his face pressed to the ground for several minutes. I thought he was weeping bitter tears, but even if I had been closer I would not have been able to tell if what wetted his face were tears or drops of olive oil. That is certainly as he wanted it.

EIGHT

DEATH BY EARTHQUAKE

The dumplings at Joe's Shanghai, a wonderful dive hidden on a small street in the heart of New York's teeming Chinatown, have a cult following. They are made with a dollop of sauce inside, and you have to be careful how you eat them to avoid having the sauce spurt out as you bite. Nothing more serious than that was on my mind as I worked my way through dinner on a sticky summer evening. I took no special notice when the clock passed 8:11.

Half a world away, in Turkey, clocks at that moment read 3:11 A.M. Most people in the industrial boomtowns of Izmit and Adapazarı and the seaside resorts of Gölcük and Yalova were sleeping as calmly as I was eating in New York. But that was the moment when a murderous terror, mean and hateful, ascended suddenly from the depths. The earth began to shake, and for forty-five seconds buildings swayed and fell. Millions of people awoke and fled onto the streets, where they stood and watched in horror as the air around them filled with dust and screams. Thousands were killed as they tried to escape. Many others, most of them elderly and devout, simply pulled blankets over their heads and waited for fate to take its cruel course.

Hours later on that awful day, August 17, 1999, I was at Kennedy Airport checking in for a flight back to Istanbul. A man passing by stopped and stared at the Turkish Airlines sign above the counter where I was waiting.

"My God," I heard him mutter to his companion. "Who would want to go to Turkey now?"

No one yet knew how serious the earthquake had been. Turkish news agencies were reporting a death toll in the hundreds, and that was enough to cast a pall over the passengers on my flight, many of whom were Turks rushing home to search for friends or relatives. After we landed in Istanbul, I was waiting for my luggage when I noticed a young man ambling around the arrival lounge, carrying a clipboard and looking disoriented. He was sizing up passengers and approaching some of them. Soon it was my turn.

"Are you here for the earthquake?" he asked me. I was, of course, but it turned out that he was looking for relief workers. Rescue teams were already arriving, but evidently the authorities had no idea who they were, so the only way to find them was to grab them at the airport.

This was but a taste of what Turkey would live through over the next few days. Prime Minister Ecevit fell into a prolonged state of shock; instead of immediately jumping on a helicopter to survey the disaster area and then ordering his aides into action, he spent days telling whoever would listen that everything was under control and there was no need for concern. Army commanders who might have been expected to deploy thousands of soldiers to the stricken region also sat on their hands. Quickly it became clear that although Turkey lies above some of the world's most dangerous geological faults and is shaken by earthquakes every few years, its government had no plan for dealing with them, no disaster-relief agency, no civil-defense network, not even an official designated to take charge at such moments. In what seemed like a very cruel joke, the government's earthquake-relief fund was found to contain the equivalent of just four dollars and forty-five cents.

The quake's epicenter was barely fifty miles east of Istanbul's city limits, near the shore of a pretty bay at the edge of the Sea of Marmara, and it wrought death and destruction far greater than was first reported. In towns across the region whole blocks of buildings had collapsed, killing thousands instantly and trapping thousands more who died slowly while government officials stumbled aimlessly about, unable to grasp the dimensions of the catastrophe. Prime Minister Ecevit later sought to excuse the government's slow response by saying that roads were too clogged to allow rescue teams to reach devastated towns. Television teams had no such trouble, though, and soon all of Turkey was watching survivors clawing at the rubble with their bare hands and even fighting over shovels and the few available bulldozers. Most television stations dropped their normal programs and broadcast live, day and night, from the disaster zone. Turks by the millions were glued to their screens, watching scenes of heartrending devastation and streams of interviews with enraged survivors, the intensity of whose anger was shocking in a country where exaggerated respect for the state has always been part of the national psychology.

Ecevit and the generals who ran Turkey with him finally responded, but only after a week, and even then they devoted most of their energy to blaming the press. One television station was ordered shut for seven days as punishment for broadcasting reports that vividly conveyed the chaos of the official rescue efforts. The top military commander, General Hüseyin Kıvrıkoğlu, called a handful of Turkish newspaper editors to his office and told them that the main problem had been not the relief effort but irresponsible journalists who emphasized its failures over its successes. He singled out five foreign correspondents as having been especially responsible for feeding these distortions to the world, myself among them, and charged that we had placed ourselves at the service of unnamed subversive "interests." Essentially, his complaint was that we had reported the truth without thinking of what effect it might have on the prestige of the Turkish state.

Earthquake victims, meanwhile, faced a host of horrors. Survivors with loved ones buried beneath rubble bore the most painful burdens. For days, thousands of them could do nothing but sit helplessly before the piles of debris. Power shovels and other heavy equipment, much of it sent voluntarily by private companies, finally arrived in the ruined towns, but only after hopes of finding anyone alive had faded, and they were worked at a pace that survivors naturally found intolerably, heartbreakingly slow. Some nurtured hopes for days, but as time passed most accepted reality and waited only to claim bodies.

On the fifth morning after the quake, I sat among survivors who were maintaining a vigil in front of an apartment complex in the sea-side town of Yalova, to which thousands of upwardly mobile Turks had moved in recent years, lured by the prospect of cheap apartments, fresh sea air and proximity to Istanbul. A fifty-foot-high pile of rubble at which they gazed had once been a handsome apartment building. Giant yellow power shovels were clawing at it, ripping away floors and ceilings that had "pancaked" when the quake struck—fallen on top of one an-other as supporting walls collapsed, crushing scores of victims as they slept. Several bodies had already been pulled from the debris, and the stench that filled the hot, sticky air was a grim signal that more still lay entombed.

As the power shovels worked, the flotsam of human lives tumbled down through the dust—clothes, mattresses, bookshelves, carpets, a tel-evision, a washing machine, a radiator, a toilet, a set of the works of Balzac translated into Turkish. The roar of machines found an eerie counterpart in the absolute silence of onlookers, who fixed their gazes on this horrific scene as beads of sweat dripped down their faces.

Shortly before noon, one group of workers cried out. A shovel had broken into a bedroom and they could see a body inside. The big ma-chine backed away, and workers began to pull away slabs of concrete by hand. Half an hour later they freed the bloated body of a young woman, wrapped it in a blanket, zipped it into a green plastic bag and carried it to a waiting ambulance, which sped away with its siren blaring.

A few minutes later one man sitting near me began to turn pale and breathe heavily. He broke into sobs and then suddenly started scream-ing. "Thirteen years old!" he shouted. "Buried under there! Just a baby! Just thirteen!" With both his hands, he began violently ripping up the grass around him. Relief workers wiped his brow with wet cloths and managed to calm him after a while, but he refused to be led away, pre-ferring to maintain his awful watch.

What made this hellish scene so especially and outrageously tragic was that all around stood buildings that had been damaged either lightly or not at all. These were structures that had been built by responsible contractors using decent materials, and the people who lived in them had survived unhurt while their neighbors had been horribly crushed to death in their beds. Earthquakes are often described as natural disasters, but seismologists like to say that it is buildings that kill people, not the quakes themselves. So it was here. The victims cursed not just the violent earth beneath their feet but also builders like Veli Göçer, who had built the collapsed edifice before which I spent that Sunday.

Lynch mobs tried to find Göçer in the days that followed the quake, but, like other contractors whose buildings had become tombs, he had disappeared. A week later he spoke by telephone with a German newspaper. "There's no reason for me to have a guilty conscience," he said. "Naturally I sympathize with the victims and their families. But I don't understand why they're making me into a scapegoat. I started building the Bahçekent complex in Yalova about six years ago. Naturally I didn't have any idea about construction. I studied literature in school. I'm a poet, not a structural engineer. I remember visiting my first construction site. I saw workers using beach sand to make concrete. When I asked about it, the architects told me that this was completely normal. Only later did I learn that this is a completely wrong and dangerous technique. So I ordered a stop to that disgusting practice. Unfortunately half the complex was already finished."

Several days later Göçer was arrested at a house in Istanbul where he had been hiding. More than a dozen other contractors had already been jailed pending investigations, but Göçer, whom the press had branded "the contractor of death," was the focus of public outrage. Three lines of police officers surrounded the station where he was booked, and when he was brought to prison he had to be isolated to protect him from other inmates, several of whom swore to kill him at the first opportunity.

For weeks after the earthquake, much of northwestern Turkey continued to be shaken by aftershocks, some of which qualified as small quakes in their own right. Dozens of people were injured as they jumped from shaking buildings. In Adapazarı, a town that had been heavily damaged on the first day, a woman died of a heart attack as she rushed from a building she thought was about to collapse. This panic reflected something beyond the culture of exaggeration that traditionally leads Turks to dramatize imminent perils. It showed how unsettled they had become, how deeply their collective psyche had been wounded by the shock of the August 17 disaster and the state's inability to cope with it.

Among journalists it is a truism that covering natural disasters is a colossal waste of time. They take a heavy emotional toll because they force us to confront horrible tragedies, but in essence they are alike; even the most pitiful stories about children dying and families being decimated are almost identical. Worst of all, in the larger scheme of things disasters mean nothing. When the earth stops shaking or the floodwaters recede or the flames are extinguished, people pick up what remains of their lives and go on as best they can. For those interested in the fate of nations, disasters are only distractions.

The Turkish earthquake, however, shattered that cliché just as completely as it devastated towns, cities and human lives. Few natural disasters in modern history have had such a profound political, social and cultural effect. Some Turkish intellectuals went so far as to suggest that when the history of the Turkish Republic is written years or centuries from now, it will be divided into two periods, pre-earthquake and post-earthquake. The quake led millions of Turks to question institutions they had never questioned before, and to accept the necessity of changes they had resisted for years. Survivors saw that thousands had died needlessly—been murdered, some said—because their homes had been built with materials and construction techniques that could not withstand a quake. They knew without being told that this was not simply the fault of contractors like the wretched Veli Göçer but the result of a political system that tolerated corruption and contempt for human life. The self-perpetuating Turkish elite that calls itself "the state" had maintained itself for generations by the fiction that it alone could guarantee people's safety and security. But when the quake struck, this vaunted "state" was nowhere to be seen. Now it blazed in people's consciousness as the institution that allowed unscrupulous contractors to build big housing developments directly above one of the world's most active fault lines.

A flood of images conveyed the Turkish state's failures. Among the most memorable were the white-faced Prime Minister Ecevit, spending the post-earthquake period wandering around as if in a daze; military rescue workers racing frantically to dig out officers lying under the debris of a naval base while ignoring the plight of anguished civilians outside the gates; and the florid President Demirel visiting devastated towns after a very long delay, a trip that turned into a fiasco because all roads in and out of the area were closed to traffic, including relief convoys, for hours before and after his tour, every moment of delay meaning that more trapped victims were dying awful deaths beneath the rubble. No one realized this more than survivors, whose anguish quickly turned to outrage at the institutions they had long considered sacred. When Demirel finally acknowledged the government's failings but warned that "the state is an institution you cannot replace with anything else," he sounded as if he were speaking from another planet.

The official who dominated most news reports in those days was not the president, prime minister or chief of staff. He was one Osman Durmuş, an obscure politician who since the formation of Ecevit's coalition government a few months earlier had been minister of health. Since taking office he had concentrated mainly on the quiet work of dismissing bureaucrats and hospital administrators so that they could be replaced by cronies from his far-right political party, Nationalist Action. Then, in the days after the quake, he showed himself to be one of those narrow-minded nationalists who have done so much over so many years to keep Turkey locked inside its fantasy-world shell. First he declared that Turkey needed no foreign aid for earthquake relief because it could handle everything perfectly well by itself. Then he said that even if aid was accepted, none should come from Armenia; that earthquake victims should be especially careful to refuse any blood sent from Greece; and that there was no need for portable toilets in the devastated region because many mosques had sanitary facilities, and anyway the Sea of Marmara was close by. These comments provoked a fury, including calls for his resignation, but he proudly stayed in office. No senior figure reprimanded him. The closest he came to an apology was to concede that if he were one day on the edge of death, he would be willing to accept blood from a Greek or Armenian donor.

Durmuş's mindless chauvinism did not represent the feelings of most government leaders. But along with many other examples, it conveyed the impression of a government and "state" that were hopelessly out of touch with the needs of its restive people. The earthquake showed Turks that something was fundamentally wrong with the way their nation and political system had developed since the end of military rule in 1983.

Until then, Turks had suffocated under a host of restrictive laws and regulations that effectively cut them off from the world but also insulated their country against corruption. National leaders valued propriety above economic growth, and most ordinary people followed their example. That changed with the emergence of Turgut Özal, a towering political figure and the most revolutionary leader Turkey had seen since Atatürk. As prime minister from 1983 to 1989 and then as president until his death two years later, Özal lifted hundreds of restrictive rules and urged Turks to ignore those he could not repeal, freeing what proved to be the enormous energies of Turkish entrepreneurs. Within a very few years of his rise to power, this profoundly important campaign brought Turkey into the international mainstream. But as Özal urged Turks to free themselves from the outmoded rules that had held them back for so long, he also sent a not-so-subtle message that rules in general were bad. Some ambitious Turks understood him to mean that getting rich was so important that it didn't matter how one accomplished it.

What sort of business could an unschooled and capital-poor Turk launch that would put him on the road to wealth? Hundreds chose to start construction companies, relying on the help of friends in local politics to win contracts. In a wide-open economy that was growing at dizzying rates, many of these do-it-yourself contractors quickly became rich. The price Turkey paid for their rapid rise to wealth became tragically clear when the earthquake turned many of the apartment blocks they had built into tombs.

If the anger that Turks felt had been directed only at contractors and the inspectors they bribed, if the tragedies of the earthquake had been seen as isolated failures, all might have been slowly forgotten and the country might have returned to its old ways. Instead, a new dawn seemed to burst over the country. People of every social class and political persuasion began to understand how dangerous it was to build a country on a social system in which everything is negotiable and *devlet baba*—"daddy state"—is always presumed to know best.

Respect for the state had begun to crumble with the Susurluk scandal in 1996, though with great effort military commanders and political godfathers had managed to put the lid on it before the full truth could emerge. Now they tried frantically to cover up their failures in the earthquake-relief effort. General Kıvrıkoğlu went so far as to demand names of journalists who were not writing glowingly enough about the army's work. But these efforts were fruitless because the relief effort, or what passed for one, had unfolded in full view of an already dubious public. Visceral and intense disgust sparked a civil uprising unlike anything modern Turkey had ever experienced.

Turks correctly saw the state's failures as the logical and even inevitable result of a system in which human life had always been considered a low priority. They learned that the state's traditional relief agency, Kızılay, a local branch of the Red Cross–Red Crescent, had become a dumping ground for incompetent and greedy hacks who spent their budget mainly on lavish trips and stays in luxury hotels. The few tattered old tents it scrounged up when the quake struck quickly became symbols of the government's incompetence and apparent callousness.

While wandering through a waterfront park where several hundred homeless earthquake survivors were living in leaky Kızılay tents, I met a carpenter who told me he had drawn a moral from all this. "I worked as a laborer in Europe, and later I lived in Israel for eighteen months," he said. "That's where I realized that in other countries, protecting human life comes before anything. We don't think like that here. If our leaders cared about human life they would have been ready for this earthquake, but it just isn't a priority for them. That's the main thing that has to change here."

The superb performance of private rescue and relief groups that raced to the earthquake zone to help victims only increased the anger at the state's failure. Twelve hours after the quake struck, a group of mountain climbers and practitioners of extreme sports who had banded together into an emergency-response team were already digging victims out of the rubble, and private charities and individuals were distributing food and blankets to the homeless. They were hard at work while government officials were still giving interviews claiming that their relief columns could not move along jammed or ruined roads to the devastated area. Politicians and generals in Ankara quickly realized that earthquake victims were becoming grateful to the wrong people. They responded by forbidding several religious charities from collecting or distributing relief aid, by urging donors to send their cash only to Kızılay or to an official fund at a government-owned bank and finally by trying to require private groups to transfer their aid to the army so that it could be distributed by soldiers. The cynicism of these maneuvers only emphasized the state's moral blindness.

To this day no one can say with even remote certainty how many people perished in the 1999 earthquake. The authorities stopped counting when they reached eighteen thousand, but thousands more were probably washed into the sea or bulldozed away with wreckage. No definitive list of the dead was ever drawn up.

Even before the pain of the tragedy had faded, another complex of emotions surged across Turkey, beginning with outrage at the government but then moving on to jubilant self-discovery. The generous and effective actions of ordinary people and private groups made millions of Turks realize, many for the first time, that they could take responsibility for their own lives and collective future without guidance from above. This realization introduced a genuine democratic consciousness, not through lectures or theoretical instruction but by events immediately and personally assimilated. It thrilled intellectuals and other reform-minded Turks who had been driven to despair by years of frustration and disappointment.

Private television stations, which Turgut Özal had legalized barely a decade before, rushed to offer exhaustive coverage from the devastated region, broadcasting unforgettable images that made the state's failures undeniable and also gave voice to hundreds of angry survivors whose words were heavy with emotion. Many, weeping openly on camera, talked of friends or relatives still alive under the rubble. The most commonly repeated cries of frustration were *"Devlet nerede?"* and *"Asker nerede?"* Where is the state? Where is the army?

The failure of the army, supposedly Turkey's indispensable institution, was a special shock. In the wake of this disaster, it was nowhere to be seen. Ecevit did not summon it to action and its own commanders did not volunteer troops. Tens of thousands of soldiers who were garrisoned within a few hours' ride of the earthquake zone were not moved from their barracks for days. When they finally did show up in ruined towns, most were assigned to provide security and distribute goods rather than help with rescue efforts. How could this institution defend the state if it was unable to protect the lives of Turkish citizens? The Susurluk scandal had shown that the state's priority was to guard an established order, not to serve individuals, and now it was displaying the same impulses in the earthquake-relief operation.

Had the quake devastated a remote Kurdish city like Erzincan, where Turkey's worst quake of the century hit in 1939, it might not have struck such a raw nerve. But this one destroyed densely populated towns just a short ferry ride from Istanbul, towns that were built around factories owned by people in Istanbul, towns where Istanbul residents went on their vacations. Millions of ordinary people in the Istanbul area lost friends or relatives, and thousands of them rushed to the region on the first day to try to help. The middle class led the civic uprising that followed, an uprising that was in some ways as shattering as the earthquake itself.

Perhaps the greatest surprise of all was people's response to the work of foreign relief agencies, whose energy and resourcefulness posed such a stark contrast to the Turkish government's paralysis. Teams from abroad appeared almost immediately, flying from their homelands, making their way to devastated towns and setting to work while the Turkish authorities were still lost in slumber. For generations Turks had been taught to believe that they were surrounded by enemies, that at every moment evil forces were plotting against them and their nation. But if more than seventy countries sent rescue and relief workers who saved victims who otherwise would have perished, how could it be true that, as nationalists had long asserted, "The only friend of the Turk is the Turk"?

The Turks' perception of Greece changed most vividly and remarkably, wiping away generations of resentment in a matter of days. Several months before, following the scandal that surrounded the capture of Abdullah Öcalan, Greek leaders had rid their government of powerful Turk-haters. Now, on the very day of the quake, the quick-witted Greek foreign minister George Papandreou telephoned his Turkish counterpart, Ismail Cem, to offer whatever help Turkey needed, and then quickly sent rescue workers, ships and planes loaded with relief supplies, and streams of messages pledging solidarity with the victims. Even more important, Greek television crews rushed to the ruins and began broadcasting live. Countless Greeks shared the grief of parents whose families had been destroyed, the suffering of those who waited tearfully for rescue workers to find their loved ones and the exhilaration of watching victims being pulled alive from the rubble. This was a deeply intimate experience that shook Greeks to their emotional core.

Then, only twenty-seven days later, an earthquake struck in Greece—a smaller one, but powerful enough to give Turks and Greeks a sense of shared fate. Now it was Turkish volunteers who flew to the rescue, and clever Greek officials directed them to help in places where they knew victims were alive and could be helped. Televised pictures of Turks saving the lives of Greek children melted hearts on both sides of the Aegean. Soon the two nations, caught up for years in senseless animosity, found themselves embracing each other with the fervor of lovers who realize they have been separated far too long.

Whenever I told a Turkish friend about my ambition to swim across the Bosphorus, the reaction was the same: "Why?" Each gave me a different warning. The Bosphorus is too dirty, its currents are too unpredictable, the giant tankers and freighters that traverse it are too dangerous. On top of all that, it is illegal to swim anywhere but along the shore.

I was not dissuaded. No one can live near the Bosphorus and see it every day without falling in love with it. I wanted to immerse myself in it, possess it, make it mine.

Istanbul may or may not be the world's most magnificent city, but it is certainly the most magnificently situated. Over the centuries it has been described as the pole to which the world turns, the envy of kings, city of the world's desire. "O city of Istanbul, priceless and peerless!" rhapsodized the eighteenth-century Ottoman poet Nedim. "I would sacrifice all Persia for one of your stones."

This is the only city that straddles two continents, and the Bosphorus is what divides and unites it. Without this strait Byzantium/Constantinople/Istanbul would be unimaginable. It would not have been so enormously important over so many centuries, so eagerly sought after by so many of history's greatest conquerors. Nor would it be nearly so rich, beautiful or romantic.

The Bosphorus is the link between the Black Sea to the north and the Sea of Marmara and Mediterranean to the south, so since time immemorial it has been the key to empires. The sixteenth-century French scholar Pierre Gilles described it as "the strait that surpasses all straits, because with one key it opens and closes two worlds, two seas." It winds and twists for nineteen incomparable miles. I never tire of seeing it, walking along its shores or sailing on it. Every day it has a different color, a different texture, a different mood. It is a world unto itself.

Many scientists now believe that the Bosphorus did not slowly swell to its present size as a river might, but was flooded in a single day seventy-five centuries ago. What a day that must have been! Ten cubic miles of water are thought to have surged northward through what was then a dry valley, and then ten more cubic miles every day for months, coursing into the Black Sea and submerging vast regions along its shores. This cataclysm may well have been the great flood described in the Bible, the Gilgamesh epic and other ancient texts.

The name Bosphorus is said to derive from an ancient Greek word meaning "cow's ford." It was given to this waterway because of the ancient myth about a beautiful maiden, Io, whose love affair with Zeus arouses the anger of his wife, Hera, and whom Zeus then tries to hide from Hera's wrath by turning her into a cow. But Hera discovers the truth and sends a gadfly to torment the cow, which, trying to escape, swims across this waterway.

Some of the first adventurers to sail through the Bosphorus were Jason and his legendary Argonauts, among them Hercules, Theseus and Orpheus, who were on their way to what is now the Black Sea coast of Georgia in search of the golden fleece. In 512 B.C. the Persian emperor Darius built a pontoon bridge across the Bosphorus at its narrowest point, barely seven hundred yards across, so that he could march his army of seventy thousand men into Europe. Overlooking that same spot, Sultan Mehmet II built the breathtaking fortress called Rumeli Hisarı, from which he set out to conquer Constantinople in 1453. It still stands, the most exquisite and delicately shaped piece of military architecture on earth.

Rumeli Hisarı is the crown jewel of the Bosphorus, but its shores are crammed with scores of other extraordinary edifices built directly on the water. The most magnificent among them are ornate Ottoman palaces, most of them designed in the nineteenth century by a gifted family of Armenian architects, the Balians. Each is layered in history.

Beylerbeyi Palace was a favorite summer retreat for nineteenth- and early-twentieth-century European monarchs, among them Empress Eugenie of France, Tsar Nicholas II of Russia, Emperor Franz Josef of Austria and King Edward VII of Great Britain. Çırağan Palace served as a sumptuous asylum and prison for Sultan Murat V, a lunatic who was forced from office after just three months in 1876 and then lived amid its splendor for nearly thirty years. Dolmabahçe Palace, the most overwhelming of them all, is a temple of excess whose construction is said to have bankrupted the empire. It has a marble facade the length of three football fields, two hundred eighty-five rooms, a staircase made of crystal, more than a square mile of handwoven silk Hereke carpets and the world's largest chandelier, which weighs four tons.

Almost as imposing and far more human in scale are the scores of mansions called yalıs that line the shores, set below groves of jacarandas that burst into violet bloom each spring. Classic yalıs are built of wood in styles ranging from neoclassical and baroque to art nouveau and eclectic arabesque, and painted in beautiful pastel colors. Many have been lovingly preserved or restored, either by members of the old upper crust or by the newly rich. Most have docking space for boats. Each has a name: Egyptian Yalı, Snake Yalı, Pink Lion Yalı, Writers' Yalı, even Mad Fuat Pasha Yalı, named for a nineteenth-century Ottoman noble who was bold enough to denounce the repressive rule of Sultan Abdülhamid II. Lord Byron was transfixed by these homes: "Each villa on the Bosphorus looks a screen / New painted, or a pretty opera-scene."

In past eras, sultans, viziers and ambassadors gave grand illuminated parties at their palaces and yalıs. It is still fashionable to be married beside the Bosphorus, and weddings are usually accompanied by fireworks, an old tradition. Often the main dish at these celebrations is fish, because fish caught in the Bosphorus and the nearby seas are as tasty as any in the world. Menus vary with the season since each species has a different temperature tolerance and migrates between the Mediterranean and Black Sea at a different time. My favorite is palamut, a gourmet cousin of the mackerel that appears in late autumn, but others prefer the flaky and delicate lüfer and wait impatiently for summer because that is when it shows up at markets and on restaurant menus.

The Bosphorus is not only a place of surpassing beauty but also Istanbul's heavily trafficked main street. Ferries cross it and shuttle among its villages a thousand times a day. They and the hundreds of skiffs from which fishermen ply their trade are reminders that a great city depends on this artery for its daily life. It is also the world's busiest commercial waterway. About one hundred fifty vessels, lumbering Russian and Ukrainian rust buckets or giant tankers carrying oil and liquefied natural gas from the rich fields of the Caspian, pass through it each day. Under clauses of the 1923 Lausanne treaty and another signed in Montreux thirteen years later, the Turkish government has no control over them and cannot require them to take on pilots or even to prove that they are insured. Many are not, like a Lebanese freighter that sank in 1992 with a cargo of ten thousand sheep and goats and lies at the bottom to this day.

How much else could be found at the bottom of the Bosphorus! I imagine not just sunken treasures and evidence of a thousand crimes but the weighted sacks into which royal plotters or unfaithful harem women were sewn before being thrown to their watery deaths. The novelist Orhan Pamuk once wove a fantasy of the day the Bosphorus dries up and becomes "a pitch-black swamp in which the mud-caked skeletons of galleons will gleam like the luminous teeth of ghosts." Besides fields of jellyfish and soda-pop caps, he expects that "among the American transatlantics gone to ground and Ionic columns covered with seaweed, there will be Celtic and Ligurian skeletons open-mouthed in supplication to gods whose identities are no longer known."

To me, the Bosphorus fantasy that burned most brightly was that of swimming across. After entertaining it for far too long, I finally found a friend with a boat who was willing to accompany me. He advised that we start before dawn, since traffic is lighter then and the waves and currents more predictable.

We set out from near my home in Tarabya, a village near the north end of the Bosphorus, and motored northward toward the entrance to the Black Sea. I wanted to swim westward from Asia to Europe because that is the direction of Turkish history. We found a small inlet below *the ruins of Anadolu Kavağı, a twelfth-century Byzantine castle on the Asian side, and there, after waiting for a freighter to glide silently by, I started.*

The sun had not yet risen and the waves of the Bosphorus were rippling gently. Its water was warmer and cleaner than I expected. I felt exuberant as I made my way steadily across, thinking of Jason, Darius and Mehmet the Conqueror. Other than my friend's small boat and a couple of jellyfish, I was alone, and grateful to be in this place. To orient myself I focused on a green shape on the shore that I first thought was a yalı but turned out to be a fishing vessel docked at Yeni Mahalle, the northernmost settlement on the European side. I swam to it and past it. Just thirty-nine minutes after setting out, having covered a distance of slightly more than a mile, I touched the seawall. No moment of my life in Turkey filled me with such rich and complex satisfaction.

NINE

AEGEAN DAWN

Visiting Athens is an odd experience for someone who lives in Istanbul. So much there is familiar to anyone accustomed to Turkish life. Greeks and Turks eat the same food and wash it down with the same liquor while listening to the same music and laughing at the same jokes. They have the same emotions, the same outsize passions. They dance through the night and seal lifetime friendships in an hour. Even their ingrained fatalism does not dampen their lust for life.

Greeks and Turks are bound to each other by history, culture and, as the earthquakes showed, magnificent but also terrifying geography. For half a millennium Greeks and Turks lived together under Ottoman rule and shared what has been called "one of history's most intensive cultural symbioses." But things went badly wrong between them and they became bitter rivals.

A few weeks before the fatal earthquakes I was strolling along a main avenue in Athens and met a gentleman in a natty suit who turned out to be a retired chemist named Evangellos Katsaounis. He was willing to take a few minutes to explain his country's problems with Turkey, and he did so in classic fashion. It was a terrible shame, he said, but there was nothing to be done.

"Turkey wants to take control of the Aegean and grab our islands," he told me sadly. "It's a militaristic country. We want to be their friend, but they don't want our friendship."

This is what most Greeks today were brought up to believe, and most Turks believe exactly the same thing: that their leaders have made countless peace overtures toward their troublesome neighbor, all without success. "It's time for Greece to stop being so hostile toward us," said a man in Istanbul who sells lottery tickets from behind a cardboard stall. He sighed with an air of resignation. "No matter what they do to hurt us, we always react calmly. They should stop rejecting our good will."

Atatürk's crushing defeat of Greek forces in 1922 brought under Turkish control lands along the Aegean coast that had been culturally Greek for thousands of years and that even during the Ottoman period had been populated mainly by Greeks. This trauma has only begun to recede in the Greek consciousness. During the last decades of the twentieth century, tensions between Greece and Turkey led the two nations to a series of angry confrontations, several of which took them to the brink of war. Yet their hostility was actually an aberration. It was a modern phenomenon, a product of rising nationalism and the search for identity on both sides of the Aegean. There was nothing natural or inevitable about it, and it never settled into the soul of either people. That is why, after a cataclysmic nudge from nature, it began to dissolve so quickly.

When the Turks captured Constantinople in 1453, they put an end to a Byzantine empire that was in essence Greek. Yet their farsighted leader, Sultan Mehmet the Conqueror, showed remarkable tolerance and even admiration for Greeks. Less than a year after the conquest he named a learned monk, George-Gennadios Scholarius, to the long-vacant post of Orthodox Patriarch, and allowed Gennadios to rule not only the Greek community's religious affairs but its temporal ones as well, supervising an autonomous legal system with its own judges, laws and prisons.

Greeks contributed inestimably to the growth of Ottoman power, and when reformers began to modernize the empire in the mid-nineteenth century, they took special pains to guarantee the equality of Muslims and non-Muslims. Afire with the spirit of the Enlightenment, they prodded the sultans Abdülmecid and Abdülaziz to issue a series of decrees guaranteeing equal treatment for "all our subjects, of whatever religious sect they may be." All were to have equal access to education, to be taxed equally and to be considered equally for civilian and military office. When the first Ottoman constitution was promulgated in 1876, it proclaimed that "all Ottoman citizens are equal before the law . . . without distinction as to religion." Greeks sat in the Ottoman Senate elected in 1877 and served as ambassadors in Berlin, London, St. Petersburg and even Athens. Many were skilled artisans and others became prominent physicians, engineers, lawyers, bankers and traders. By 1914 half of all capital invested in the Ottoman Empire was Greek.

While Ottoman Greeks in Turkey flourished, their cousins in Greece took up arms in the 1820s to fight for independence. Istanbul's Greeks looked down on these revolutionaries as ignorant ruffians unable to appreciate the empire's cosmopolitanism, but many Europeans fervently embraced their cause. Lord Byron's rapt elegies to their heroes, and his own death of fever in the Greek town of Missolonghi while the rebellion was at its peak, symbolized the conflict as Europeans saw it: the heirs of Plato and Sophocles throwing off the yoke of Muslim oppression. Several episodes in which Ottoman soldiers massacred Greeks with unspeakable cruelty cemented this lurid stereotype.

Greeks won their independence by overthrowing Turks, and a century later, in a remarkable historical turnabout, Turks won theirs by overthrowing Greeks. Their victory came in what Greeks still call "the catastrophe in Anatolia," the decisive 1922 battle in which Atatürk's forces literally pushed thousands of Greek soldiers into the sea at Smyrna. These two neighboring countries fought their definitive wars of liberation against each other. Each had to defeat the other's army in order to become a modern nation-state. The world knows no other such case.

Following the 1922 conflict, Greece and Turkey agreed to carry out a "population exchange." Although by modern standards this solution was in some ways repugnant, and although it caused great suffering, it was actually a relatively humane way of solving what then seemed an otherwise insoluble problem. In the exchange, about a million and a half Turkish citizens who were Orthodox Christians and thus called "Greeks" were uprooted from their homes and sent to Greece, though many spoke no Greek and had no wish to abandon communities where their families had lived for generations. Suddenly they were refugees, many of them penniless and disoriented, trekking over mountains and spilling out of cargo holds at Attic seaports. Another mass of unfortunates, nearly a million Muslims in Greece whose parents and grandparents had known only Greece but who were now suddenly "Turks," were shipped in the other direction. The travail of these displaced masses was as spiritual as it was material, a human tragedy in a conflict that had until then been political and military.

Yet even these dramatic circumstances did not condemn Greece and Turkey to hostility. Both nations were under the leadership of brilliant statesmen, Atatürk in Turkey and Eleftherios Venizelos in Greece, visionaries who realized that their peoples' long common history offered great opportunities. They embraced the challenge with typically Mediterranean passion and, within an amazingly short time, had set their nations on the road to reconciliation and friendship. In 1934 Venizelos went so far as to nominate Atatürk for the Nobel Peace Prize, praising him as "a great reformer" whose gestures toward Greece were "a precious contribution to the cause of peace."

Later, however, instead of preaching the benefits of cooperation, many Greek and Turkish politicians chose to pursue votes by embracing and even fomenting aggressive nationalism. Their prejudices inevitably bore bitter fruit, the bitterest being the decimation of the Greek population of Istanbul. For centuries Istanbul been one of the world's most tolerant cities, and it had been specifically exempted from the population exchange because of the vital role Greeks had played there since time immemorial. "There are two great centers of Hellenism, Athens and Constantinople," the nineteenth-century Greek prime minister John Collettis had asserted in a famous speech. "Athens is only the capital of the kingdom; Constantinople is the great capital, *the* city, the attraction and the hope of all Hellenes."

But after 1934, when a law was passed that banned them from practicing professions including law, dentistry and pharmacy, Greeks began to trickle out of Istanbul. A far heavier blow against their community, and also against the city's thriving Jewish and Armenian communities, came eight years later with the enactment of the insidious *varlık vergisi*, or wealth tax. Turkey was then suffering from serious economic troubles, some the result of war profiteering, price speculation and hoarding, and food shortages reached alarming levels. The temptation to squeeze money from the city's non-Muslim merchants was too great, and the government decided to demand large and immediate payments from them. Most were required to come up with between half and three-quarters of their 1941 income, and to do so within fifteen days. Finding that much cash in such a short time was all but impossible, and so the property of many of them was seized. Others were arrested or deported. Later the levy was repealed and the government apologized for its excesses, but terrible damage had been done. Non-Muslim merchants no longer felt secure doing business in Istanbul, and Turkey's reputation for religious tolerance was permanently damaged.

Still, despite this assault on their community, many Greeks remained in Istanbul; the city's 1950 census showed more than one hundred thousand of them. But in September 1955, when Turkish chauvinists learned that their Greek counterparts had set fire to Atatürk's birthplace in Thessaloniki, they seized upon this pretext to vent primitive hatreds and launched what amounted to a pogrom, terrorizing Greek neighborhoods in an orgy of arson and violence. The government may not have organized the outburst, but to its shame did nothing to stop it, and it raged for several days. When it was over, many Orthodox families who had helped build Istanbul and whose ancestors had loved it passionately for centuries reluctantly concluded they could stay no longer. Their departure accelerated the spiral of mistrust and hostility that was slowly enveloping Turks and Greeks. It turned out that Atatürk's house had not been burned at all, but that hardly seemed to matter any more. The rioting and anti-Greek passion, one historian later wrote, "marked the beginning of the end of the historic Greek community in Turkey."

A final blow to Istanbul's Greek community, if one was needed, came in 1965 when the Turkish Parliament passed a law forbidding ethnic Greeks to remain in Turkey so long as they held Greek passports, which many of them considered the last and vital link to the land of their forebears. More important, the law served notice to them that the authorities considered them outsiders, fifth-columnists and potential traitors.

Thousands departed sadly for Greece, leaving behind only remnants of a community that had made immeasurable contributions to the Ottoman Empire from the time of the first sultans and to the Turkish Republic for forty years.

Although both nations had treaty obligations to honor the rights of their respective minorities, neither lived up to them. Greek officials subjected Muslims in areas near the Turkish border, whose ancestors, like the Greeks in Istanbul, had been exempted from the population exchange, to all sorts of petty harassment, restricting their right to buy land, maintain their mosques or even obtain licenses to drive tractors. Turks closed the century-old seminary at Heybeli (known to Greeks as Halki), a placid island in the Sea of Marmara, which was Turkey's only remaining school for Orthodox clergy.

The natural friendship between Greeks and Turks might nonetheless have been slowly rebuilt had it not been for the conflict that burst over the Mediterranean island of Cyprus in 1974. The island, which lies less than fifty miles from Turkey's southern coast and five hundred miles from the Greek mainland, had been tense since the 1950s, when Greek nationalists launched a campaign to turn it into a province of Greece. It was then a British colony, and the British, unable to suppress the spreading violence, granted it independence in 1960 under a delicate constitutional arrangement designed to give its Greek and Turkish residents proportional shares of power. Greek thugs, however, continued to terrorize Turkish Cypriots, hoping to force them to emigrate. In 1974 the island's elected government was overthrown by Greek militants backed by the right-wing colonels then in power in Athens. In response, Turkey, acting under the terms of a treaty that allowed it to intervene in Cyprus if the Greek-Turkish balance there was upset, felt compelled to send in troops. Turkish leaders argued that their operation was a rescue mission designed to defend their ethnic cousins against Greek depredations, but Greece called it an illegal invasion of a sovereign state. The episode was a triumph of ethnic nationalism, and it bound both countries into a cycle of recrimination and suspicion. Greek leaders like the demagogic Andreas Papandreou, who was prime minister from 1981 to 1989 and then again from 1993 to 1996, portrayed it as proof that Turkey was a profound threat to everything Greek, while their counterparts in Turkey made no less use of it to whip up chauvinistic fervor. Each side blamed the other rather than face its own responsibility for the crisis.

In subsequent decades Turkey and Greece grew apart in important ways. For most of the twentieth century both had been weak and marginal to world affairs, and neither had international ambitions. Greece enjoyed an intangible advantage because it had been favored and even romanticized for so long by the West, which identified it with the glory of ancient times. But as time passed, the relative importance of the two countries began to shift. Turkey, already more populous, became far more powerful economically and master of a far more potent military machine. Competition between the Western and Soviet blocs, and later the collapse of the Soviet Union and the emergence of radical regimes in Iraq and Iran, made Turkey a vitally important NATO ally. The opening of the Turkish economy in the early 1980s released the pent-up energy of a young and ambitious generation of entrepreneurs. When the Turkish army embarked on an intensive program of modernization, emerging with a large, well-equipped and battle-hardened force of soldiers, Greeks naturally felt increasingly inferior and vulnerable.

But the tide of history did not run only in Turkey's favor. The unhappy years of military dictatorship in Greece, 1967 to 1974, convinced many Greeks that their country needed to grow up, renounce authoritarianism and commit itself to democracy. In what was probably its most important step in modern history, Greece joined the European Community (now the European Union) in 1981. Often the Greeks acted petulantly in European councils, but slowly and inevitably they adjusted to European standards, even taming their chaotic economy enough to join the European Monetary Union. Military influence over politics was reduced to zero. Courts functioned independently and the legal system became a reliable guarantor of individual rights.

Which country can then be said to have emerged from the twentieth century more happily? According to the United Nations, which prepares a "human development index" ranking nations according to the health care, education and economic opportunities they offer their citizens, Greece ended the century as the world's twenty-fifth most successful nation, just behind Singapore. Turkey, which for years has been unable to

cope with its uncontrolled population growth and the migration of millions of poor villagers to big cities, came in dismally at eighty-fifth, with
development levels equivalent to those of Sri Lanka and Oman. By the
standards of the world gone by, in which the success of nations was
measured by military and geopolitical power, Turkey was triumphant.
But in the world of the twenty-first century, the real winners are countries where voters are the supreme authority, where courts function
freely, where people live peacefully together and where good health
care and education are available to all.

As the old century ended, Greece was prevailing in the contest for
world sympathy. In the West, although occasionally a prickly ally given
to anti-Western outbursts, it was believed to hold the moral high
ground. That claim to moral superiority was devastated in 1999, however, when Abdullah Öcalan was found to have been living under the
clandestine protection of Greek diplomats in Kenya. Here, Turkish leaders bitterly asserted, was proof of what they had been saying for years:
that Greece was supporting a mass murderer in an effort to sow chaos in
Turkey and ultimately tear it apart. What better proof could there be of
Greece's perfidy? President Demirel called Greece a "rogue state that
has to be put on the list of countries supporting terrorism and harboring
terrorists" and warned darkly that Turkey would make use of its "right
to legitimate self-defense" if Greece did not mend its ways. General
Kıvrıkoğlu, the chief of staff, asserted that Greece "has been caught red-
handed" and as a result "has nothing to say, nowhere to run." Foreign
Minister Ismail Cem called Greece's actions "incredibly frightening,
merciless and irresponsible."

In the summer of 1999, at the height of this verbal assault, I had
lunch with Cem at a fashionable restaurant in Ankara. After we had each
enjoyed a couple of drinks, I asked him how he was feeling about
Greece these days. To my surprise, he began to wax nostalgic.

"When I was a student in Switzerland," he began, pausing for a sip of
vodka to allow the sweet memories to flow more freely, "I felt quite
alone for a while. Those Swiss can be very cold people, you know. They
can make a Turk feel that he comes from another planet. Then one day
I met a Greek guy who was studying in the same university. We hit it off
right away, we shared everything, we were best friends. That was very

natural, because we had so much in common. And this was not an isolated case. Whenever a Greek and a Turk find themselves outside their own countries, they become great friends. We get along wonderfully as individuals, just not as nations."

A few days later, in Athens, I repeated what Cem had told me to his Greek counterpart, George Papandreou. "It's absolutely true," he said, shrugging with an air of both sadness and resignation. "My brother's roommate at Princeton was a Turk, and they were very close. But in the political arena, unfortunately, this kind of warmth fades away very quickly."

Many Greeks did indeed instinctively sympathize with Öcalan, among them more than one hundred members of Parliament who had signed a petition asking that their government grant him political asylum, even though they had no special love for Kurds. Yet simply blaming "Greece" for sheltering Öcalan was to oversimplify the issue. A highly aggressive form of national chauvinism, blessed by the Orthodox clergy, infects Greek political parties across the ideological spectrum, much as rigid Kemalism does in Turkey. Over the years, this chauvinism led to the formation of a clique of Greek politicians, secret-police agents and retired and perhaps active military officers who operated beyond the reach of government—Greece's own version of Turkey's "deep state." This clique was tolerated and probably even encouraged by the long-time Prime Minister Andreas Papandreou. When Papandreou died in 1996, he was replaced by the more moderate but politically weaker Costas Simitis, whose nationalist credentials were never strong enough to satisfy militants in his own party. Simitis undoubtedly knew that a shadowy core of influential figures in and around his government was working with Öcalan's guerrillas, perhaps even financing them and helping them obtain arms. These activities were an outrageous breach of the solidarity that is supposed to bind military allies, and Simitis cannot be excused for having tolerated it. Yet his own political power was limited, and he was not strong enough to confront the state-within-a-state that was nourishing the Kurdish rebellion.

Öcalan's capture in Kenya was a disaster for Greece, not only because its government had failed to shield someone to whom it had pledged protection but because it had allowed him to fall into the hands of the hated Turks. Öcalan's comrades naturally blamed Greece for the entire fiasco. The Greek ministers of justice, interior and foreign affairs, together with the head of the intelligence service, all of them hard-liners who opposed détente with Turkey, were forced to resign. Their successors could not have been more different, most notably George Papandreou, Andreas's son, whose view of the world was infinitely more rational and progressive than his father's. The scandal also led to the indictment and trial of eighteen pro-Öcalan figures on the fringes of Greek politics, including some who had flaunted their ability to make foreign policy on their own. Never again, it seemed safe to assume, would Greek agents embark on provocative adventures like sheltering a man who is the most wanted fugitive in a neighboring country.

The Öcalan crisis created a magnificent opportunity to begin the historic work of repairing Greek-Turkish relations. Greece was finally under the control of serious-minded men and women committed to modernity and with at least a modest amount of room to maneuver. Turkey had achieved its great goal of capturing Öcalan. To the judicious mind, this would have seemed an ideal time to knock on a neighbor's door and say, "We've got a lot of complaints about the way you've been behaving. Let's sit down and see if we can talk some of these things through."

When I visited Athens after Öcalan's capture, I found Greeks in a confused and depressed but also reflective mood. Everyone agreed that something had gone very wrong. If they were not ready to blame themselves, they were at least open to ideas they might previously have rejected out of hand. I spent one evening with an elder statesman of Greek politics, Minister of Defense Apostolos Tsohatzopoulos, a nationalist never known for sympathy with anything Turkish. Even he turned out to be hopeful that the shock of the Öcalan affair might lead to new dialogue across the Aegean.

"This was a very heavy blow to Greece, and it created a political and ethical crisis here," Tsohatzopoulos said. "I see it as a chance to change the bad perceptions that exist. With Turkey it should be possible to discuss many things. We have to enter a new period, a new phase. Many things can now be changed. I don't know what or how, but we have many reasons to do it."

Rather than extend a hand of friendship to Greece at a time when Greece was at an obvious political disadvantage, however, Turkish leaders chose the course of triumphant self-congratulation. No dialogue with the offender was possible, they insisted, until the Greek government begged forgiveness and offered a self-abasing apology. They even chose this moment to wave a red flag, reviving the notion that some traditionally Greek islets in the Aegean Sea lay in "gray zones" and might actually be Turkish. By choosing this moment to make these claims, they gave the Greeks more evidence to buttress the old conviction that Turkey was relentlessly expansionist, incurably militaristic and beyond the pale of civilization.

Turkey could have used its newfound position of moral superiority to declare victory and make peace overtures to its temporarily disadvantaged neighbor. By failing to do so, it allowed Greece to maintain its position as the more sophisticated of the two countries. Although still caught in the grip of some unfortunate strains of chauvinism, Greece has moved with increasing enthusiasm toward the norms of Europe. Turkey has moved much more erratically, when at all, and when criticized for its reluctance has angrily challenged the right of outsiders to judge it.

I wanted to argue with Thanos Veremis, a professor of political history at the University of Athens, when he made this point to me over a bottle of red wine one day at a café near his office, but I found myself unable to do so. "What divides Greece and Turkey is the incompatibility of the two states as such," he told me. "Greece may not be the most developed state in Europe, but it is part of the European system with a full democracy, civilian control of the military and a population whose basic aspirations are no different from those of the average European. Turkey is a very faulty democracy with deep economic problems, great disparities in income and a megalomania that has given it the idea that it is a global power, as if size and population and weaponry rather than democracy and human rights and social peace are what makes a state powerful."

Through all this conflict and bitterness, however, ordinary Greeks and Turks never forgot all that binds them together. I realized this one night when I was riding a taxi through Istanbul, crawling at a snail's pace because we could not pass an oversize bus ahead of us. After twenty minutes of this frustration, I noticed that the bus had a Greek license plate.

"Ah, it's from Greece," I told the driver with a smirk. "That's the problem. Greece is always making life difficult for Turks!"

The driver spun around, suddenly agitated. "*Yunanistan'la problem yok!*" he said, shaking his finger at me. "*Yunan halkı ile problem yok! Problem politik!*" Greece is not the problem. Greek people are not the problem. Politics is the problem.

For a while I doubted whether that cabdriver really reflected the views of many Turks and Greeks, but after the two earthquakes not much doubt remains. What happened in their wake amazed the leaders of both countries and exceeded the expectations of even the most fervent advocates of Greek-Turkish reconciliation. Within hours of the big quake in Turkey, telephones at the Turkish embassy in Athens began to ring. Lines were jammed as ordinary Greeks, many of them sobbing and overwrought, called to say how upset they were about what had happened and ask what they could do to help. Hundreds lined up the next day to give blood for the victims. Thousands donated money to a fund drive organized by the Greek Red Cross or dropped donations at depots set up by the mayor of Athens. One man even volunteered to donate a kidney if an earthquake survivor needed it.

The Greek government also jumped into action. In the first two days after the quake, more aid arrived from Greece than from any other country: two C-130 transport planes laden with blankets, canned food and medical supplies; two mobile emergency teams whose members included eleven doctors; two planes and a helicopter equipped for firefighting, for help in extinguishing the blaze at the Izmit oil refinery; twenty-five soldiers trained for emergency relief work, with four trucks specially designed to serve as first-aid clinics; and more than a dozen sniffer dogs trained to catch the scent of people trapped under rubble.

"The catastrophe from the earthquake drained us emotionally," the Greek government spokesman said in Athens when asked to explain the phenomenon. "In these situations there is no need for ulterior motives. You try to help someone who is in need, someone who is facing a difficult situation."

Before dusk had fallen on the day of the quake, teams from just about every television station in Greece had flown to Turkey and begun broadcasting live from the devastated region. Greeks watched the same excruciating scenes that Turks were watching, and suddenly found it impossible to maintain the old stereotype of the Turk. No longer was he a brute waving a scimitar and waiting for the chance to grab some Greek island. Instead "he" was a wailing mother whose lifeless child had just been pulled from beneath a pile of rubble.

"We have been taught to hate the Turks for years," wrote Anna Stergiou, a prominent Greek newspaper columnist. "But their unbelievable pain gives us no joy. We were moved, we cried as if the age-old hatred disappeared at the sight of dead babies."

The days and weeks that followed turned into a veritable love fest between the two countries, the suddenness and intensity of which were almost frightening. Wherever Greek rescue and relief workers went in the earthquake zone, they were jubilantly welcomed. A handful of doctors from Greek Cyprus, who were at first afraid even to leave Istanbul, were met with kisses and tearful embraces rather than the cold hostility they had expected. Could such a radical turnaround in public attitudes be serious, or was it just a wild mood swing in the psyches of two peoples known for their emotional volatility?

Relations between the two neighbors had been improving, albeit slowly, for several months before the quake. Their foreign ministers had met several times during the Kosovo war, which had been a vivid warning to both countries of how easily local hatreds can spiral out of control. But the crisis sparked by the seizure of Abdullah Öcalan was the real breakthrough because it led to the fall of the Greek officials most resolutely opposed to détente with Turkey, disgraced the handful of retired military officers who harbored ultra-nationalist views and forced the firing of the chief of the Greek intelligence service, who for years had connived with those officers in nasty anti-Turkish plots. The contrast between the overstuffed foreign minister Theodore Pangalos, who liked to describe Turks as "thieves and rapists," and his slim, soft-spoken successor, George Papandreou, could not have been sharper or more felicitous.

Undoubtedly it was a humanitarian impulse that moved Papandreou to telephone Ismail Cem as soon as he heard news of the Turkish quake and offer all the help that Greece could provide. He could not have failed to realize from the first moment, however, that this was also a chance to move his political agenda forward.

After the quake, hardly a day passed without some new sign of the growing warmth between Greece and Turkey. The commander of the Greek navy toured devastated towns in Turkey and then made a moving call for peace at a ceremony marking the retirement of his Turkish counterpart. While he was there, a Greek naval vessel called at a Turkish port for the first time since the Cyprus clash of 1974. The mock dogfights between Greek and Turkish fighter jets that had vividly expressed the tension between the two countries suddenly ended. The Greek army called off its annual autumn naval maneuvers, the purpose of which was mainly to kick sand in Turkish faces.

Soon afterward, Greek and Turkish business leaders agreed to revive a cooperation council whose activities had been suspended several months earlier in the wake of the Öcalan scandal. Greek and Turkish officials signed a series of agreements to encourage trade, begin cultural exchanges and cooperate in tourism, environmental protection and other areas. The Turkish education minister announced that he had directed aides to compile a list of negative references to Greece in Turkish textbooks, with an eye to removing them in future editions. Turkey's best basketball player signed a multimillion-dollar contract to play for a Greek team, and in the same week the Greek Parliament approved construction of the first new mosque to be built in Athens for more than a century.

The annual ceremony marking Turkey's victory over Greek occupiers on September 9, 1922, was eloquent proof of how fully the Greek-Turkish relationship had changed. Normally the day was marked by an outburst of chauvinism in Izmir, where the victory was won. Turkish soldiers in period costume would symbolically bayonet scores of actors dressed in Greek uniforms, throw others into the sea and then tear down a Greek flag from the pole above the city hall, gleefully shred it and stomp on the tatters, all to the wild cheers of excited spectators. This time, though, there was nothing more than a solemn wreath-laying and singing of the national anthem.

"I have been writing a 'Greek-Turkish' piece almost every September 9 for twenty-five years now," one conservative Turkish columnist wrote in an Istanbul paper. "I pulled them all out of the archives. I tore them all up and threw them away. I am now starting a new September 9 series. This is the real starting point, a fresh beginning, the first step toward the twenty-first century."

The night after the 1999 earthquake in Greece, I was in an Athens hotel room watching live television coverage of the rescue effort. Announcers struggled unsuccessfully to contain their emotions as a team of Turkish volunteers worked to free a buried child. "It's the Turks!" one of them cried as he described the scene unfolding before him. "They've got the little boy! They saved him! And now the Turkish guy is drinking from a bottle of water! It's the same bottle the Greek rescuers just drank from! This is love! It's so beautiful!"

A couple of days later, when there was no longer any realistic hope of finding more survivors, I was chatting with a couple of exhausted Athens police officers who were on duty in front of an appliance showroom that had collapsed in the quake. A giant power shovel was at work behind them, clawing through the debris in search of bodies. I asked the officers what they were thinking, but one answered only in brief monosyllables while the other said nothing at all. As I was about to shut my notebook and take my leave, the second suddenly spoke.

"I want to say something," he said loudly enough to draw the attention of several dozen onlookers. "It's hard to love your enemy in times of joy. But when he's hit by a tragedy, when he's crying and suffering, you can't think of him as your enemy anymore." There were several moments of silence, and then people in the small crowd behind us began to nod in agreement. Some applauded softly, and a few others muttered: "True, true."

There were of course skeptics, like the Turkish newspaper columnist who warned of "idiotic optimism" and asked whether Turks were ready "to unilaterally surrender our vital interests in the Aegean and Cyprus in the name of friendship." Even the two foreign ministers felt called upon to issue gentle warnings. When Cem said in one television interview that the process of improving relations between the two countries had run out of his control and claimed to believe that was a good thing, he didn't sound entirely convincing. For his part, Papandreou warned people on both sides of the Aegean not to presume "that all of a sudden everything has been solved."

Still, within a year Turkish assault troops had landed on a Greek beach as part of a joint military maneuver, and even more wonderfully, Greece had dropped its opposition to Turkey's entry into the European Union. The Greek government canceled plans to spend $4.5 billion for new fighter jets, saying it would use the money to increase pensions and expand social welfare programs. Papandreou visited Ankara and declared that Greece and "the friendly Turkish people" had "a historical opportunity to create a peaceful future for the two peoples." In reply, Cem said they had already "achieved in a year what had not been achieved over the last forty years." In dozens of negotiating sessions, one irritating bilateral problem after another was solved. But as they fell away, the conflict over the Aegean, including not just disputes over the ownership of islands but also the rights to the skies above them and the riches under the seabed around them and, even more dauntingly, the conflict over Cyprus, continued to loom like dark clouds on the political horizon.

Both of these volatile issues are laden with exaggerated symbolism. Over the years outside mediators have come up with reasonable formulas for resolving them, but at every juncture nationalist passions have overwhelmed reason. Still, the climate between Athens and Ankara has never been so warm, and if the leaders of both countries can break away from the grip of history, they can place their hostility behind them and build a Greek-Turkish axis around which one of the world's most volatile regions could revolve.

My favorite Turkish writer is everyone's favorite, Nazım Hikmet. By universal agreement he is the greatest literary figure the Turkish Republic has produced. Poet, playwright and novelist, extravagantly gifted and fervently patriotic, he was also a Communist who spent much of his life in jail and died in exile in 1963 after having been stripped of his Turkish citizenship. Every Turk knows his name, but to this day his works may not be taught in public schools. His life and literary creations exemplify Turkey's glories and frustrations, its audacious beauty and its paralyzing fears.

Nazım—his admirers always call him by his first name—was born in 1902 in Salonika, the same city where Atatürk had been born twenty years earlier. Unlike Atatürk he came from a well-to-do family, but like the Great Man he decided as a youth that he could best serve his country by making a career in the military. When illness forced him to leave the naval academy, he chose to follow his other passion, poetry. On a trek across Anatolia in his late teens he met several Turkish Communists. Impressed with their idealism and fascinated by the promise of bolshevism, a conviction that deepened after he visited Moscow in 1922, he joined the Communist party. He saw no contradiction between his love of Turkey and his Marxist convictions, but the authorities did. His talent proved no defense against persecution, and he spent the rest of his life in trouble with the law.

Turkey shared a tense border with the Soviet Union, and for years Soviet leaders plotted to bring it into their sphere of influence or even to seize it and incorporate it into their empire. In this climate it was too much to hope that a Turkish poet could get away with writing rhapsodic elegies to Marxism and bitter condemnations of oppression in Turkey. Nazım was in and out of prison on a variety of charges, but at the same time he flowered as a poet. His style was as revolutionary as his politics. Until he picked up a pen, Turkish poetry had for centuries been heavily stylized and effete. He was the first writer to produce poetry in conversational, colloquial Turkish, and although his books were banned for years, he was the first to touch the hearts of ordinary Turks. In his approach to literature and life he was comparable to Walt Whitman, a poet of the common man who scorned conventional patriotism but still insisted that he loved his country beyond all reason. The heroes in his poems, he once wrote, were not "generals, sultans, distinguished scientists or artists, beauty queens, murderers or billionaires; they were workers, peasants and craftsmen, people whose fame had not spread beyond their factories, workshops, villages or neighborhoods."

At another time he explained his ambition this way: "I want to write poems that both talk only about me and address just one other person and call out to millions. I want to write poems that talk of a single apple, of the plowed earth, of the psyche of someone getting out of prison, of the struggle of the masses for a better life, of one man's heartbreaks. I want to write about fearing and not fearing death."

The works Nazım produced in the 1930s have lost none of their freshness. Today they speak to Turks as poignantly as ever, like this one written in the Istanbul House of Detention:

> *I love my country:*
> *I've swung on its plane trees,*
> *I've slept in its prisons.*
> *Nothing lifts my spirits like its songs and tobacco . . .*
> *My country:*
> *goats on the Ankara plain,*
> *the sheen of their long blond silky hair.*

The succulent plump hazelnuts of Giresun.
Amasya apples with fragrant red cheeks,
olives,
   figs,
      melons,
and bunches and bunches of grapes
           all colors,
then plows
and black oxen,
and then my people,
   ready to embrace
      with the wide-eyed joy of children
anything modern, beautiful and good—
my honest, hard-working, brave people,
half full, half hungry,
      half slaves. . . .

Nazım was strongly attracted to the epic form, and he first embraced it in a long elegy to Sheik Bedreddin, a fourteenth-century mystic whose egalitarian ideals led him to foment an ill-fated rebellion against the Ottoman sultan. When military cadets were found to be reading it in secret, Nazım was arrested and sentenced to twenty-eight years in prison on charges that he was inciting the army to rebel. He spent the next thirteen years in jail, producing not only a stream of poems but also translations of Italian librettos for the Ankara State Opera. This was a wonderful example of how the Turkish state worked and sometimes still works; while one branch of government was imprisoning him, another was paying him to help bring masterpieces of European culture to eager Turkish audiences.

As Nazım's health deteriorated, leftists organized a worldwide campaign for his release that was supported by admirers including Sartre, Picasso, Robeson, Yevtushenko and Neruda. After Adnan Menderes won his shocking victory at the polls in 1950 and became Turkey's first democratically elected prime minister, he decreed a general amnesty under which the poet was finally freed. The army, however, was not through with him. Soon after his release he was ordered to report for military service despite the fact that he was forty-eight years old and sick. Surmising that he would never survive his service, he fled across the Black Sea to the Soviet Union, where he lived for the rest of his life. There he was embraced by Communist leaders and wrote crass poems in homage to Lenin and Stalin. After the Turkish authorities stripped him of his citizenship, though, he alienated his hosts by turning down their offer of Soviet citizenship and accepting a Polish offer instead, honoring a Polish ancestor who had fought in anti-Russian uprisings during the eighteenth century.

In his prison poems, Nazım had often reflected on the possibility that he would one day be sentenced to die and summarily executed:

> Death—
> a body swinging from a rope.
> My heart
>   can't accept such a death.
> But
> you can bet
>   if some poor gypsy's hairy black
>   spidery hand
>   slips a noose
>   around my neck,
> they'll look in vain for fear
>   in Nazım's
>   blue eyes!

As it turned out, however, he died in Moscow, never having been allowed to return home to the land he loved. Admirers have started a campaign to bring his body back, but not every Turk likes the idea.

"Let him stay there!" my friend Altemur Kılıç, a fierce nationalist whose father was a compatriot of Atatürk's, once spat at me. "Hikmet was our evil genius. He was no doubt a very good poet, a very good wordsmith and not a negligible man. I would even admit that he was a patriot in his own way. His poems about our War of Liberation are magnificent. But he wanted Turkey to become liberated so it could become a satellite of Soviet Russia. He did great harm to Turkey. I cannot consider him a hero of democracy, as some people do today."

During the 1960s Nazım's poetry books, which had already been translated into dozens of foreign languages, began to reappear in Turkey. Today new editions of his works stream off the presses, theater companies present his plays to sold-out houses and pop stars turn his poems into hit songs. The Nazım Hikmet Foundation, based in Istanbul, organizes exhibitions related to his life and work and publishes a thick pocket calendar each year filled with pictures of him and excerpts from his writings. But the fact that the education ministry still forbids school-teachers to present his poems to their students reflects a lingering bitterness toward him in some circles. Staunch Kemalists, those who believe the Republic still faces dire threats, consider him to have been a traitor and do not want to see him turned into more of a hero than he already is. They see a sinister and subversive hand behind the campaign to rehabilitate him.

Nazım Hikmet called himself "a child of the twentieth century, and proud of it." His admirers are to be found wherever people read books. Denise Levertov has described him as "a supremely confident, energetic, passionate and powerfully imaginative poet." Raymond Carver called "Human Landscapes," his seventeen-thousand-line epic masterpiece, "one of the great works of modern literature." Tristan Tzara, who translated several of his works into French, said that his poetry "exalts the aspirations of the Turkish people and articulates the common ideals of all nations." In death his renown has spread, and no one now doubts the strength of his creative genius. Surely it will take no more than another generation for Turkey's ruling elite to embrace him, probably with the same tormented uncertainty that shaped his own feelings for his homeland:

> You are my imprisonment and my freedom,
>   my flesh,
>   burning like a summer night,
>   you are my country.
> You, with your green spots in golden-brown eyes,
> you are my great one, my beauty, my triumphant desire
>   that slips ever further away
>   the closer one comes to it.

TEN

THE PRIZE

An attractive and vivacious Turkish woman I know lives at home with her parents. Although she is already in her mid-twenties, she likes the arrangement, not just because Daddy pays her credit-card bills but also because her family is close-knit and loving. This is quite a normal situation in Turkey. It is assumed that parents will guard their daughters' virtue, and keeping them close by is the best guarantee. But this woman has in fact been sleeping with boyfriends since she was in high school. So have most of the women she knows. Their parents have no idea how far they have ventured from conservative tradition, or are so deep in denial that they refuse to see how different the new generation of Turks is from all generations that have come before.

That solicitous but remote entity called *devlet baba* is as far out of touch with the Turkish people as these parents are from their daughters' real lives. It is trying to run a country that no longer exists, to make decisions for people who are now quite able to decide for themselves. Young Turkish men and women are doing what birds do and bees do, but they and their compatriots are not allowed to do what Estonians and Taiwanese and Uruguayans do: shape their own future. What makes Turks different? Why should they not be trusted with the responsibilities of self-government? Are they too reckless, too emotional, too stupid? Ever more of them are asking these questions, and ever more urgently. Answers that satisfied their parents and grandparents do not satisfy them. Weaned on Atatürk's revolutionary rhetoric, they are now impatient to realize his dream. For the first time it is truly within reach. All that remains is for the ruling elite, which was shaped in a very different era, to face the reality that its sons and daughters have grown up and deserve the rights of mature adults and a mature nation.

Turkey will certainly change in time, but Turkey does not have time. At the beginning of the twenty-first century it is presented with an opportunity that does not come often in the lives of nations. For nearly all of its existence Turkey has been a country on the fringe. It was in a distant corner of Europe, on the outer edge of Asia, near but not actually in the Middle East, the Balkans and the Caucasus. Suddenly, following the collapse of the Soviet Union and the emergence of a new world geopolitics, Turkey finds itself not on the fringe of anything but in the middle of the world. The distinction between Europe and Asia, an artificial construct of Europeans looking for ways to define their superiority to the presumed barbarians east of them, has fallen away. Today the Eurasian land mass is understood as the single entity it is, and one of the great challenges of the new century is to break down the barriers of development and perception that have divided it for so long. Geographically, culturally and historically, Turkey is ideally placed to be a key player in this emerging world. But to become such a decisive agent of change, it must itself change. If it does not do so soon it will lose its chance for greatness. By the second half of the twenty-first century, Turkey will be politically and socially developed enough to serve as a model for countries from Morocco to Macedonia to Malaysia, but that will be too late. Those countries will long since have found other models, perhaps much less positive ones. That will be an incalculable loss not just to Turkey and the Turkish people but also to the world.

Lagging behind the world is nothing new for Turkey. The first Ottomans, like their counterparts in Tabriz, Samarkand and other centers of Islamic scholarship, were writing immortal poetry and discovering the secrets of mathematics and astronomy at a time when most Europeans were living in primitive ignorance. They correctly concluded that they had nothing to learn from Europe, so they turned inward. As Europeans climbed out of the Dark Ages and began to progress, however, the sultans refused to adjust their world view. Europe raced past them while they remained stuck in a form of denial much like the one that now imprisons the leaders of modern Turkey. They waited three hundred years after the invention of the printing press before allowing one to be brought to Istanbul, and resisted the ideals of democracy for almost as long. So when today's ruling elite worries that Turkey will sink into anarchy if it is allowed to embrace universal standards of freedom and human dignity, it is acting as heir to a long tradition. That tradition is Turkey's enemy. Turks are clamoring to break away from it, but their leaders are afraid to let them. Imprisoned by their fears, they are depriving their nation and the world of something that could be both beautiful and profoundly important. They are poised to show the world how fully tradition can coexist with freedom, Islam with democracy, unity with diversity, prosperity with equality. But they are afraid to do it.

Three fault lines lie close beneath the surface of Turkish society: the ethnic one dividing Turks from Kurds, the religious one dividing Sunni Muslims from Alevis, and the political one dividing those who believe there is a place for religion in public life and those who do not. Although every Turk is aware of these divisions, for many years it has been considered bad form even to acknowledge them, much less to discuss how they can be healed. For decades Turkish leaders have chosen the course of denial, and the collapses of the Soviet Union and Yugoslavia have reinforced their resolve. They know what a rich mosaic Turkey is but pretend not to, even going to the extreme of jailing citizens who dare to assert that they are different from some of their neighbors. Whatever logic that pretense might have had in the past, today it is not just laughable but pernicious. Turks have a strong sense of patriotic unity, and their state will not be threatened if they are allowed to revel in their various identities and beliefs. On the contrary, it will be immeasurably strengthened because it will become a state based on openness and honesty rather than subterfuge and pretense.

Generations of Turks grew up learning that there is no virtue more perfect than obedience. They never questioned either their leaders' wisdom or legitimacy, and were not simply dutiful subjects but genuinely grateful for the privilege of being ruled. The revolution that replaced sultans with zealous reformers wiped away many traditions, but not this one. Atatürk found it invaluable because it allowed him to impose his revolution from above. Many Turks accepted him and his ideas simply because he was in power. When sultans told them to fear God, subjugate women and scorn the European infidel, they did so because they knew instinctively that the man in power must be right. When Atatürk told them to do the opposite, they submitted just as eagerly and for the same reason.

Atatürk's heirs have eagerly taken advantage of this tradition. Today they find to their horror that it is collapsing, and very quickly. The face of Turkey and the consciousness of Turks have been reshaped by a technological, educational and demographic revolution every bit as shattering as the political one that Atatürk led. Two-thirds of Turks are under the age of thirty-five, and the country is becoming younger and more sophisticated every day. People do not obey the way they used to. They are impatient for change and impatient with leaders who are preventing it. Their country's huge potential is staring them in the face, and they want to fulfill it.

There are reasons why Turkey's leaders resist the growing clamor for democracy. They fear losing their own power, not simply because they like it for its own sake but because they believe they are using it to steer Turkey away from mortal dangers. Many are genuinely convinced, as they and their ancestors have been for three-quarters of a century, that free speech will mean debate that could ultimately tear the country apart. They fear the modern world and the individual conscience. Although they claim to be modern, they are still gripped by two ancient Middle Eastern taboos. One is the taboo against change, which they equate with admitting failure. The other is the taboo against dialogue, compromise and negotiation. Turks are tired of conflict and look enviously at countries that are on the path of reconciliation. They believe their society can be unified if it reaches out to embrace those, like Kurdish nationalists and devout religious believers, who have in the past felt excluded and victimized. Their leaders disagree. They seek national unity as fervently as anyone but still cling to the old view that it can be achieved only by repressing what they consider divisive voices.

For many years Turkish leaders have been obsessed with the twin dangers of separatism and religious fundamentalism. They are absolutely justified in these obsessions. Movements aimed at tearing Turkey apart, as the long Kurdish rebellion showed, bring only blood and tears, and if one were ever to succeed it would probably be to the detriment of all parties. Fundamentalism is also just as profound a danger as the most radical Kemalists believe it to be, since it would rob Turks of their freedom and their future. It is not only appropriate but necessary for the state to take urgent measures to combat these threats. The way to do that, however, is not to pretend that every patriotic Turk is happy with the status quo. Much more effective would be to bring social cleavages into the open, discuss them freely and work to bridge them. Kurds who think of themselves as Kurds, or believers who want to wear head scarves, can love Turkey as much as anyone else. They begin to resent the state only when it tells them, as it has for too long, that they must conform to an artificial stereotype or else be stigmatized and excluded from society.

The Turkish establishment is only beginning to understand the virtues of self-criticism. Although those who point out flaws in the political or social system are often suspected of evil intent, many Turks agree that some facts of national life need to change if Turkey is to become truly modern. The educational system needs to evolve from one based on rote memorization to one that encourages free inquiry and unorthodox thought. University faculties, which after the 1980 coup were disastrously purged of professors suspected of leftist leanings, need to return to their mission of encouraging open debate and unrestricted research. The press must move away from sensation and political bias toward responsible and impartial reporting. Urgent attention must be given to the problem of income distribution so that the fruits of Turkey's economic boom do not remain concentrated in the hands of wealthy families and developed regions. Taxes must be collected fully and fairly. Judges and prosecutors need to become more independent from the state apparatus and, like newspaper editors, begin to think of themselves as servants of the nation rather than of the state. Corruption, not just in government but also in private business, must be recognized as a force that saps too much of the country's wealth and energy.

Another root of Turkey's problems is that its political system has produced remarkably poor leaders, many of whom have spent years and even decades holding their country back. Even Turks who have devoted their lives to government service acknowledge this sad truth. Once while traveling in Europe I visited a Turkish embassy and spent an afternoon with the ambassador, who was then one of his country's most senior diplomats. He was approaching retirement and told me he couldn't wait to be free of the petty politicians who had run Turkey for most of his career. "In other countries, crises produce leaders," he lamented. "In our country, leaders produce crises."

Undoubtedly the Turkish politician who made the least of the greatest opportunities was Süleyman Demirel. After a record seven terms as prime minister starting in 1965, followed by seven years as president, he should have been able to retire with immense satisfaction. Instead his achievements are almost exclusively negative. During the years he dominated Turkey, countries from Portugal and Ireland to South Korea and Thailand zoomed to prosperity and democracy while Turkey remained stuck in the mud of mediocrity. One American ambassador to Turkey told me he considered Demirel the political equivalent of a surfer. I couldn't grasp the analogy, so he explained: "A surfer is always on top of the waves. He doesn't ever get to what's underneath. He skips along on the surface trying to keep his balance, but never affects the way the currents run."

Bülent Ecevit must also bear much of the blame for Turkey's failure to break through into the world elite. In an act of supreme irresponsibility he kept Turkey out of the European Community when the prospect of membership first emerged in the 1970s, and during the same period he allowed his ideological prejudices to prevent the national economy and hence the nation itself from integrating with the world. Later in his career he atoned for these sins by turning halfheartedly toward Europe, but his dogged defense of laws that restrict freedom, the absolute dictatorship he exercised over his political party and his militant refusal to consider Kurdish grievances mark him as the second of modern Turkey's gravediggers. The third is Tansu Çiller, who in the early 1990s could have pulled a newly self-confident nation toward greatness but instead dragged it down into brutality, corruption and economic crisis. Of all the leaders Turkey has had in the post-Atatürk era, only Turgut Özal grasped the scope of the country's potential and tried to realize it. He was flawed but also imaginative, bold and audacious. Today there are more than a few men and women in Turkey whose vision is as grand as his was. The nation's success in the new century depends on their ability to pull the reins of power away from the tired old elite.

The issue that hung so terribly over Turkey during the last decade of the twentieth century, the one that terrified the political elite more than any other, was the challenge of Kurdish nationalism. The long Kurdish war lies at the root of many of the nation's problems. Because of the war, dispossessed migrants flooded out of their villages into already overcrowded cities. Because of the war public dialogue was censored, peaceful dissidents were imprisoned, jailhouse torture became routine and many foreigners came to view Turkey as a bastion of repression. Now that it has ended, the state needs to be magnanimous in victory. By granting Kurds the rights for which everyone in Turkey is clamoring, rights that are essential features of every democracy, it can end this age-old conflict forever. But the fear of seeming weak, the fear that enemies of Turkey will seize on even the slightest concession for their base ends, blocks the path of conciliation.

As Turkey grapples with these challenges, it has huge assets that augur well for success. Kurdish nationalists have toned down their demands and no longer yearn for anything more than what the state can quite safely give them; the fact that there has never been communal violence between Turks and Kurds, even at the height of the war, suggests that this conflict can be solved if the elite in Ankara truly want to solve it. The evolution of the religious political movement has been equally encouraging. As recently as the mid-1990s it was heavily influenced by a cadre of angry and resentful fanatics who barely managed to conceal their contempt for the secular state. Now, chastened by experience, it has matured enormously and lost its fascination with foreign ideologies. Reformers are challenging aged reactionaries for leadership, and it is only a matter of time before the movement is theirs. Then it can become an enormously positive force in Turkish society, drawing conservative believers into the political system and thereby serving the cause of national reconciliation.

For most of the Turkish Republic's short history its people have been content to think of themselves as subjects, but no longer. Their new-found assertiveness, which is the product of education, travel, television and the Internet, naturally disturbs the entrenched elite, but it bodes well for Turkey. The human-rights cause is becoming a national obsession. Non-governmental organizations are springing up like mushrooms, and many insist on playing a political role instead of confining themselves to charity work. Not just ordinary people but many of the country's richest industrialists, masters of far-reaching conglomerates, are viscerally dedicated to the cause of social and political change. The economy is rich enough to support a crash program that can turn Turkey into a fully developed country within a relatively few years, if only taxes are honestly collected and the proceeds wisely used.

Even cynics who believe that Turkey is hopelessly imprisoned by its fears were astonished in the spring of 2000 when Parliament refused to amend the constitution so the septuagenarian Süleyman Demirel could serve a second term as president, and then proceeded to elect one of the country's most outspoken reformers, Ahmet Necdet Sezer, to replace him. Sezer, who at the time of his election was chief justice of the country's highest court, had burst into prominence a year earlier by delivering an astonishing speech in which he denounced the 1983 constitution as fundamentally undemocratic, called for repeal of all laws that restrict freedom of speech and said the government had no right to ban education or broadcasting in the Kurdish language. In his inaugural address he declared that Turkey could not become truly modern until it abandoned "structures and regulations that bring to mind a police state." Once in office he took a series of steps that convinced even the most skeptical of Turks that he would not be sucked into the sterility of traditional political discourse. His power is limited, but he symbolizes his country's thirst for change, for true liberty, for a place among the world's most advanced and successful countries. Since his election, according to opinion polls, the presidency has displaced the army as Turkey's most popular institution. Now no one can claim that only a few crackpots want to change the country's political system radically and permanently.

The financial shock that hit Turkey in the spring of 2001, sending the stock market into a steep fall and wiping out billions of dollars in private savings, was a product not only of economic factors but of the clash between the dying old order and the emerging new one. It was triggered by a confrontation between President Sezer, who is passionately devoted to the rule of law, and Prime Minister Ecevit, a dinosaur desperate to preserve the political traditions that have been sapping Turkey's lifeblood for decades. Sezer pressed Ecevit to cleanse his government of profiteers and other sharks, but Ecevit demurred during a meeting of the National Security Council. When Sezer asked him, "Why are you so hesitant to crack down on corruption, my prime minister?," Ecevit stormed out of the meeting, claiming he had been intolerably insulted. Money markets went into momentary panic. The crisis was serious, not just because of the pain it inflicted on ordinary people but because it strengthened, at least temporarily, the arguments of pessimistic Turks who believe their country is caught in a permanent cycle of political irresponsibility and economic shock. It was also, however, a salutary birth pang, a sharpening of the titanic conflict between the geriatric establishment and the growing numbers of Turks determined to re-invent their country.

Conditions abroad are also highly favorable for Turkey. Its enemies are weak or, in the case of Greece, no longer enemies at all. Its friends, especially the United States, passionately support the forces of domestic reform because they know that when those forces triumph, Turkey will become immeasurably more influential and powerful. The Muslim world is splintered and looking for an inspiring example. Countries that emerged from the ruins of the Soviet Union are being energetically courted by Moscow but are also willing and in some cases even anxious to be seduced by a more appealing suitor. If Turkey can become appealing enough, if it can shed its complexes, liberate the energy of its people and complete its march to democracy, it can become that successful suitor.

The brightest star in the constellation that shines over Turkey, however, is the one that beckons from Europe. When the European Union agreed in 1999 to name Turkey as a candidate for membership, every calculation changed. An overwhelming majority of Turks believe their country must do whatever is necessary to join, for two reasons. The first and most obvious is that membership in the European Union is as close to a guarantee of prosperity and freedom as there is in this world. But something else about the prospect especially excites Turks. For two hundred years they have been marching westward, albeit with varying levels of enthusiasm. Their national hero, Atatürk, was also the greatest proto-European in Turkish history. What the European Union now demands of Turkey is no more or less than the embodiment of Atatürk's dream. The drive to join has become Turkey's orienting principle because it crystallizes the hopes that for years have fired the nation's imagination.

Europe is not simply a destination for Turks but also a tantalizing model. Although Turkey started late in its drive toward modernity, so did Europe. Within living memory much of Europe was under the rule of uniformed barbarians. Only a few centuries before that, Turks were more advanced than Europeans by almost any standard. Why, Turks dare to ask, could that not happen again? If allowed to soar as high as they can, could they not reach European levels of development and then go even further? Is any other country so perfectly poised not simply to embrace the European ideal but to spread it to peoples who today hardly dare contemplate it?

For each of the more than a dozen countries that are waiting to join the European Union, the appeal of membership is political, social and economic. For Turkey it is also psychological. The central question facing Turks today is whether their country is ready for full democracy, but behind that question lies a more diffuse and puzzling one: who are we? The Ottomans knew they were servants of God and lords of a vast and uniquely diverse empire. The true heart of their empire, however, was not Anatolia but the Balkans. It was in that long-peaceful cauldron of nationalities that they felt most at home, where they built many of their loveliest mosques and bridges, where many of their viziers and the mothers of many of their sultans were born. But by caprice of history the founders of the Turkish Republic found themselves bereft of the Balkans and masters instead of Anatolia. To make matters worse, through a series of twentieth-century tragedies Anatolia lost most of the Armenians, Greeks and Jews who had given it some of the same richness that made the Balkans so uniquely appealing.

In an attempt to shape his Anatolian people into a new nation, Atatürk, himself a child of the Balkans, developed the concept of Turkishness. This was something new; in Ottoman times the word "Turk" had been an insult, used to label rural bumpkins and other primitives. Certainly most citizens of the Republic, then as now, had no Turkish tribal blood whatsoever in their veins. They were and are Kurds, Arabs, Georgians, Azeris, Chechens, Armenians, Russians, Bulgars, Macedonians, Albanians, Bosnians, Montenegrins or some combination thereof. Atatürk told them they were all Turks, noble people whose past was Central Asian and whose future was European. To this day, however, Turks are not sure who they are. It takes no deep psychological insight to see that beneath their veneer of racial and ethnic pride, which some of them take to absurd lengths, lies a strong sense of uncertainty and even inferiority. Their new drive toward Europe dates only from the European Union's historic 1999 summit at Helsinki. It has given them a unifying focus that holds the promise of finally resolving their long identity crisis.

Since the morning after the Helsinki summit, Turks have been obsessed with the question of when they might actually join the European Union. Some dare to hope they could be at least close by 2010 or 2015. The real answer, though, is both more and less specific. Turks can join almost whenever they want. It will take them time to tame inflation, cut the size of their agricultural workforce and make the thousands of legal changes the union requires. But they can reach European levels of freedom as soon as they choose to. Embracing rather than denying ethnic diversity, encouraging rather than repressing dissent, decentralizing power rather than holding it all in Ankara, giving ultimate political authority to Parliament rather than to military commanders—these are steps that require only political will. The Turkish people have that will. They are waiting for their leaders to vault over psychological barriers and give them the freedom they want and deserve.

When the Turkish Republic celebrated its seventy-fifth anniversary in 1998, the country was plastered with signs that read CUMHURIYETI VE DEMOKRASIYI SEVIYORUZ—We Love the Republic and Democracy. That slogan so perfectly encapsulates the aspirations of most Turks that when the celebration ended, many of the signs were left in place. One can still be seen on an ornate arch outside the Çıragan Palace in Istanbul. Every time I drive under it I wonder whether it was written by a clever subversive or whether the country's leaders fail to grasp its true meaning and implication. Actually it is an ideal slogan for the impatient masses. They hunger for democracy and believe the Republic owes it to them. Standing in their way is an ideology built on abstractions rather than on a desire to make citizens happy, which is after all what governments are for. Pretty concepts like secularism, unity and even democracy itself are only means to this end. People embrace them because they are ways to happiness. Once they become tools with which people are threatened, divided or made unhappy, they lose all their value. For years Turkish leaders have believed that the best way for them to show their love of democracy was to repress people, ideas and movements that they consider anti-democratic. They can no longer do so and still claim to love "the Republic and democracy."

One of my friends is a foreign diplomat who spent three years in Turkey and then moved on to another post. Protocol required him to leave a memo with advice for his successor. This is what he wrote: "Never violate the four commandments. Thou shalt not express sympathy for the Kurds. Thou shalt not use the g-word [genocide] when discussing what happened to the Armenians in 1915. Thou shalt not question the legitimacy of the Turkish Republic of Northern Cyprus. And most important, thou shalt not mention the religious beliefs of the Turkish people or suggest that people have not completely embraced Atatürk's reforms." I asked him if he really defined his job this way, and he laughed. "I could have made it ten or twenty commandments," he said, "but I decided to stop after four."

There is no good reason why at this point in its history, Turkey must still be defined by its taboos and its fears. Turks chafe more and more impatiently under the rule of those whose job it is to say no. They know what they and their nation can be, and hate to see it where it is. When Nelson Mandela refused to come to Ankara to receive the country's highest peace prize, evidently because he thought Turkish leaders lacked moral authority to single out peacemakers, the political elite complained bitterly that he had been manipulated and misinformed by enemies of Turkey. Many ordinary people, however, understood and sympathized. The episode gave them a new way of formulating their national dream: to become the kind of country from which Nelson Man-

dela would happily receive an honor. That means a country where tolerance, compromise and conciliation are the main tools of statecraft—the
Turkey of Turks' dreams.

It is easy to rattle off all the benefits that will accrue to Turkey if it
becomes that kind of country. Its leaders must also recognize, however,
that dangers lie ahead if they do not change. Turkey cannot stand still. If
it remains trapped in political immobility, its people will become dangerously polarized. By nature they are polite people who dislike confrontation and contradiction, but their frustration is beginning to build.
They cannot be ordered around the way their parents and grandparents
could. Their desire for a breakthrough to modernity is reaching critical
mass. If their leaders do not respond to it, there may be trouble.

The Turkish Republic is a new nation, very much a work in progress.
Only a brave soul would dare to predict what direction it will take in the
years ahead. But it takes very little imagination to posit some of the alternatives. In the worst case, it falls under ever harsher rule by a tiny
clique that clings to a reactionary form of Kemalism, backed by an angry
and repressive military and barely tolerated even by its friends in the
world. That scenario seems all but impossible because the Turkish people would at some point rebel against it. They are galloping toward the
new world and will get there no matter how furiously the old elite tries
to hold them back.

The brightest scenario may also be the most likely. In it, Turkey's
leaders break out of their denial and recognize how fully their people
deserve democracy. Political parties and the military command, renewed and invigorated by generational change, join to lead the race
toward modernity. They break away from their fears and commit themselves to building a country in which every citizen is free to speak, write,
worship and organize. In a land of such magnificent diversity, this freedom liberates enormous energy. Religious believers, Kurdish nationalists, human-rights advocates and freethinkers of every stripe unite to
demand that Europe open its doors to such a richly colorful nation.

This is not a far-fetched prospect. Turkey is entering the most profound period of self-examination in its history. It has resisted change for
as long as it can. For generations Turks have agreed with their leaders
that no sacrifice made in the name of stability was too onerous. They be-

lieve that no longer. They are stepping out. Youthful, vigorous and enthusiastic, they can become a force that will help shape the new century. If they manage to transform their country into a modern democracy, they will become happier and richer than they have ever been. That will make them a unique model for the developing world and an invaluable ally of all who work for peace and freedom.

Every Saturday night for three years, radio listeners in Istanbul could hear a voice speaking in heavily accented Turkish that welcomed them to another evening of blues music. "Yalnız gerçek blues çalıyorum," the voice would say as each show began. I play only real blues.

That voice was mine. I got a great kick out of being the "blues baba," or blues daddy, on Turkey's hippest radio station. Mine was hardly the first or only blues show in the country, but as far as I know I was the first American to host one, the first disc jockey in Turkey who not only featured artists like Lightnin' Hopkins, Alberta Hunter, Roosevelt Sykes, Big Joe Turner and Muddy Waters but had actually had the privilege of hearing them perform live.

A generation of Turks grew up hearing blues-influenced musicians like Eric Clapton, Johnny Winter and the Blues Brothers. But I never played their music. I was interested only in "real blues," music that many Turks had never heard before.

When I first planned the show, I resolved that any artist I featured would have to fit two categories: black and dead. I eased up on the second restriction a bit but never allowed myself to cross over into blues-rock or other derivative styles. The reason for this was not any kind of exclusionary elitism. My mission was to broaden the knowledge and taste of my audience. I wanted to let them know that Mick Jagger did not write "Little Red Rooster" and that "Hound Dog" was not an Elvis Presley original.

In my bilingual commentary I always tried to tell something about the lives of the artists whose music I played. I also explained the rudiments of blues history, working under the assumption that many Turks liked this music but didn't know much about it. Listeners sometimes told me they loved my show and then asked, "What is blues anyway?" To help orient them, I often talked about the Southern roots of blues music and how it moved north and went electric. Most of my listeners had probably never heard phrases like "Jim Crow" or "Parchman Farm," nor could they understand why so many blues songs are about leavin' home and ramblin'. I tried to present the cultural background against which blues music emerged, explaining how the forces of poverty and racism produced such rich musical expression.

After a while, I began to sense that many Turks found my explanations remote and hard to grasp. What I really needed to do, I realized, was to explain this music in terms Turks could easily understand. After all, African-Americans are hardly the only people in the world who feel the blues. They developed a richly evocative way to express those emotions, but the emotions themselves are universal.

I didn't want my radio station—which was always skirting the edge of the law anyway—to find itself in trouble because of something I broadcast, so I never delivered my imagined monologue on the air. If I had, it would have gone something like this:

You say you're a Kurdish villager out tending your sheep one day when some PKK guys show up and demand food. You're a Kurd and maybe you're scared, so you feed them. The next day an army patrol arrives in your village, curses you and your neighbors and gives you an hour to move your belongings. You have no choice but to obey, and an hour later the village that is the resting place of your ancestors and the repository of all your memories is set afire. What's the matter? Blues got you.

You say you're that Kurdish villager's son. You saw the fire, and naturally you're filled with resentment for the army and the state it repre-

sents. You've become one of the millions of refugees who lost everything in this dirty war. But you're smart enough to realize that violence is no answer and there's no point throwing your life away by picking up a rifle and taking to the mountains. So you go to school, study hard and spend your evenings talking with your Kurdish friends about paths of peaceful change. The cops find out you're having these meetings and one night they swoop down on your group, take you to jail and start beating you. What's the matter? Blues got you.

You say you're a Turk who is curious about Kurds and their lives. As a first step, you decide to try learning the Kurdish language. You can't do it at a language academy because it is forbidden to offer courses in Kurdish. Finally you hear that a Kurdish intellectual who lives in your town is going to offer a course. You sign up. When you arrive for the first session, you find the door locked with a police seal and a notice on the door saying that the course has been banned and the teacher arrested. What's the matter? Blues got you.

You say you're a thinker who has decided there are some things you don't like about your country. The army has too much power, religious and political freedoms are unconscionably restricted and police officers torture prisoners. Maybe these complaints are valid, maybe not. But as a patriotic citizen you feel free and even obligated to write and speak of them. You quickly find your book banned and yourself facing a prison term. What's the matter? Blues got you.

You say you've been elected to Parliament or as mayor of a town or big city. To represent your voters, you have to speak your mind. But in your mind are ideas that might not please the ruling elite. You can either give an honest speech and risk going to jail or betray your voters and yourself by remaining silent. What's the matter? Blues got you.

You say you're a pious Muslim and want to educate your children in the faith of their forefathers. You spend an hour each evening discussing the Koran with them. After a while, some of the neighbors' kids start dropping by to listen. One night police officers arrive, accuse you of illegally teaching religion and haul you off for interrogation. What's the matter? Blues got you.

You say you're an ambitious young woman who revels in the freedom Turkey offers to those of your sex. You enroll in medical school, but on your first day you find a guard standing outside the classroom. He won't let you in because you're wearing a head scarf. Despite Turkey's promise of gender equality, you find yourself in a predicament like those facing women in Yemen and Saudi Arabia. What's the matter? Blues got you.

You say you're a police officer. You spend your time arresting troublemakers—people who don't accept the rules of Turkish society. To make sure they realize how serious you are, you treat them the way prisoners have always been treated in your part of the world. But suddenly you find foreign do-gooders calling you a torturer and an enemy of humanity. Maybe they'll even force the authorities to prosecute you for doing your job. What's the matter? Blues got you.

You say you're an army general. You see the knaves and fools who are elected to Parliament, and you lie awake nights worrying that they are exposing Turkish democracy to mortal threat. Religious fanatics are attacking it from one side, Kurdish separatists from another. Feeling noble Atatürk's cold glare from the portrait hanging in your office, you know you cannot remain silent while his life's work is attacked. You spring to action to defend Turkey's secular and united state. For your pains you are condemned by democrats at home and around the world. What's the matter? Blues got you.

You say you're a judge or a prosecutor or a security officer or a nationalist politician or a senior bureaucrat. For the better part of a century you and people like you have managed to keep Turkey quiet and stable. Suddenly you find yourself and your ideology under siege. The whole nation is clamoring for freedom. Terror in the Kurdish region has subsided and tension with Greece is dissolving. The European Union has promised Turkey a brilliant prize if it can complete its march to modernity. You can barely recognize your own nation. Heresy is everywhere. You feel yourself surrounded as if by a prairie fire. The state is slipping from your grasp, the people marching away from you. A new Turkey is being born before your eyes. What's the matter? Blues got you.

INDEX

A

Abduction from the Seraglio (Mozart), 7

Abdülaziz, Sultan, 203

Abdülhamid II, Sultan, 37, 197

Abdülmecid I, Sultan, 203

Abdülmecid II, Caliph, 42, 44

Achilles, 53, 54, 55, 105

Adapazarı, Turkey, earthquake in, 183, 187

Aegean coast, 201–16; Greek-Turkish hostilities on, 39, 40, 201–11, 213; Greek-Turkish ties along, 173, 211–16, 231; Turkish territory of, 39, 41, 202

Afghanistan, fratricidal conflict in, 17

Afyon, Turkey, court trial in, 153–54

Ağca, Mehmet Ali, 98

Agence France-Presse, 149

Ahlat, Ottoman cemetery at, 106

Akmeşe, Hamza, 177

Alevi Muslims, 63–64, 225

Alexander the Great, 54–55, 105

Alı Riza Bey, 35

Anatolia: ancient sites of, 107; Greek catastrophe in, 203; nomadic Turks in, 32; Turkish territory of, 39, 40, 165, 232

Ani (Armenian capital), 106–7

Ankara: government moved to, 44; governors appointed from, 48; Hittite symbolism of, 107; Hizbullah hideout in, 100

Ankara State Opera, 219

Ankara Symphony Orchestra, 75–76

Ankara University, theology department in, 62

Anti-Terror Law, 147–48

Arabic language, prayers in, 46, 62

Arabic script, 45

archaeology, 103–7; culture ministry and, 107; diverse civilizations uncovered by, 104, 107; Hellenic discoveries of, 104–6; Roman discoveries of, 103–4, 105; Trojan discoveries of, 53–56; Zeugma discoveries of, 103–4

archers, mounted, 179–80

Argentina, 93

Armenians: diaspora of, 90–93; massacre of (1915), 88–94, 102, 114, 149; PKK supported by, 112; and Turkish territory, 39, 41, 173

Collettis, John, 204

Commandos of the Armenian Genocide, 91

Committee of Union and Progress, 38

Communist party: anti-Communists versus, 174; deported members of, 46; Hikmet as member of, 217–20; Marxist ideologies of, 63, 111, 118, 217–20; threat of, 146

Constantinople: Byzantium renamed as, 55; conquest of, 4, 55, 202; renamed Istanbul, 4; *see also* Istanbul

Crusades, 4, 55, 106

culture ministry, 107

Curio, Augustino, 5

Cyprus: earthquake relief from, 213; Greek-Turkish conflict over, 206, 215, 216; independence of, 206; Ottoman capture of, 4

D

D'Alema, Massimo, 120, 121

Damascus, Ottoman capture of, 4

Dardanelles: and city of Troy, 54, 56; international control of, 39, 40, 57; value of, 56

defense ministers, 19–20, 166

Demirel, Süleyman: democratization resisted by, 76, 160, 228; and earthquake devastation, 188–89; and Erbakan, 69, 70, 76; on Greek-Turkish hostility, 208; limits on tenure of, 230; and PKK, 131

democracy: constitution versus, 14, 21; deliberate development of, 18, 19, 129; European Union and, 22, 24, 25–26, 211, 232, 233; fear of, 12, 17–18; as goal of the people, 16, 192, 229–36; Islam and, 24, 231; modernity and, 12–13, 24, 172, 232, 235; NATO and, 76; political parties in, 17–18, 48; resistance to, 14, 18, 48, 74, 80, 160, 165, 167–76, 225, 226,

228, 231; role of individual in, 11, 26; role of military in, 164, 175–76; role of religion in, 61, 81; as social system, 19, 165, 173, 229–30; Turkey's potential for, 10, 12–13, 17–18, 24–26, 68, 129–30, 134, 229–36

Dereli, Toker, 80

devlet, meanings of, 26–28, 127, 145

Dimitrov, Philip, 92

Disraeli, Benjamin, 7

divorce, repudiation versus, 45

Diyarbakır, Turkey: author's arrest in, 137–38; Hizbullah in, 100; Kurds in, 109–10, 114–15, 154

dolma, 31

Dolmabahçe Palace, 197

Dörpfeld, Wilhelm, 55

Dostoevsky, Fyodor, 5

drugs, smuggling of, 171

Duran, Ragıp, 149–50

Durmuş, Osman, 189

E

earthquakes, 183–94; army's response to, 185, 188, 190–93; corrupt contractors as contributors to damage of, 187, 188, 190; foreign aid for, 189, 193–94, 212–13; as God's vengeance, 148; government's inadequate response to, 184–85, 189–93; and Greek-Turkish relations, 189, 193–94, 212–15; media coverage of, 185, 191, 192, 193–94, 213, 215; rescue efforts in, 185, 188, 191, 193, 213

Ecevit, Bülent: democratization resisted by, 160, 228, 231; and earthquakes, 184, 185, 188, 192; and European Community, 228; and Öcalan's arrest, 122, 125, 128; and torture, 155

education: change needed in, 227; functions of, 170, 230; Kurdish-language, 132–33; religious schools of, 61, 62, 64, 65, 72, 76; of women, 78–80

Edward VII, king of Great Britain, 197

Egypt, Islam in, 44

Eichmann, Adolf, 126

Elbiye, Cengiz, 181

Enlightenment, 18, 36, 202

Erbakan, Necmettin, 63–66, 68–78; author's interview with, 72–74; and Islam political movement, 63, 64–65, 68, 70, 72, 73, 74–77, 80, 175; military coup against, 75, 76–77, 165, 166, 175; and National Order party, 63; and National Salvation party, 64–65; as prime minister, 69–75, 166–67; and religious fundamentalism, 64, 65, 66, 70, 74–75; and Virtue party, 77–78; and Welfare party, 65–66, 68–69, 72, 77

Erdoğan, Recep Tayyip, 77

Erdoğan, Tülay, 79

Erkaya, Admiral Güven, 145

Ertep, Ismet, 83

Erzincan, Turkey, earthquake in, 193

Eugenie, empress of France, 197

Euphrates River, mosaics near, 103–4

Europe: Allied forces of, 39–41, 56–57; anti-Semitic pogroms in, 5; armies in, 170; calendar of, 45; Crusaders from, 4, 55, 106; freedom of speech in, 146; heroin smuggling in, 171; Kurdish exiles in, 112, 129, 130–31; map of, 23; Ottoman threats to, 4–5, 41; political influence of, 48–49, 159–60, 172, 231–32; Turkish laborers in, 160, 161; Turkish Republic as part of, 24, 41, 71, 73–74, 133–34; Turkish Republic formed against, 11, 16–17, 41–42

European Monetary Union, 207

European Union: criteria for membership in, 175; Greece as member of, 207, 211; human-rights issues and, 172; Turkey's potential entry into, 22, 24, 25–26, 170, 173, 175, 216, 228, 231–32, 233

Evren, Kenan, 95

Evrensel, 153

F

fez, banning by Atatürk of, 44

food and drink, 29–33, 59–60, 197–98

France: freedom of speech in, 146; Muslim raids on, 4; "zone of influence" for, 39, 41

Frank, Anne, 146

Franz Josef, emperor of Austria, 197

Frederick II, king of Prussia, 5

freedoms: *devlet* and, 27–28, 127, 145; *istiklal* and, 9, 28; open debate on, 150; restriction of, 14, 16–18, 27, 144, 145, 147, 152, 156, 167, 190, 226, 228, 230; *see also* human rights

G

Gagik, King, 88

Galatasaray University, 149

Gallipoli, battle of, 38–39, 56–57

Germany: freedom of speech in, 146; Kurds in, 129, 130–31; Turkish alliance with, 38–39, 158; and World War I, 38–39

Gilles, Pierre, 196

Göçer, Veli, 187, 188

Göktepe, Metin, 153–54, 155

Gölcük, Turkey, earthquake in, 183

Greece: archaeological discoveries of, 104–6; Byron's death in, 7, 203; and Byzantine Empire, 4, 202; and Cyprus, 206, 215, 216; and earthquakes, 189, 193–94, 212–15; in European Union, 207, 211; independence of, 203; military dictatorship in, 207; and Öcalan's exile, 122–23, 208, 209–11, 213, 214; and Ottoman Empire, 4, 201, 202–3, 206; PKK supported in, 112, 122; population exchange with, 41, 203–4, 206; Salonika conquered by, 37; Trojans versus, 55, 57; Turkey's hostility toward, 201–11, 213; and Turkish territory, 39, 41, 202; Turkish ties with, 173, 212–16, 231

Gül, Abdullah, 81

Gulf War, 166

H

Hanim, Zübeyde, 35, 37, 49

Hasan (translator), 137–38, 141–42

Hatay, 119, 173

Hellespont, 54

Herodotus, 54

heroin smuggling, 171

Hikmet, Nazım, 217–21

Hindemith, Paul, 45

Hitler, Adolf, 91–92

Hittite culture, 106, 107

Hizbullah scandal, 99–101, 102

Holy Land, conquest of, 3–5

Homer, on Trojan War, 53–56

Hopkins, Lightnin', 237

horsemanship, 179–80

human rights: and author's interrogation, 141; constitutional restrictions of, 14, 147; doctors' testimony about torture, 154–56; emergency rule versus, 112; foreign opinions about, 25–26, 48, 74, 113, 118, 132, 144–47, 151, 156, 172, 173, 229, 234; Hizbullah scandal, 99–101; judicial system and, 124–25, 127, 128, 144, 151–56; legal protection of, 21, 167, 190, 226, 228; in Middle East, 17, 145; military excesses versus, 17, 21, 63, 94–95, 101, 113, 118–19; non-governmental agencies for, 230; police interroga-

tions versus, 124, 144, 151–52, 154–56, 229; value of, 114, 149

Human Rights Watch, 149

Hunter, Alberta, 237

I

Imam Bayıldı, 31

Ingres, Jean-Auguste-Dominique, 7

Iran: author's visit to, 15; Council of Guardians in, 15; domestic conflict in, 173; government of, 15, 16; Jerusalem Day in, 74–75; Kurds in, 110, 173; radical regimes in, 207; theocracy of, 16, 60, 65, 70, 172; Turkey compared to, 15–16

Iraq: isolation of, 17, 173; Kurds in, 110, 112, 128; radical regimes in, 207

Ishak Pasha castle, 106

Islam, 60–65; Atatürk versus, 61–62; caliphate of, 42, 44; call to prayer of, 46, 62; Christians versus, 3, 4; coexistence with democracy, 24, 231; in Egypt, 44; Erbakan and, 63, 64–65, 68, 70, 72, 73, 74–77, 80, 175; Feast of Sacrifice of, 61; fundamentalism of, *see* religious fundamentalism; Kemalists versus, 63–64, 69, 72, 78, 81, 175; Koran and, 60, 62, 65, 75; moral authority of, 60; Sunni vs. Alevi, 63–64, 225; in Turkish constitution, 45; uprisings in the name of, 46; *see also* Muslims

Islamoğlu, Mustafa, 148

Israel, 134

Istanbul: and the Bosphorus, 195, 198; Constantinople renamed as, 4; Greeks driven from, 204–6; international control of, 39; Istiklal Boulevard in, 9–10, 72, 143; mayor of, 77; tourism in, 6; wealth tax in, 205

Istanbul University, 79–80

istiklal, meanings of, 9, 28
Italy: Muslim raids on, 4; Öcalan in, 120–22; and Turkish territory, 39, 41
Izmir, Turkey (Smyrna), assassination plot in, 46
Izmit, Turkey, earthquake in, 183, 212

J
Jagger, Mick, 238
James I, king of England, 5
James VI, king of Scotland, 5
Jandarma (police), 139
Janissary corps, 172
Jerusalem Day, 74–75
John Paul II, Pope, 98
journalists: at Afyon trial, 153–54; conflicting attitudes toward, 20, 47, 147; earthquakes covered by, 185, 191; Erbakan's interviews with, 72–73; and Greek-Turkish relations, 215; imprisonment of, 21, 140, 141, 149–50, 152, 167; legislation for control of, 147–49; in Öcalan's trial, 125–28; restrictions on stories of, 14, 47, 96, 101, 149–51; skepticism of, 215
Julius Caesar, 55, 106

K
Karabulut, Songül, 130–31
Karatepe, Şükrü, 77
Katsaounis, Evangellos, 201–2
Kavakcı, Merve, 78
Kayserı, Turkey, mayor of, 77
Kemal, Mustafa, 37–42, 44–48, 57; *see also* Atatürk, Mustafa Kemal
Kemal, Namık, 37
Kemal, Yaşar, 131
Kemalism, 35–36; and democracy, 48, 74, 76; and Islam, 63–64, 69, 72, 78, 81,

175; opportunities for women in, 78–80; opposition crushed by, 46, 47, 63, 77, 101; rigid principles of, 169; ruling elite of, 76–78, 132 (*see also* military commanders); statues to, 49–50; of traditional politicians, 76, 227, 235
Kenya, Öcalan in, 122–23, 208, 209–10
Khatami, Mohammed, 15
Khoumeni, Ayatollah, 74–75
Kiliç, Altemur, 220
Kırışcı, Kemal, 95–96
Kıvrıkoğlu, General Hüseyin, 185, 191, 208
Klose, Hans-Ulrich, 121
Kocadağ, Hüseyin, 97, 98
Konya, Turkey: bus ride from, 163–64, 167; Hizbullah hideout in, 100; whirling dervishes in, 163
Koran, 60, 62, 65, 75
Korea, North and South, 134, 157–59
Korean War, 157–59, 161, 174
Korelis, 157–61
Korfmann, Manfred, 55
Kurdish language, 131, 132–33
Kurdistan, 71, 110, 118, 129
Kurdistan Workers Party (PKK), 111–15, 117–21, 124, 126–32
Kurds, 109–35; and Armenian massacre (1915), 89–90; army campaign against, 112–15, 117–19, 135, 171, 174; assimilation into society of, 132–34, 227, 229; in diaspora, 129–31, 173; in Diyarbakır, 109–10, 114–15, 154; ethnic identity of, 118, 129, 133; and freedom of the press, 150; Hizbullah scandal and, 99–101; jailhouse beatings of, 154; Medes as ancestors of, 87; nationalism of, 95–97, 100, 102, 109–15, 129, 131, 135, 147–48, 167, 226, 229; Öcalan and, 111, 112, 114, 118–28, 129, 130–31, 149–50; as oppressed minority, 148; in Parliament, 113; populations of, 110; and Turkish territory, 39, 41; uprisings of, 11, 14, 17, 19, 46, 74, 95–

96, 109, 111, 115, 134–35, 146, 151, 166, 171, 174, 209, 227; in Van area, 87–90

Kuriş, Konca, 100

Kutlular, Mehmet, 148

L

Lake Van, 87–88, 106

Lausanne, treaty of, 41, 198

Lebanon, fratricidal conflict in, 17

Levertov, Denise, 221

Lewis, Bernard, 47

Libya, Erbakan's visit to, 71

Lice, Turkey, Kurds in, 115–17

Lloyd George, David, 39

Luther, Martin, 4, 62

M

Mahmut II, Sultan, 172

Mandela, Nelson, 234

Manisa, Turkey, teenagers tortured in, 154, 155

Manuel (architect), 88

Marlowe, Christopher, 5

Marthoz, Jean-Paul, 140–41

Marxist ideologies, 63, 111, 118, 217–20

Mater, Nadire, 96–97

Mecca, pilgrimages to, 62

Medes, 87

media: earthquake stories covered by, 185, 191, 192, 193–94, 213, 215; freedom of, 96, 144, 147, 150; government control of, 21–22; modernity introduced via, 230; *see also* press

Mediterranean Sea: Bosphorus as link to, 196; Italian forces on, 39, 40; Muslim pirates on, 4

Mehmet the Conqueror, Sultan, 39, 55, 199, 202

Mehmet II, Sultan, 196

Mehmet VI Vahidettin, Sultan, 42

Mehmet's Book (Mater), 96–97

Melville, Herman, 84

Menderes, Adnan, 17, 62–63, 219

Mesopotamia, 110

Mexico, Zapatista rebels in, 134

meyhane, 31–32, 33

meze, 31–32

Middle East: heroin smuggling in, 171; human rights in, 17, 145; map of, 23; power and confrontation in, 133; predatory neighbors in, 12, 119–20, 145, 149, 168, 172–73; Turkey's location in (map), 23

military: civilian control of, 14, 164, 166, 175, 211, 233; in democracy, 164, 175–76; modernization of, 174; and "mystery killings," 100; political involvement of, 164; size of, 170; standards of behavior in, 163–64, 167–68, 169, 170; universal male conscription in, 17, 170–71, 172, 174

military commanders: appointment of, 20; authoritarian rule by, 13, 16, 20–21, 65, 165–66, 233, 235; change resisted by, 169–72, 225; constitution written by, 13–14, 21, 166; defense ministers and, 20, 166; democracy resisted by, 149, 167–76, 226; and earthquakes, 185, 188, 190–93; and formation of Republic, 16–17, 60; and National Security Council, 14–16, 76, 165; people's respect for, 16–17, 165, 171, 172, 173; versus PKK, 112–15, 117–19, 135, 171, 174; political coups of, 13, 16, 17, 21, 63, 65, 76–77, 94, 164, 165, 175; political vacuum filled by, 14, 17, 22, 166–67, 169; populace mistrusted by, 10, 16, 146, 149, 165, 167, 176, 226; power of, 48, 63, 133, 174, 226; solemn oath taken by, 175–76; stability provided by, 16, 17–22, 67–68, 76–77, 94, 165, 167, 173; tragic excesses of, 17,

14; and Greek-Turkish ties, 193, 209, 213–14, 216

Parliament: city officials chosen by, 48; and constitution, 230; human-rights committee of, 153, 155; Kurdish members of, 113; members' moral character in, 20, 21; military domination of, 165–66, 167; multiparty elections for, 13, 48; prime minister chosen by, 15, 48, 69; role of, 15, 233

Pasha, Enver, 38

Pecevi, Ibrahim, 85

People's Democracy, 131

Perinçek, Doğu, 148

Peter, Saint, 106

Peter of Bracheaux, 55

Phaselis ruins, 105–6

Picasso, Pablo, 219

Pişkinsüt, Sema, 155

PKK (Kurdistan Workers Party), 111–15, 117–22, 124, 126–32

plebiscite, 10; *see also* democracy

Presley, Elvis, 238

press: official review of stories in, 151; as platform for civil society, 147; responsibilities of, 227; restrictions on, 14, 16, 21, 47, 96, 101, 148–50, 151; structure of, 21; *see also* journalists

prime ministers: as chosen by Parliament, 15, 48, 69; military control of, 166; *see also specific prime ministers*

61, 81, 225; separation of government and, 61, 81; taught in schools, 61, 62, 64, 65, 72, 76; *see also specific religions*

Religious Affairs Directorate, 60–61

religious fundamentalism: and Erbakan, 64, 65, 66, 70, 74–75; and Hizbullah, 100; and Jerusalem Day, 74–75; Kemalists versus, 16, 63–64, 69, 72, 78, 81, 146; modernity versus, 24, 59–60, 64–65, 67, 78, 226–27; Sunni versus Alevi, 64, 225

Republican People's Party, 62

Rhodes, Ottoman capture of, 4

Robeson, Paul, 219

Roman Empire: archaeological discoveries of, 103–4, 105, 106; and Constantinople, 4

Roman mosaics, 103–4

Rose, Brian, 55

ruling elite: change resisted by, 10, 11–13, 22, 81; as decision makers, 10, 13–14; detachment from the people of, 12, 118; and *devlet*, 27–28; dissidents destroyed by, 21, 27; of Kemalism, 76–78, 132; media controlled by, 21–22; modernity as expressed focus of, 12–13; on people's readiness for democracy, 10, 28, 48, 149; politicians controlled by, 21–22, 133; as self-perpetuating, 27, 188; *see also* military commanders

Rumeli Hisarı, 196–97

Q

Qaddafi, Muammar el-, 71

R

radio, *see* media

rakı, 29–33

religion: freedom of, 45, 175; as political force, 63–66, 68–78, 229 (*see also* religious fundamentalism); role of,

S

Salonika: Atatürk's birthplace in, 37, 205, 217; Greek conquest of, 37; Hikmet's birthplace in, 217

Samsun, Turkey, 27

Şanlı, Selahattin, 161

San Salvador, national reconciliation in, 134

sarma, 31

formed against European powers, 16–17, 41–42; judicial system of, 148; Kemal as first president of, 42; Korean War veterans from, 157–59; military coups in, 13, 16, 17, 21, 63, 65, 75, 76–77, 94, 164, 165, 166–67, 175; Ottoman Empire as foundation of, 7–8, 41, 164, 225–26; as part of Europe, 41, 71, 74, 133–34; political isolation of, 158–61, 165; political parties in, 21, 46–47, 48, 65, 77, 167; population exchange with, 41; poverty in, 11, 41; secularism in, 10, 60–62, 64, 65, 67, 69–70, 71, 76, 79–80; seventy-fifth anniversary of, 233

Turks: duality of, 6, 7; in families or clans, 26, 47–48; as general enemy, 3–8; Holy Land as conquest of, 3–5; in literature, 3, 5–7; names of, 47–48; new generations of, 48–49; nomadic, 32; obedience as way of life for, 11, 19, 225–26, 230; patriotic unity of, 225, 226; ruling elite as detached from, 12, 118; social goals of, 11, 16, 229–36

Turner, Big Joe, 237

Tzara, Tristan, 221

U

United Nations (UN), 158, 207–8

United States: freedom of speech in, 146; in Gulf War, 166; political influence of, 48–49, 159, 174, 231; separation of church and state in, 81; weaponry from, 174

Urartu, kingdom of, 87, 89

Urban II, Pope, 4

V

Van, Turkey, 87–90

Venizelos, Eleftherios, 204

Veremis, Thanos, 211

Versailles, treaty of, 39

Vienna, Ottoman threat to, 4

Virtue party, 77–78, 81

Voltaire, 5

W

water pipe smoking, 83–86

Waters, Muddy, 237

Welfare Party, 65–67, 68–69, 72, 77

whirling dervishes, 163

Whitman, Walt, 218

Wilhelm, Kaiser, 38

Winter, Johnny, 237

women: demonstrations by, 143–44; education of, 78–80; head scarves of, 60, 72, 75, 78–81, 169, 227; marriage laws for, 45; political activism of, 46, 66; veils of, 44–45; voting rights for, 46; in younger generation, 223

World War I: emergence of Kemalism after, 36; fall of Turkey in, 38–39, 56–57, 158, 165

World War II, 158

X

Xenophon, 111

Xerxes, Persian army of, 54

Y

Yağmurdereli, Esber, 148

Yalova, Turkey, earthquake in, 183, 186

Yazar, Mehmet Vahi, 148

Yeltsin, Boris, 120

Yerevan, Armenia, Genocide Museum in, 91

Yevtushenko, Yevgeny, 219
Yılmaz, Mesut, 69, 70
Young Turks, 13, 38, 61
Yugoslavia, collapse of, 17, 225

Z
Zarakolu, Ayşe Nur, 148–49
Zeugma, archaeological discoveries of,
103–4